Understanding Tropical Coastal and Island Tourism Development

This book contains a collection of articles that include both case studies and theoretical insights applicable to the tourism development challenges of tropical coastal and island destinations throughout the world. Topics include: the shortcomings of (eco)tourism in Madagascar; collaboration theory and successful multi-stakeholder partnerships on Indonesian resort islands; resilience theory and development pressures on a Malaysian island; results and implications of a detailed survey of cruise passengers in Colombia; perceptions of underdevelopment as limiting factors in Costa Rica; conflicts of perception and reality through the literary myths of Pitcairn Island; residents' attitudes toward tourism in the Cape Verde Islands; and 'slow tourism' as a soft growth alternative to mass tourism development in the Lesser Antilles. As a collection, not only do the chapters provide readers with a broad overview of the range of issues found in tropical coastal and island tourist destinations, but they also offer tourism managers and planners insights into both the positive and negative aspects of alternative tourism development in tropical destinations.

This book was based on a special issue of *Tourism Geographies*.

Klaus J. Meyer-Arendt is a Professor in the Department of Environmental Studies at the University of West Florida (Pensacola, FL). His research interests include coastal tourism, tourism impacts in coastal environments, hurricane impacts and sustainability of coastal (eco)tourism.

Alan A. Lew is a Professor in the Department of Geography, Planning and Recreation at Northern Arizona University where he teaches courses in geography, urban planning and tourism. His interests and writings focus on tourism in Asia, particularly China and Southeast Asia, and tourism in the American West.

Understanding Tropical Coastal and Island Tourism Development

Edited by
Klaus J. Meyer-Arendt and Alan A. Lew

LONDON AND NEW YORK

First published 2015 by Routledge

2 Park Square, Milton Park, Abingdon, Oxon, OX14 4RN
605 Third Avenue, New York, NY 10017

Routledge is an imprint of the Taylor & Francis Group, an informa business

First issued in paperback 2020

British Library Cataloguing in Publication Data
A catalogue record for this book is available from the British Library

ISBN13: 978-1-138-79285-2 (hbk)
ISBN13: 978-0-367-73997-3 (pbk)

Typeset in Times New Roman
by RefineCatch Limited, Bungay, Suffolk

Publisher's Note
The publisher accepts responsibility for any inconsistencies that may have
arisen during the conversion of this book from journal articles to book chapters,
namely the possible inclusion of journal terminology.

Disclaimer
Every effort has been made to contact copyright holders for their permission to
reprint material in this book. The publishers would be grateful to hear from any
copyright holder who is not here acknowledged and will undertake to rectify any
errors or omissions in future editions of this book.

Contents

Citation Information

The following chapters were originally published in *Tourism Geographies*, volume 15, issue 1 (February 2013). Some chapters were published in other issues of the same journal. When citing this material, please use the original page numbering for each article, as follows:

Please direct any queries you may have about the citations to
clsuk.permissions@cengage.com

New Perspectives on Tropical Coastal and Island Tourism Development

KLAUS J. MEYER-ARENDT* & ALAN A. LEW**

*University of West Florida, Pensacola, Florida, USA
**Geography, Planning and Recreation, Northern Arizona University, Flagstaff, Arizona, USA

ABSTRACT *This special issue is presented as a thematic issue devoted to tropical coastal and island tourism. Included in the issue are articles on (eco)tourism in Madagascar, collaboration theory and tourism partnership models on an Indonesian island, development pressure and resilience on a Malaysian island, a survey of cruise passengers in Colombia, perception and limits to development in Costa Rica, and perception and reality on Pitcairn Island. Placed within theoretical or conceptual frameworks, these case studies can be applied to development challenges of tropical coastal and island destinations worldwide.*

Just as the great explorations of the nineteenth and early twentieth centuries strove to fill in the last blank areas on the world map, the frontiers of tourism have rapidly expanded over the past few decades to the remotest corners of the world. Among the most popular of these have been the sun, sand, and sea destinations of tropical islands and coastlines. Tourists in ever growing numbers seek out their warm temperatures, sandy beaches, and tropical waters. As a result, tropical shorelines the world over have been impacted by infrastructural development to accommodate both stayover tourists and cruise tourists.

In spite of the abundance of scattered literature on tropical coastal and island tourism in sources such as *Tourism Geographies*, there exists a relatively small volume of books or special collections devoted exclusively to the topic. Following a successful conference on 'The Changing World of Coastal, Island and Tropical Tourism' held in Martinique, French West Indies, in January 2011, as well as two paper sessions on Coastal Tourism at the Association of American Geographers annual meeting in Seattle, Washington, in April 2011, the idea for a special issue of *Tourism Geographies* was born.

This special issue contains articles that address a cross section of topics related to tourism development in tropical islands and coastal areas. Bruno Sarrasin (2012)

1

explains how (eco)tourism falls a bit short in its purported role to protect natural resources in impoverished Madagascar, specifically at Ranomafana National Park, Madagascar. Sonya Graci (2012), examines successful multi-stakeholder partnerships through the lens of collaboration theory and tourism partnership models on Gili Trawangan, Indonesia. Mark Hampton and Amran Hamzah (2012) document development pressures on a small Malaysian island using insights from resilience theory as opposed to classic resort evolution models. Juan Gabriel Brida and his co-authors (2012) describe the results and implications of a detailed survey of cruise passengers in Colombia. Eric Nost (2012) uses Costa Rica to examine how perception of a place as underdeveloped can define and limit development efforts. Maria Amoamo (2012) similarly looks at conflicts of perception and reality through the literary myths of remote Pitcairn Island.

These articles provide useful case studies and theoretical insights that can be applied to the development challenges of tropical coastal and island destinations throughout the world. Grounded in tourism models and theories, together they also make a valuable contribution to the conceptual side of tourism development.

References

Amoamo, M. (2012) (de)Constructing place-myth: Pitcairn Island and the 'Bounty' story. *Tourism Geographies*, DOI: 10.1080/14616688.2012.699093.

Brida, J. G., Pulina, M., Riaño, E., and Zapata Aguirre, S. (2012) Cruise passengers in a homeport: a market analysis. *Tourism Geographies*, DOI: 10.1080/14616688.2012.675510.

Graci, S. (2012) Collaboration and partnership development for sustainable tourism. *Tourism Geographies*, DOI: 10.1080/14616688.2012.675513.

Hamzah, A. and Hampton, M. P. (2012) Resilience and non-linear change in island tourism. *Tourism Geographies*, DOI: 10.1080/14616688.2012.675582.

Nost, E. (2012) The power of place: tourism development in Costa Rica. *Tourism Geographies*, DOI: 10.1080/14616688.2012.699090.

Sarrasin, B. (2012) Ecotourism, poverty and resources management in Ranomafana, Madagascar. *Tourism Geographies*, DOI: 10.1080/14616688.2012.675512.

Notes on Contributors

Dr Klaus J. Meyer-Arendt is a professor in the Department of Environmental Studies at the University of West Florida (Pensacola, FL). His research interests include coastal tourism, tourism impacts in coast environments, and sustainability of coastal (eco)tourism.

Alan A. Lew is a Professor in the Department of Geography, Planning, and Recreation at Northern Arizona University where he teaches courses in geography, urban planning and tourism. His interests and writings focus on tourism in Asia, particularly China and Southeast Asia, and tourism in the American West.

Ecotourism, Poverty and Resources Management in Ranomafana, Madagascar

BRUNO SARRASIN

Department of Urban and Tourism Studies, University of Quebec at Montreal (UQAM), Montreal, Quebec, Canada

ABSTRACT *This paper explores how the protection of natural resources is managed in Madagascar in order to understand how and why tourism development is part of the strategy to safeguard these resources. Based on a heterodox political economy approach and using documentary analysis as well as exploratory interviews, this paper focuses on the specific case of Ranomafana National Park showing how the environment, economic growth and poverty alleviation strategies are instrumental to a 'development framework' that envisions the rural poor population as a problem as well as a solution with respect to resource depletion. The analysis concluded that tourism is far from being an 'axis of development' for the Malagasy economy, and, thus, an insufficient alternative to address the destructive practices described in this paper. The case study shows that ecotourism creates few work opportunities for local people and does not absorb the job seekers who rapidly revert to survival techniques and anarchic use of resources, thereby threatening the integrity of the forest and the long-term survival of ecotourism activities. In this context, the place of tourism in general and of ecotourism, in particular, appears to have been highly exaggerated in Madagascar as the direct economic benefits of tourism at the local level remain minimal.*

Introduction

Madagascar is an island located southwest of the Indian Ocean (Figure 1). It is among the 10 *hotspots* of global biological diversity and counts itself among the 12 so-called 'mega-diverse' countries, being home to 80% of the planet's biological diversity (MEF & UNEP 2010). Madagascar's insularity has encouraged a great diversity in its topography, its landscapes and climate, and has a remarkable variety of vegetal and animal species living in diverse natural habitats. This geographical isolation coupled with diverse microclimates has allowed for the development of archaic life forms that have moulded the island's terrestrial ecosystems, resulting in

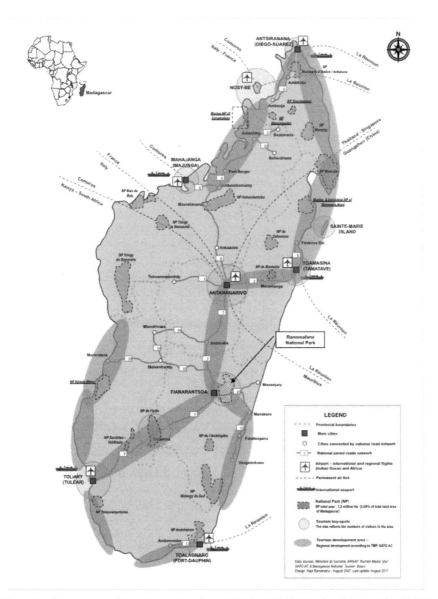

Figure 1. *Data sources*: Ministére du Tourisme, PNM-ANGAP, Tourism Master Plan GATO AC & Madagascar National Tourism Board. *Design*: Haja Ramahatra – August 2007. Last update: August 2011.

some of the rarest forms of biodiversity in the world (FEM 2005). However, this biological diversity, particularly the virgin forest cover, is seriously threatened by numerous conditions, including man-made activities, ranging from the burning of the flora to the chaotic exploitation of the soil. Slowly but inexorably, the land area of Madagascar's natural habitats is decreasing annually, intensifying the threat of extinction of certain endemic animals and flora that depend on these ecosystems. While there has been a slowing down in the degradation of the island's forest cover since 2003, national data nevertheless show a mean decrease of 200,000 hectares of forests per year (MEEFT 2008). If the rural population is generally identified as being responsible for this degradation (Cleaver & Schreiber 1998; Carrière & Bidaud 2012), actions taken in the last 20 years, particularly in the three stages of the Environmental Action Plan (*Plan d'action environnemental*: PAE), do not seem to have met their objectives: to stop environmental degradation of the natural resources in general, and to reverse the spiral of deforestation in particular. While the present analysis is not an assessment of the PAE, we will explore how the protection of natural resources is managed and organized in Madagascar, and attempt to understand how and why tourism development has proven to be unsuccessful as part of the strategy to safeguard these resources.

In Madagascar, tourist sites and activities are still geographically uneven and poorly distributed (see Figure 1). The allocation of accommodation establishments corresponds to the principle tourism vacation areas (key tourism spots in Figure 1) with the exception of the capital Antananarivo, which, despite being the main point of arrival for foreign travellers, serves mainly as a transition point as tourists make their way to their final destinations – either for nature or discovery tourism (*Antsirabe, Fianarantsoa, Ambatolampy, Moramanga, Ranomafana*) or for seaside tourism (*Nosy be, Fort Dauphin, Saint Marie, Tulear, Morondava, Diego, Majunga, Tamatave, Antalaha, Sambava, Manakara, Mananjary*). The image of Madagascar as an ecotourism destination (tourism based on nature and discovery) is confirmed by the development of the axis to the South – Tourism Development Area in Figure 1 (oriented to encourage the discovery of the national parks and other natural sites) – which outperforms the North (which is more oriented towards the seaside). However, the demand for seaside tourism is evidenced by the important variety of tour operator options for those who prefer sightseeing tours that combine both seaside and nature tourism. Overall, the tourism demand and supply in Madagascar is located in large part in seaside locations and has been developed around a few secondary cities that are accessible from the capital city.

Conceptual and Methodological Approach

Our approach uses a macro analysis within the context of ecotourism development in Madagascar, using as an anchor the heterodox approach to international political economy (IPE) developed predominantly by Susan Strange (Stopford *et al.* 1991;

Strange 1996, 2002). Discussions of political economy are generally focused around issues relating to 'the relative power of states and markets and their respective ability to define the rules of the global economic and social game' (Chavagneux 1998: 25, our translation). The advantage of the approach proposed by the heterodox branch of this field of study is the challenge to analytical and conceptual separation that has traditionally been established between, first, national and international spheres and, second, issues defined as economic and considered to be political (Teivainen 2002).

According to the approach developed by Strange, the contemporary economic system 'results from the confrontation of a set of diffuse multiple authorities continuing negotiations with each other to impose their preferences' (Chavagneux 1998: 25, our translation). These negotiations take place within the context of specific structures that define, at a given moment and within a particular area of IPE, the procedures for the exercise of power by different authorities. Each of the structures also has fundamental values that give it legitimacy (prosperity, justice, equity, security, etc.). Taking into account the values preferred by those who hold power in a particular area can help to address the structures and agreements that characterize these values and to update inherent weaknesses. Equally important in the heterodox approach is the concept of power that, in this case, is not only *relational* (the power of an actor to change the behaviour or preferences of another), but also *structural* (the power of an actor to shape structures and define the rules, to which the behaviour of other actors must conform). From this perspective, and to expand the understanding of the benefits of protected areas beyond a purely economic analysis, we hypothesize that ecotourism in Madagascar, and the case of the national parks in this study, be considered as part of these basic structures, as proposed by Strange, and acknowledge the ways in which various forms of structural power can have not only economic but also social and environmental consequences. The inclusion and exclusion of some of the values underpinning these structures can have important consequences on the feasibility and impact of a proposed conservation and development project through the ecotourism development of natural resources.

Our hypothesis is grounded in empirical research that is based on a qualitative analysis method. The process of collecting data consisted of two principle approaches. First, to clarify multilateral economic and national policies – favouring an expansion of ecotourism in the region of interest – we chose a methodology that consisted of analytical and deductive examinations of documentary sources, based on the review of working papers, research reports and articles. This step allowed us to obtain an overall picture of the key issues in the development of ecotourism in Madagascar and the context in which this has happened in the Ranomafana National Park. This was supplemented by 21 semi-structured interviews administered at the site of the National Park, in the Ranomafana region and in the capital Antananarivo. Table 1 presents a brief typology of these interviews.

Interviews with members of the Malagasy government and administration took place in the capital city, Antananarivo, specifically in the Ministry of Environment,

6

Table 1. Types of interviews

Location of the interview	Type of respondent		
	Malagasy Government and administration	Member of an NGO	Rural population
Antananarivo	3	2	0
Ranomafana	4	2	10

Forestry and Tourism, in the National Environment Office (*l'Office National de l'Environnement*: ONE) and in the offices of Madagascar National Parks (*Parcs Nationaux de Madagascar*: PNM, known prior to 2001 as l'*Agence National des Aires Protégées*: ANGAP) during May 2007. Local representatives of PNM and *Faritany de Fianarantsoa* were the subjects of interviews, as were non-governmental organization (NGO) representatives of *Tany Meva*. Representatives of Conservation International and WWF (World Wildlife Fund) were interviewed in Antananarivo. An individual representing the ecolodge 'Domaine nature' on the outskirts of the National Park was also interviewed and appears in the table as an NGO. All interviews with members of the rural population were administered in or around the National Park. The interviews were conducted during workdays, over a period of 2 weeks. The approach is exploratory and no specific sampling was used. Respondents were identified based on their proximity to the protected area and their (actual and potential) behaviours within this area. All of the respondents were economically poor, where 70% of them were farmers (representing seven respondents) and the remaining three respondents practised other types of food agriculture activities. We administered interviews as informally as possible, using a list of open questions. The main objective was to establish a trusting relationship with the respondent, within the limits of an interview. They were conducted individually, except with the rural population where an interpreter was present at all times. This method recognizes the particular importance of the interviewee to be able to properly address the themes proposed by the interviewer.

An Overview of Madagascar's Biodiversity

The ecosystems of the *Grande île* can be broken down into four major categories. Firstly, one finds the virgin formations (the original ecosystem) representing about 16% of the territory, characterized by substantial biological diversity of flora and fauna with a high level of endemism. The secondary formations are found in 63% of the island's land area and represent different forms of the virgin forest degradation (at different evolutionary stages, ranging from the ligneous stage, such as trees and shrubs, to the grassland stage, such as savannas and steppes). One also encounters specific formations that result from specialized vegetal formations regulated by ecological conditions in different regions of Madagascar. In this third category, one finds rock outcroppings – very important in the granitic domes in the central region (with very striking cases of micro-endemism), marsh and wetland vegetation (0.5% of the island) and mangroves (0.6% of the island) – and littoral forest formations consisting of very particular vegetation adapted to the environment with the flow of the tides. The humid zones (river systems of more than 3,000 km in length and numerous lakes, marshes and peat bogs) and the marine and coastal ecosystems make up about 420,000 hectares of marshes, 300,000 hectares of mangroves and more than 2,000 km^2 of reefs. Finally, the fourth major category is made up of man-made plantations and cultures, particularly land reforestation (0.5% of the island) that consists mainly of fast-growing exotic species (eucalyptus and pines) and different types of food production: rice farming, cash crops and market gardening (ANGAP 2001; MINENVEF 2005). Each of these ecosystems contains biological diversity, the details of which extend considerably beyond the objectives of our presentation. This overview nevertheless highlights the importance of natural resources in this country as well as the stakes involved in their conservation.

PNM is an NGO with the mandate to encourage and manage biodiversity conservation in the country. By 2005, the first stage of PNM's mission led to the creation and the classification of a national network of 46 protected areas (18 National Parks, 5 Complete Natural Reserves or *Réserves Naturelles Integrales*: RNI) and 23 Special Reserves (*Réserves Spéciales*: RS). In 2007, the Commission for the System of Protected Areas in Madagascar (*Système des Aires Protégées de Madagascar*: the 'Commission SAPM') counted 20 new Protected Areas that had already been created (since 2005) or were in the process of being formed. These represent a land area of nearly 2 million hectares. We present a brief overview of these territories classified as 'eco-regions', in order to provide a perspective on the development stakes involved.

Madagascar's Eco-Regions and the Threats They Face

Despite the adoption of an Environmental Charter in 1990 and the PAE, which has been endorsed by the various funding agencies (PAE, 1993–2008 [2011]), in recent decades there has been a continuing deterioration of the quality of the environment as well as a quantitative decline of national landmarks in numerous eco-regions, particularly in the virgin forest, where many flora and fauna that make Madagascar unique are found. The country continues to experience a high level of damage in its biodiversity, mainly in its forest cover, which is disappearing at an annual rate of 150,000–200,000 hectares (FAO 2005). Regardless of the numerous strategies contained in the various protection and conservation programmes, this trend does not seem to have significantly changed, as the annual deforestation rate was 1% from 1990 to 2005 (Freudenberger 2010). The United Nations has estimated that in the last

60 years, 75% of the forest cover has disappeared – 10% of the total loss occurred in the 1990s. The clearing of forests has had a number of direct consequences, among them are the loss of biodiversity, the reduction of the soil's fertility, erosion and the silting of riverbeds and estuaries. From 1990 to 2000, a yearly average of 24,466 hectares of forests were burned for agricultural development (of which 74% were concentrated in the *faritany* of *Diego* and *Tamatave*). Meanwhile, the logging industry increased exponentially during this period (ONU & République de Madagacar 2003). Many factors may account for this environmental damage but only the principal causes, those most frequently mentioned for their high impact on the forest cover of the eco-regions, are discussed for the purpose of this analysis.

Firstly (acknowledging that this practice occurs in a framework that goes far beyond its agricultural dimensions; Kull 2004, 2012), the *tavy* practice of wood-clearing has been identified as a principal cause of degradation. It affects an average of 350,000 hectares per year (this number is underestimated as it only represents *authorized* clearing and most *tavy* practices go unrecorded). *Tavy* is a traditional farming practice of slash-and-burn practised by the majority of the rural population (itself made up of small-scale, extremely poor farmers). In addition, as there is no other means of farming to replace this practice – a fact that the PAE does not seem to have considered – the pressure on natural resources will continue to increase in the short and mid terms (Sarrasin 2005). Soil erosion due to the increase of cultivated land, particularly involving *tavy*, results in an annual net loss estimated at US$ 100–300 million in agricultural potential (Rarivomanana 2000).

Secondly, bush or grass fires increase erosion and reduce the impact of reforestation initiatives. The clearing of the undergrowth for cattle raising and for the increase of the national livestock – a centuries-old tradition in Madagascar – puts continuous pressure on the virgin forest ecosystems. Bush fires destroy an average of 650,000 hectares per year of primary or secondary plant cover (Freudenberger 2010). Logging and the collecting of firewood to produce charcoal are considered to be other important causes of deforestation in Madagascar. In most countries of the South, ligneous resources meet domestic energy needs and the need for raw materials for house construction. Population agglomerations, growing at faster rates, are major wood consumers; moreover, the peri-urban forest areas that surround the population centres and the Protected Areas suffer major damage since they are the first to be exploited (Thibaud 2005). Hence, population migrations cause major strains on the forests because of the excessive exploitation of sawn lumber for greater demands of energy and increased construction requirements (CEPF 2000); migration also threatens forest resources in areas around settlements and increases the potential risk of invading the Protected Areas and neighbouring classified forests.

Lastly, hunting and commerce are threats which weigh particularly heavily on certain protected species that are illegally exported to La Réunion Island. Altogether, hunting (including poaching) should probably be considered as an even greater threat to the fauna than the commercial traffic of wild animals, since it affects several of the larger and more threatened species. While the ecological loss due to the degradation of natural habitats – particularly the forest cover – has yet to be fully assessed, it is undeniable that there is a very high level of erosion in Madagascar's biodiversity. If degradation rates remain at current levels, the recent forecasts of the *Center for Applied Biodiversity Science* (CABS) for Conservation International could be confirmed and the forest cover of Madagascar will completely disappear in the next 20 years. Therefore, questions are still being asked: How, in these conditions, can degradation be effectively slowed down? How should one act on the principal causes of degradation mentioned above? For the Government of Madagascar and the international funding agencies, the answers lie in the relationship between poverty, economic growth and the protection of natural resources. So, with the creation and management of the Protected Areas, the logical and main source of pressure weighing on the biodiversity comes from the activities of the poor population. This logic is based on a set of relationships and hypotheses which can be summarized as follows (World Bank 2010, 2011b): Madagascar is one of the poorest countries in the world; 85% of the poor live in rural areas and they depend largely on natural resources; their way of living (way of surviving) and their production system contribute to environmental degradation and the accelerated loss of forest cover; this situation, in turn, further increases the vulnerability of the poor population living in rural areas, given the increase and frequent occurrence of natural disasters. This logic is not new, since for the last 20 years it has provided the structure of how 'environmental problems' are envisaged and the solutions that are offered in sub-Saharan Africa as in other countries in the South (Sarrasin 2005). By briefly looking at the characteristics of the 'development framework' presented by the international financial institutions – particularly the World Bank – we propose to examine, from a political economy perspective, how and why tourism development has become part of the strategy to safeguard natural resources, and the apparent failure of this approach.

Structural Adjustment and Poverty Alleviation as Neoliberal Environmental Management

During the 1980s, having been under structural adjustment since 1983, the Government of Madagascar went from being firmly entrenched in socialist policy to becoming a 'star pupil' of the International Monetary Fund (IMF) and the World Bank by adopting the prescribed neoliberal strategies such as promoting exports, reducing the role of the State and promoting comparative advantage and foreign investment – what Susan Strange refers to as 'fundamental values'. In terms of international financing, this had the particular consequence of a sevenfold increase, from 1980 to 2009, in the volume of World Bank loans that the Government of Madagascar received (World Bank 2011a). Structural Adjustment Programs (SAPs) became the vector for the fight against poverty and from the start their social consequences have been hotly disputed (Cornia *et al.* 1987). A central pivot was outward-oriented for economic growth in

Africa in general, and in Madagascar in particular. The 1994 World Bank report on sub-Saharan Africa specifically stated that 'adjustment is the necessary first step on the road to sustainable, poverty-reducing growth' (Banque Mondiale 1994: 15, our translation). This logic was re-affirmed more or less explicitly in the institution's subsequent analyses on the ties between poverty and the solution to alleviate it (World Bank 2002, 2004, 2011b; Arbache *et al.* 2008). Since the World Bank mentioned that the majority of poor people live in rural areas and that structural adjustment sought specifically to 'reposition' the agricultural sector as the core for economic growth, measures aimed at raising the prices of exports should benefit the poor whose labour was tied to this sector of the economy. Structural adjustment has gradually incorporated the fight against poverty as a fundamental value in response to criticism. The ultimate objective of the poverty alleviation strategies via adjustment was based on the integration of the poor into the national production process, which itself was to be oriented towards the outside world and the inclusion of the poor in the 'formal economy'.

In 1996, the Government of Madagascar adopted a Political and Economic Document (*Document Cadre de Politique Économique*: DCPE). This text, renewed in June of 1999, declared that the decrease of poverty would be achieved mainly by setting up a socio-economic environment that would encourage economic growth within the logic of structural adjustment. This approach confirms the importance of the fundamental values of economic adjustment within the power structure that determines economic and social relations in Madagascar. This policy statement, connecting economic growth and the containment of poverty, has since been replaced by the Madagascar Action Plan (République de Madagascar 2006). The first element of this plan assumes that the rural poor benefit from the reorientation of resources towards the agricultural sector. But when prices of products destined for export rise, landowners – whose production is export-oriented – benefit more than poor plantation workers or subsistence farmers. One can therefore question whether it is the majority of the peasants who benefit from these measures (Sarrasin 1999; Campbell 2005). Because a large number of poor farmers are often excluded from such growth, the World Bank suggests complementing SAPs with transfers and programmes aimed at protecting the poor, thus allowing them to obtain rapid benefits from the growth.

The Government of Madagascar's approach falls within the scope of the World Bank's neoliberal development framework, seeking to reduce poverty so that, by 2015, only half of the island's population will remain poor (République de Madagascar 2006). This assumes a mean annual growth rate of an estimated 7% from 2000 to 2015. As the Government of Madagascar rightly emphasizes: 'These perspectives can be envisaged if the opportunities offered by the international market and the rhythm of applying reforms are respected' (INSTAT 2000: 23, our translation). However, the pattern of economic changes in recent decades shows a negative mean annual growth of –2.68% for the period between 1980 and 1990, and 2.32% between 1990 and 2000

(World Bank 2009). Despite a mean annual growth rate of 11.8% between 2000 and 2008, applying this framework reveals that this increase remains particularly fragile due to the world economic crisis and the political instability that has prevailed in Madagascar since 2009. As a result, political and economic pressures are very strong in certain sectors – particularly mining, telecommunications, manufacturing and export agriculture – in order to achieve the conditions of growth set by the funding institutions. It is in these conditions that tourism is upheld as an emerging sector with a high growth potential, one that could both contribute to poverty alleviation and reduce the degradation of natural resources (in the logic of the development framework, by offering the poor rural population an alternative source of income other than large-scale agriculture and the exploitation of forest resources). The case of the Ranomafana National Park allows us to explore some of the limits of this strategy.

The Ranomafana National Park in the Eco-Region of Eastern Madagascar: The Difficult Relationship Between 'Conservation' and 'Development'

The Ranomafana National Park was created in 1991 following the 1986 discovery of a new species of lemur – *Hapalemur aureus* – and the rediscovery of the *Hapalemur simus* a year later, which was believed to be extinct. With a land area of 41,601 hectares, the National Park is located in the Fianarantsoa province in the south of Madagascar, close to the town of Ranomafana (see Figure 1). The boundaries of the National Park were established so that no village would be located within the Protected Area, but our interviews with local representatives of PNM told us that some villages had in fact been displaced. The Park was therefore divided into three sectors (or parcels) separated by a national highway. *Parcel 1* is the largest, the least accessible (and thus the least disturbed) and contains two types of virgin forests; *Parcel 2* is the smallest of the three sectors with a tropical rainforest cover and pine and eucalyptus plantations; finally, *Parcel 3* contains the most important undisturbed virgin forest cover as well as areas dedicated to scientific research and tourism activities. The geomorphic wealth of the Ranomafana National Park allows for significant biodiversity of endemic animal species and has contributed to shaping the ecotourism image that Madagascar has developed since 1990 (ANGAP 2001; MEF & UNEP 2010).

Historically, the region's forests have been disturbed by human activities, which have principally had major impacts on the forest composition. The slash-and-burn technique or *tavy* and the exploitation and uncontrolled extraction of wood are the most important causes of forest cover degradation in the National Park (see Figure 2). The flora and fauna found in areas surrounding the rural population have been under pressure in various ways. Besides the *tavy* practice, the Park has been subjected to other sources of disruption. The exploitation of tropical hardwood is the second most important cause of disruption, and it primarily affects rare tropical woods,

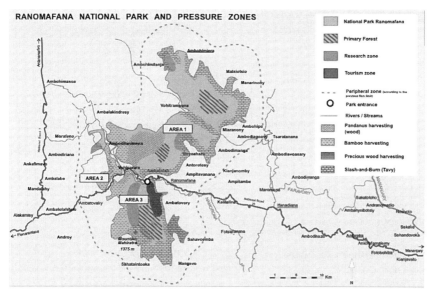

Figure 2. Adapted by Haja Ramahatra from Lappalainen 2002.

bamboo harvesting (for construction), fishing activities, honey extraction, bush fires and extracting plants (for subsequent resale; Lappalainen 2002; Andrianambinimina 2007; Freudenberger 2008). All interviews with the rural population confirmed the practice of activities presented in Figure 2, and 50% of interviewees admitted that these practices had taken place in the Park. This incessant and increasing human activity practised within the boundaries of the National Park, and in the immediate proximity of the highways that border the three parcels of the Park, not only threaten the biodiversity of the eastern eco-region but also make it difficult to protect the resources that the Park is supposed to be safeguarding.

Major Threats to Conservation

Forest resources in the region have long been depleted through the practices of *tavy* and wood removal for construction needs. Considered an ancestral practice (*fombandrazana*) by the rural population, *tavy* is said to be essential to the survival of farmers and continues to be practised due to the advantages it represents when compared with rice farming in specific locations – *tavy* requires little or no labour on the land and requires no irrigation work. This type of farming satisfies basic needs by allowing sufficient harvests and by improving the fertility of the soil without using chemical fertilizers that farmers cannot afford (Peters 1994; Kull 2004; MEF 2009). However, this practice only allows for 2 years of rice production and these parcels of land are later used for growing less demanding crops such as maize and cassava. The land is eventually abandoned.

It takes between 10 and 12 years for a *tavy* field to fully recover; this practice can be ecologically viable when the population density and/or soil fertility allows for long enough regeneration periods of the forest between harvesting cycles on the same parcel of land (Brady 1996; Woodwell *et al.* 2004). However, *tavy* re-uses the same fields after 2–5 years because of the exponential population increase in the National Park region (around 40,000 people live in the 100 villages surrounding the Park [see Figure 2]). The mean annual population growth rate is 2.8% and households typically include six to eight children (CMP 2002). Furthermore, other factors such as the scarcity of arable land and the banning of *tavy* within the National Park also account for the intense rate of land re-use. Consequently, the region's rural population has been forced to seek other forms of subsistence farming to which the neoliberal growth framework is unable to provide an alternative.

Despite the efforts of ANGAP-PNM and the promotion of awareness led by numerous NGOs with the population, the *tavy* practice remains the first cause of destruction of the region's forest cover, particularly within the regions surrounding the Park. The two principal factors that (1) limit the control of destructive practices and (2) apply alternative practices to *tavy* are to be found, first, in the marginal economic conditions and poverty of the villagers who depend heavily on cultivating new *tavy* parcels of land to survive and, second, in the resistance of the local population (particularly the *Tanala* population) to abandon this ancestral practice inherited from their forefathers, and whose abandonment would signify the loss of their cultural identity (Rakotoson 1994; Lappalainen 2002; Freudenberger 2008). Government officials, authorities and NGO respondents were unanimous in denouncing their lack of resources to convince people to change their practices and to support forest rangers in their enforcement of protected area boundaries.

The cutting and exploitation of tropical hardwood is the second most important cause of forest cover degradation in the surrounding areas and within the National Park itself (see Figure 2). It is the forest cover of the intermediate zone that is the most exposed to human pressure and to the commercial exploitation of wood (CMP 2002; Freudenberger 2008). These forests are the areas with the greatest biological diversity. Furthermore, an increase in human intrusion into the virgin forests results in a progressive deterioration in the composition of the primal vegetation and leads little by little to the mutation of the ecosystem, which will eventually become similar to the zones surrounding the Park (Ramahaitra 2006).

The large scale of the Park and the lack of resources available to PNM to monitor and enforce the regulations enable illegal exploitation of the forest despite support from several NGOs present on the ground (e.g. inhabitants of some villages travel up to 15 km into the Park to cut wood for making charcoal or leave their zebu to roam free in the Park). Although far from presenting an exhaustive portrait of the causes of the degradation of natural resources in the eastern eco-region and in the Ranomafana

National Park, the above issues (i.e. scale and lack of resources) highlight two fundamental elements in our analysis. On the one hand, we observe that the coupling 'poverty-migration' exerts significant pressure on the natural resources, particularly on forest resources. Our interviews with the rural population have revealed that this has added an important political dimension: to obtain electoral support, representatives of local authorities often 'turn a blind eye' to the practices of people in the Park – some have even been encouraged to settle there, thus negating (or at least challenging) the efforts of NGOs and local tourism operators. On the other hand, the solution favoured by structural adjustment based on farming exports seems to also increase the pressure put on natural resources, whether these resources are officially protected or not. It is particularly under these conditions that ecotourism represents a possible compromise between (1) the need for local sources of income, (2) the balance of payment equilibrium (structural adjustment) and (3) the protection of natural resources that are essential for building up the 'tourist supply'.

These conditions are part of both the liberalization programme implemented in Madagascar in the 1980s and the definition of 'development' proposed by the World Bank – which is based largely on an 'opportunity to seize' – and they are responsible for poor economic growth, particularly in sub-Saharan Africa (Killick *et al.* 2001). It is within this logic that we find the development of ecotourism in Madagascar: a relationship that links the economy, the environment and the fight against poverty, which clearly involves rural inhabitants at every level. This 'development model' attempts to balance the growth of exports (ecotourism) that helps to reduce poverty and protects biodiversity (by providing employment to the rural poor). This, in turn, raises a number of issues that our exploratory interviews have touched upon: Which export sectors must be favoured in a context of declining terms of trade? To what extent does the 'rational use' of resources (i.e. cost-effective use, a fundamental value of the model) fit into the relationship between space and land that sustain farmers in Madagascar (their own fundamental values)? By what means do you 'convince' rural inhabitants to change their production methods and why have they not done so already? How should the start-up costs be financed in order to ensure the transition from extensive to intensive agriculture? And the costs of even more complex projects such as the transition from the primary sector (agriculture) to the tertiary sector (tourism)? In Madagascar in general, and in the region of Ranomafana in particular, the answer to these questions is sought through the logic of the fundamental values of structural adjustment, in which ecotourism is instrumental.

Ecotourism as a Poverty Alleviation and Conservation Strategy: A Few Lessons

During the last 15 years, Madagascar as a tourist destination has become increasingly associated with ecotourism. The profile study on non-resident tourists shows that 55% of foreign travellers chose ecotourism as their first choice of activity during their stay in Madagascar. Ecotourism remains the fastest-growing segment of the

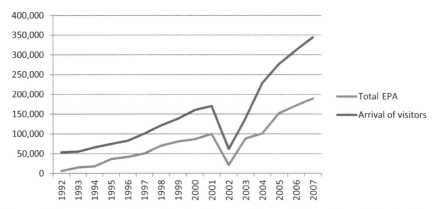

Figure 3. The evolution of Entry fees into Protected Areas (EPA) and the arrival of visitors to Madagascar (1992–2007). *Sources*: Parcs Nationaux de Madagascar; Office National du Tourisme de Madagascar; Ministère de l'Environnement, des Eaux, des Forêts et du Tourisme.

tourism industry, with an annual increase of 10%–30%, compared with an overall 4% increase in a year for Madagascar as a whole (Christie & Crompton 2003; ONT 2008). Closely dependent on the network of existing Protected Areas that make up the 'raw material' of the tourist product, one can understand that the various causes of degradation that we have presented constitute economic activities that 'compete' with ecotourism and represent a major problem for ANGAP-PNM (which spent considerable efforts increasing the attractiveness of sites having a high ecotourism potential). Thus, we find that a total of 150,000 visitors were registered in 2009 (a decrease of more than half from 2008 figures), 86% of whom were concentrated in the six most important National Parks of the network: *Montagne d'Ambre*, *Ankarana*, *Andasibe*, *Bemaraha*, *Isalo* and *Ranomafana* (ESAPP 2005; ONT 2010).

Although the statistics on the National Parks entries have been compiled by the ANGAP-PNM since 1992 (Figure 3), it seems difficult to have similar statistical data from 2005 onwards. However, with partial data released in 2008 and 2009 as well as the historical data from 1998 to 2004, it is possible to make a portrait of the importance of ecotourism in Madagascar. Thus, the data show that, proportionately, tourists' interest in visiting the Protected Areas is still present. Nevertheless, the number of entries into Protected Areas does not follow the increase in the number of tourist arrivals. For instance, the political instability that prevailed in 2001–2002 (especially evident in the first 6 months of 2002) had a negative effect on tourist arrivals, specifically for ecotourism. In 2004, the proportion of ecotourists declined, representing only 44.19% of international tourist arrivals; nevertheless, the desired number of 100,000 ecotourists in 1 year was attained for the first time during this same year, with 101,102 visitor entries into the Protected Areas. According to our estimates, on average, the Visitors of Protected Areas (VPA) represent approximately half of the tourist arrivals in Madagascar. Given that the number of tourists was 160,000 in 2009, the VPA would account for 75,000 (compared with 175,000 in 2008), a performance level comparable with 1998 which results from 2009 political instability (ONT 2010; Madagascar Hotels Online 2011).

The great majority of tourists and ecotourists come from Europe, representing more than 72% of arrivals. If we include the regional market (mainly from La Réunion), the French market only accounts for 70% of tourist arrivals in Madagascar. As mentioned previously, the historical data indicate that, independently of the countries of origin of the visitors, the proportion of the VPA represents altogether half of all international arrivals. According to the available data, of the 47 Protected Areas for which ANGAP-PNM keeps statistics, 10 or so Protected Areas account for 96% of the ecotourism market. In this context, tourism itself could constitute a potential threat to the Protected Areas. The three National Parks most visited are *Andasibe*, *Isalo* and Ranomafana – mainly because of their accessibility but also because they are on the *Antananarivo-Toliaro* axis (the road most frequented by tourists). According to the Madagascar Ecotourism Development Master Plan (*Plan directeur du Développement de l'Écotourisme à Madagascar*) – a complement to the tourism master plan and sectorial study drawn up by the World Bank – Madagascar's positioning as an ecotourism destination depends on a number of factors: a multiplication of investment efforts in ecotourism infrastructures; the adoption of an aggressive marketing policy in the principal markets from which tourists are drawn; and a multi-disciplinary and participative approach, particularly with local communities, in elaborating the ecotourism offer (ESAPP 2005). These objectives have been articulated in three principal phases of development which cover the period 2004–2013, with the goal of increasing the number of ecotourists from 100,000 (the 2004 figures) to 370,000 in 2013. Moreover, the number of eco-lodges should rise from 6 to 57 in the period between 2004 and 2013, for an average capacity of 3,400 additional beds. The cumulative amount of investments needed to support these objectives is calculated at US$ 16 million. Current political instability has had dramatic consequences on the tourism industry in Madagascar, and although the representatives of the Tourism Department and the national office of tourism remain confident in the ability of the tourism industry to rebound following the crisis, the objectives laid down for 2013 appear unrealistic.

This brief description of ecotourism in Madagascar allows us to note another element that supports our analysis. While tourism has evolved positively during the decades we have studied, it is far from being an 'axis of development' for the Madagascar economy that is sufficient to represent a real alternative to the destructive practices we have described. Under these conditions, should it be acknowledged that ecotourism is not, in fact, economically significant? If so, why is ecotourism presented as a preferred means for resolving the economic growth objective, alleviating poverty and protecting Madagascar's biodiversity? The case of the Ranomafana National Park shows that, despite 12,354 visiting tourists in 2009, ecotourism creates few local employment opportunities, and these are opportunities mainly for guides who speak other languages (generally French or English) and who have a level of education that allows them to understand the biodiversity characteristics of the National Parks. These jobs are also very well paid compared with the standard of living of public servants, for example. Among the park guides who were interviewed, one (male) interviewee's situation clearly revealed this pay discrepancy: during the tourist season (June–October), he earned five times more than his wife, an English teacher in a public school. However, this example should not disguise the lack of access to these jobs for local people. The interviews conducted around the Protected Area suggest that daily inflow of new migrants to the zone around the Park does not allow ecotourism to absorb (even marginally) job seekers, who thus rapidly revert to survival techniques and anarchic use of resources, thereby threatening the integrity of the forest and the long-term survival of ecotourism activities. In fact, the overall receipts generated by tourism in the Protected Areas are estimated at US$ 2.1 million in 2008, representing 2.5% of total tourism receipts for Madagascar (Madagascar Hotels Online 2011). According to the ONE, the overall receipts generated in 2000 by tourism in the Protected Areas were US$ 5.8 million, representing only 4.7% of total tourism receipts for Madagascar (ONE 2002). This estimate includes the entry fees to the Protected Area (*Droits d'entrée à l'Aire protégée*: DEAP), the services of guides, porters, various purchases and lodging on an average stay estimated to be 2.4 days (Table 2).

The amount of the DEAPs corresponds to about 7.6% of the operating and maintenance expenses of the Protected Areas, thus representing an insignificant contribution by tourists visiting these zones. Essentially, the financial contribution of ecotourists who visit National Parks such as Ranomafana (which occupies the third place in terms

Table 2. Entrance fees to PNM

Entry fee rates to the Protected Areas (DEAP) according to category.
Categories of Protected Areas
A: Isalo – Ranomafana – Andasibe/Mantadia – Montagne d'Ambre – Ankarana – Bemaraha – Ankarafantsika
B: Protected Areas open to visitors that are not included in category A.
Entry fees (in US$ at 23 August 2011 rates):
• Adult foreigner

Length of stay	1 day	2 days	3 days	4 days
Category A	12.79$	18.93$	20.47$	25.59$
Category B	5.12$	7.68$	10.23$	12.79$

• Adult, non-foreigner: 0.52$/day/park
• Child (foreigner or non-foreigner): 0.10$/day/park

Note: The majority of National Park visits last between 1 and 2 days. Rates accurate for 29 August 2011: 1,947 MGA (Ariary) = 1 US$.
Source: http://www.parcs-madagascar.com/madagascar-national-parks.php?Navigation = 30.

of the number of visitors) fails to cover the costs of managing and protecting the site, as declared by ANGAP-PNM and the Water and Forests Department. However, interviews with public administrators in the capital of Madagascar and in park locations confirmed that 50% of the amount of DEAP allocated to finance local operations of PNM (personnel and material) has never been paid to ANGAP-PNM. In addition, the direct economic benefits of ecotourism at the local level remain minimal since local employment opportunities are often appropriated by people who come from other regions of the country, where access to education and training programmes are more readily available, and who are thus better qualified for the available positions. The rural zones around the Protected Areas shelter populations with low levels of tourism skills, with illiteracy rates often as high as 90%. The principal economic benefits largely correspond to the occasional increase in the sale of local products. Few ecotourism operators are actively involved with local communities, particularly when it comes to providing training (Paquier 2002).

Our interviews ultimately showed that perception, opportunity and/or the ecotourism 'problem' are established at the individual level. In the context of survival, individuals are prepared to make many compromises to improve personal conditions. However, the characteristics and perceptions common to all members of the rural population allow us not only to focus on the relevance of such a group but also to identify some limitations concerning the mobilization of this sector. One such aspect concerns the relationship of the rural population with its environment (or its living space). In rural areas of Madagascar, space is not only inhabited and used, but it is also an object of thought, material for (and a source of) representational systems which, in turn, shape perceptions, attitudes and behaviour. This means that ecotourism initiatives, in a park such as Ranomafana, that modify and remodel space have an impact on the social, cultural and economic worlds of rural populations. For example, we found *fady* (taboos) places that directly affect the relationship between physical space and the world of the ancestors. This is certainly a fundamental value for the rural population that seems difficult to reconcile with tourism development and promotion initiatives.

Conclusion

This paper does not claim to provide a definitive view of the management of natural resources in Madagascar. The number of actors involved, the diversity and the breakdown of natural resources found on the island continent, and the complexity of threats to the biodiversity necessarily limited the scope of the analysis that we have studied. While we have focused on the precise case of the Ranomafana National Park, our approach has remained macroscopic – in other words, we have sought to present key elements needed to better understand the stakes involved in the degradation of natural resources in Madagascar. To achieve this, we have explored how the protection of natural resources is handled in Madagascar as well as the principal causes of degradation. By focusing on the specific case of Ranomafana, we have shown how the environment, economic growth and the fight against poverty represent a 'development framework' where the rural poor population is instrumental (Scheyvens & Russell 2012). Considering the causes of degradation that we have described, the positive impact, both economically and environmentally, of tourism generally and of ecotourism specifically appears to have been highly exaggerated. As for the protection of natural resources, Bruce A. Larson (1994: 681) has suggested: ' . . . regardless of the success of actually developing a reasonable tourism policy . . . the potential country-level benefits of tourism will not have a direct impact on changing local incentives for deforestation'. So why has ecotourism been presented as an important means for conservation?

The answer to this question depends on the fundamental values that underpin ecotourism. If sponsors (international financial institutions, the Madagascar government, international and local NGOs) have a functional coherence based on a joint model of development, the position and interest of the rural population facing ecotourism is not as clear. The heterogeneity and the lack of resources do not allow this population to have a clear and unified position towards ecotourism development in protected areas, and this impacts the rural population's ability to engage in actions to mitigate the effects (and implementation) of these developments. A gap between the definition and the use of space and resources, as well as fundamental values, and between promoters and rural populations is a major limitation to the power structures that reinforce the implementation of ecotourism. Another potential barrier to engagement is economic, which is directly related to sponsors' fundamental values. It is not enough to invest in a sector – whose social and environmental impacts are also important – to create jobs (skilled or unskilled) that few villagers will be able to occupy. The logic of the fundamental values underlying the project is broken if the rural poor cannot take advantage of opportunities presented by ecotourism – particularly in terms of jobs – and they will be unable to improve their living conditions, an essential faction to support poverty reduction as well as – in the logic of the promoters – the protection of natural resources.

The main question posed to respondents was simple: In what ways could ecotourism be part of a strategy to safeguard natural resources in the Ranomafana National Park? We have shown how the proposed response is part of a particular conceptualization of development that links low agricultural productivity, poverty and the degradation of natural resources. The underlying process has therefore not resolved the problem of protecting the environment through ecotourism, but has instead proposed a set of assumptions about the fundamental values and the basic structures of power as a result. This has helped us to better understand how these values have allowed developers to present ecotourism as an opportunity for the rural population to grasp. Our analysis has shown that there is a considerable gap between the living conditions – in relation to the land and living space in particular – experienced daily by farmers, and the highly rationalized discourses of developers, both from Madagascar and elsewhere. Under such conditions, is participation and ownership of problems and solutions (with respect to poverty, agricultural production and degradation of natural resources) possible in a North/South relationship where resources are particularly unequal and references not commonly shared? This paper has shown that the rural population is often placed in the unbearable role of being both the cause of the problems and the main beneficiaries targeted by initiatives that make a project such as Ranomafana ecotourism a necessary survival opportunity, albeit an opportunity that few have the chance to seize.

Acknowledgements

The author would like to thank the anonymous reviewers – this paper is much improved as a result of their comments and suggestions. In addition, the author would like to thank Sara Cameron for her contribution to the revision and translation of this paper and to Haja Ramahatra for research assistance and figures.

References

Andrianambinimina, D. (2007) Évaluation participative de la durabilité des sites d'écotourisme. Une application au Parc national de Ranomafana, in: C. Chaboud, G. Froger, & P. Méral (Eds) *Madagascar Face Aux Enjeux du Développement Durable. Des Politiques Environnementales à l'Action Collective Locale*, pp. 135–155 (Paris: Karthala).

ANGAP, Agence Nationale pour la Gestion des Aires Protégées (2001) *Plan de Gestion du Réseau National des Aires protégées de Madagascar, (MINENVEF) Ministère de l'Environnement et des Eaux et Forêts*, (Antananarivo: ANGAP).

Arbache, J., Go, D. S., & Page, J. (2008) *Is Africa's Economy at a Turning Point?* Policy Research Working Paper No. 4519, Washington, DC: World Bank.

Banque Mondiale (1994) *L'ajustement Structurel en Afrique: Réformes, Résultats et Chemin à Parcourir* (Washington, DC: Banque Mondiale).

Brady, N. C. (1996) Alternatives to slash-and-burn: A global imperative, *Agriculture, Ecosystems, and Environment*, 58, pp. 3–11.

Campbell, B. (2005) *Qu'allons-nous Faire des Pauvres?* (Paris: L'Harmattan).

Carrière, S. M. & Bidaud, C. (2012) En quête de naturalité: Représentations scientifiques de la nature et conservation de la biodiversité, in: H. R. Ramiarantsoa, C. Blanc-Pamard, & F. Pinton (Eds) *Géopolitique et Environnement à Madagascar. Normes, Acteurs et Territoires*, pp. 33–59 (Paris: Éditions IRD), in press.

CEPF, Critical Ecosystem Partnership Fund (2000) *Ecosystem Profile: Madagascar and Indian Ocean Islands*. Available at http://www.cepf.net/where_we_work/regions/africa/madagascar/ecosystem_profile/Pages/default.aspx (acessed 7 November 2005).

Chavagneux, C. (1998) Peut-on maîtriser la mondialisation ? Une introduction aux approches d'économie politique internationale, *Économies et Sociétés*, 34, p. 25.

Christie, I. T. & Crompton, E. D. (2003) *République de Madagascar. Étude du Secteur Tourisme*. Africa Region Working Paper Series No. 63, Washington, DC: Banque Mondiale.

Cleaver, K. & Schreiber, G. A. (1998) *Inverser la Spirale. Les Interactions Entre la Population, L'agriculture et L'environnement en Afrique Subsaharienne* (Washington, DC: Banque Mondiale).

CMP, Comité Multi-local de Planification (2002) *Rapport Technique Final sur L'inventaire Biologique du Parc National de Ranomafana et du Couloir Forestier qui le Relie au Parc National D'Andringitra* (Antananarivo: CMP).

Cornia, G. A., Jolly, R., & Stewart, F. (1987) *L'ajustement à Visage Humain: Protéger les Groupes Vulnérables et Favoriser la Croissance* (Paris: Publié pour l'Unicef par les Éditions Économica).

ESAPP, Eastern and Southern Africa Partnership Programme (2005) *Développement de L'écotourisme Dans la Région de Mananara-Nord et du Triangle Bleu Rapport Final.* Documentation ESAPP E604, (Antananarivo: Ecotourism Development for Everlasting Nature (EDENA)/Development Environment Consult (DEC)).

FAO, United Nations Food and Agriculture Organization (2005) *Global Forest Resources Assessment* (Rome: FAO).

FEM, Fonds pour l'Environnement Mondial (2005) *Troisième Bilan Global: Vers des Résultats pour L'environnement,* version analytique (Washington, DC: FEM).

Freudenberger, K. (2010) *Paradise Lost? Lessons from 25 years USAID Environment Programs in Madagascar* (Washington, DC: USAID).

Freudenberger, M. S. (2008) *Ecoregional Conservation and the Ranomafana – Andringitra Forest Corridor: A Retrospective Interpretation of Achievements, Missed Opportunities, and Challenges for the Future, version 2* (Washington, DC: USAID).

INSTAT, Institut National de la Statistique (2000) *Document Intérimaire de Stratégie de Réduction de la Pauvreté* (Antananarivo, République Malgache: INSTAT).

Killick, T., Kayizzi-Mugerwa, S., Savane, M.-A., & White, H. N. (2001) *African Poverty at the Millennium: Causes, Complexities, and Challenges* (Washington, DC: World Bank).

Kull, C. (2004) *Isle of Fire: The Political Ecology of Landscape Burning in Madagascar* (Chicago, IL: University of Chicago Press).

Kull, C. (2012) L'écologie politique et la question environnementale malgache, in: H. R. Ramiarantsoa, C. Blanc-Pamard, & F. Pinton (Eds) *Géopolitique et Environnement à Madagascar. Normes, Acteurs et Territoires,* pp. 109–133 (Paris: Éditions IRD), in press.

Lappalainen, A. (2002) Combining conservation and development – Case of Ranomafana National Park, Madagascar, Helsinki, Master thesis, University of Helsinki.

Larson, B. A. (1994) Changing the economics of environmental degradation in Madagascar: Lessons from the national environmental action plan process, *World Development,* 22(5), pp. 671–689.

Madagascar Hotels Online (2011) *Investissements Touristiques 2009 et Activités 2010 pour le Tourisme à Madagascar.* Available at http://www.madagascar-hotels-online.com/actualites-tourisme/actualite-economique-touristique/181-investissements-2009-activites-2010-tourisme-madagascar.html (accessed 11 May 2011).

MEEFT, Ministère de l'Environnement et des Forêts (2008) *Déforestation, République de Madagascar.* Available at http://www.meeft.gov.mg/index.php?option=com_content&task=view&id=7&Itemid=8 (accessed 27 July 2010).

MEF, Ministère de l'Environnement et des Forêts (2009) *Données et Statistiques Environnementales de Madagascar, République de Madagascar* (Antananarivo: MEF).

MEF, Ministère de l'Environnement et des Forêts & UNEP, United Nations Environment Programme (2010) *Quatrième Rapport National de la Convention sur la Diversité Biologique* (Antananarivo: MEF and UNEP).

MINENVEF, Ministère de l'Environnement, des Eaux et Forêts (2005) *Troisième Rapport National de la convention sur la diversité biologique, République de Madagascar* (Antananarivo: MINENVEF).

ONE, Office National pour l'Environnement (2002) *Rapport D'achèvement du PE 2, République de Madagascar* (Antananarivo: ONE).

ONT, Office National du Tourisme (2008) *Les Statistiques 2008 du Tourisme.* Available at http://www.info-tourisme-madagascar.com/meft_tous.htm (accessed 26 May 2011).

ONT, Office National du Tourisme (2010) *Les Statistiques D'une Décennie*. Available at http://www. info-tourisme-madagascar.com/meft.htm (accessed 27 May 2011).

ONU, Organisation des Nations Unies & République de Madagacar (2003) *Bilan Commun des Pays (CCA) – Madagascar* (Antananarivo: ONU).

Paquier, F. (2002) *L'écotourisme à Madagascar Dans le Contexte de la Mondialisation* (New York: PNUD).

Peters, J. (1994) Reconciling conflicts between people and parks at Ranomafana, Madagascar: Management interventions and legislative alternatives. Présenté dans le cadre du National Symposium on Indigenous Knowledge and Contemporary Social Issues, 3–5 Mars, Tampa, University of South Florida.

Rakotoson, L. (1994) *La Rencontre du Décret de Création du Parc National de Ranomafana avec les Coutumes et Traditions Locales, Université de Fianarantsoa* (Fianarantsoa: Université de Fianarantsoa).

Ramahaitra, T. (2006) The effects of anthropogenic disturbances on the structure and composition of rain forest vegetation, *Tropical Resources Bulletin*, 25, pp. 32–36.

Rarivomanana, P. (2000) *L'Étude prospective du secteur forestier en Afrique (FOSA)* (Antananarivo: Ministère de l'Environnement, des Eaux et Forêts).

République de Madagascar (2006) *Plan D'action Madagascar 2007–2012. Un Plan Audacieux pour le Développement Rapide* (Antananarivo: République de Madagascar).

Sarrasin, B. (1999) *Ajustement Structurel et Lutte Contre la Pauvreté en Afrique. La Banque Mondiale Face à la Critique* (Paris: L'Harmattan).

Sarrasin, B. (2005) La construction des problèmes environnementaux en Afrique subsaharienne: La mise en place d'un 'diagnostic de Washington sur les ressources naturelles', *Revue Canadienne D'études Du Développement*, XXVI(4), pp. 799–815.

Scheyvens, R. & Russell, M. (2012) Tourism, land tenure and poverty alleviation in Fiji, *Tourism Geographies*, 14(1), pp. 1–25.

Stopford, J., Strange, S., & Henley, J. S. (1991) *Rival States, Rival Firms: Competition for World Market Shares* (Cambridge: Cambridge University Press).

Strange, S. (1996) *The Retreat of the State: The Diffusion of Power in the World Economy* (Cambridge: Cambridge University Press).

Strange, S. (2002) States, firms and diplomacy, in: R. Tooze & C. May (Eds) *Authority and Markets: Susan Strange's Writings on International Political Economy*, pp. 60–67 (Basingstoke: Palgrave Macmillan).

Teivainen, T. (2002) *Enter Economism Exit Politics – Experts, Economic Policy and the Damage to Democracy* (Londres et New York: Zed Books).

Thibaud, B. (2005) *Enjeux et Mutations des Espaces Forestiers Périurbains Dans les Pays du Sud. Exemples Comparés au Mali et à Madagascar, ICoTEM*, Université de Poitier.

Woodwell, J. C., Ramamonjisoa, N., & Sève, J. (2004) *Modélisation de la Perte en Couvert Forestier Dans le Corridor Zahamena-Mantadia, Madagascar. Les Impacts des Interventions de Développement – Implications et Perspectives* (Antananarivo: USAID, United States Agency for International Development).

World Bank (2002) *Building a Sustainable Future: The Africa Region Environment Strategy* (Washington, DC: World Bank).

World Bank (2004) *Poverty Reduction Strategy Paper. Progress Report, Joint Staff Assessment*. Report No. 30036-MG (Washington, DC: World Bank).

World Bank (2009) *Madagascar at a Glance* (Washington, DC: World Bank).

World Bank (2010) *Environment Matters. Toward Sustainable Development, 2009 Annual Review* (Washington, DC: World Bank).

World Bank (2011a) *IBRD Loans and IDA Credits (DOD, Current US$)*. Available at http://data.worldbank. org/indicator/DT.DOD.MWBG.CD (accessed 27 May 2011).

World Bank (2011b) *Madagascar Economic Update: Fiscal Policy – Managing the Present with a Look at the Future* (Washington, DC: World Bank).

Notes on Contributor

Dr Bruno Sarrasin, PhD, UQAM, is Professor at the Department of Urban and Tourism Studies at University of Québec in Montreal (Canada) and a member of the Centre Interdisciplinaire de Recherche en Développement International et Société (CIRDIS) of UQAM. His research interests focus on political economy of development, more specifically in sub-Saharan Africa and the Caribbean.

Collaboration and Partnership Development for Sustainable Tourism

SONYA GRACI

Ryerson University, Toronto, Ontario, Canada

ABSTRACT *For many years, the need to improve sustainability in the tourism industry has been widely recognized. Many destinations have attempted to move toward sustainability, but unfortunately, have been hindered in their attempts by a lack of collaboration among stakeholders that is necessary to support their sustainability agendas. Collaboration, specifically through multi-stakeholder partnerships, has been seen as an effective way to support initiatives in tourism development. Through the lens of Gray's collaboration theory and Selin and Chavez's tourism partnership model, the success of collaboration and partnerships in tourism development on the island of Gili Trawangan, Indonesia, will be examined. Through a multi-method approach consisting of an environmental audit and semi-structured interviews, this paper explores the implementation of a multi-stakeholder partnership. The partnership that has been developed, called the Gili Ecotrust, provides an example of successful collaboration, leading to the implementation of innovative sustainability initiatives on the island.*

Introduction

The island of Gili Trawangan, Indonesia, is a destination that is primarily focused on dive tourism and is currently in the growth stage and rapidly moving toward the consolidation stage of its tourism lifecycle. For many years, Gili Trawangan was primarily underdeveloped; however in the span of the last decade, the selling of land to Westerners has resulted in rapid development. The island community, which is composed of mostly Westerners and local Indonesians, has become increasingly concerned with the state of the environment on the island. Gili Trawangan and its sister islands, Gili Meno and Gili Air, are located in an area with a great deal of marine diversity. The islands are currently located in the West Nusa Dua Marine Park, however this has been largely in name only and has not resulted in any involvement from the provincial government that has authority over the marine park. Despite its marine park status, there has been no implementation of initiatives by the marine park to protect the increasingly threatened marine diversity. Increasing traffic from boats, improper anchoring, rapid development on the island and overuse through fishing, diving and glass bottom boats has led to the fast decline of the marine environment. Tourism development has led to the degradation of the coral reefs, beach erosion and a large amount of rubbish littering the island. Illegal building on the beach and lack of planning has resulted in overcrowding and pressure on the existing infrastructure. In order to combat the effects of tourism development and maintain some ecological integrity on the island, a multi-stakeholder partnership was implemented in 2002. It is through this partnership that the island has attempted to move the sustainability agenda forward. This paper will focus on the progression of this partnership to illustrate how a successful collaboration can be established.

Literature Review

Tourism is often described as one of the world's largest industries on the basis of its contribution to global gross domestic product (GDP), the number of jobs it generates and the number of people it transports. Developing countries currently have only a minority share of the international tourism market (approximately 30%), with this number continuing to grow. International tourism arrivals in developing countries have grown by an average of 9.5% per year since 1990, compared with 4.6% worldwide (Tearfund 2002). In many Lesser Developed Countries (LDCs), tourism is significant to the economy and is generally growing (Tearfund 2002). The contribution that tourism makes to national economies is also far more pronounced in LDCs (United Nations World Tourism Organization [UNWTO] 2006). As many authors and government reports have outlined (World Travel and Tourism Council [WTTC] 1995, 1999; Weaver 2001; UNWTO 2005; Goeldner & Ritchie 2006) and recent events (hurricanes, tropical storms, 2004 Tsunami) have demonstrated, there is a need to move toward more sustainable forms of development to ensure long-term viability. Many small islands, particularly those with warm climates, depend heavily on sun, sea and sand as tourist attractions, and it is these resources that their industries have traditionally been based upon. Many of the problems that small islands face relate directly to their insular geography and fragile environmental characteristics (Kerr 2005; Scheyvens & Momsen 2008), and although they are benefiting from increased economic gain from tourism, they are also experiencing many negative environmental, economic and social consequences. Some of the issues and impacts affecting destinations include dependency of a host community's economy on tourism; competition; leakage; government debt to finance development; loss of habitat areas and resources due to development and pollution; decline in biodiversity of species and ecosystems; erosion; loss of natural and archeological heritage in the face of rapid expansion; sea, land, noise and air pollution; increased congestion and strains on infrastructure; encroachment of buildings, facilities and roads to the coastline, crowding and pressure on services; and displacement of the local population (Graci

& Dodds 2010). The characteristic complexities related to planning, development and management in island destinations give rise to resource management and governance issues, particularly relating to the potential success of sustainable development planning and strategies (Douglas 2006; Scheyvens & Russell 2012). It is important for small island states, dependent on tourism, to take control and manage their tourism industries. Far too many islands are facing detrimental effects from poor planning and governance. Many islands are facing beach erosion, water pollution, waste management issues, energy crises, coral reef destruction, acculturation and leakage (Graci & Dodds 2010). Strategies to influence tourism development can and have been implemented in some small islands with success. In order to overcome the challenges with managing island destinations in a sustainable manner, innovative initiatives can help to identify practical ways in which to move forward. Innovative initiatives can consist of varying forms, and in several destinations have enabled the progression of sustainability through the principles of long-term planning, collaboration, education, the conception of dialogue and creating a cohesive vision for the destination. To move toward sustainability, island destinations require the participation of the local people, the definition of long-term strategies, a carefully designed tourism plan, intensive capacity building and training of both national public officials and management in the destination and infrastructure support (Hashimoto 2002; Fennell 2003; UNWTO 2006; Graci & Dodds 2010).

Collaboration is considered to be essential in moving the tourism industry toward sustainability. Throughout the literature, cross-sector partnerships are recommended for their likelihood to result in sustainable development outcomes (Selin 1999; Bramwell & Alletorp 2001; Bramwell & Lane 2005). A central role for sustainable destination management involves bringing together different organizations in order to establish common goals and create a framework for joint action (Berresford 2004). The UNWTO revealed that public–private partnerships are the key principle for successful destination management (Foggin & Münster 2003). Participants that have traditionally acted in isolation from each other need to learn how to cooperate (Halme 2001). As no one organization does, or can deliver tourism development, a collaborative multi-stakeholder approach is necessary.

Collaboration through partnerships is described as a loosely coupled system of organizations and individuals that belong to various public and private sectors, who come together in order to reach certain goals, unattainable by the partners individually (Selin 1999; Fadeeva 2005). Collaboration is defined by Gray (1989: 5) as 'a process through which parties who see different aspects of a problem can constructively explore their differences and search for solutions that go beyond their own limited vision of what is possible.' Therefore, a collaborative alliance is an inter-organizational effort to address problems too intricate to be effectively resolved by independent action (Gray & Wood 1991). Collaboration is the evolving process of alliances working together in a problem domain (Gray 1989; Medeiros de Araujo & Bramwell 2002; Plummer et al. 2006; Jamal & Stronza 2009). The process has the potential to allow organizations to pool their knowledge, share expertise, capital and other resources (Plummer *et al.* 2006). The groups working together may therefore gain a competitive advantage. In addition, policies, implementation and enforcement of plans and regulations resulting from collaboration may be more accepted by individuals and organizations who were involved in creating them (Medeiros de Araujo & Bramwell 2002). It has also been argued that this practice of collaboration is part of a moral obligation to involve affected parties throughout any decision-making processes (Medeiros de Araujo & Bramwell 2002).

An inclusive collaborative approach has the ability to create social capital and thus contributes to the development of more sustainable forms of tourism (Kernel 2005). As indicated by Carbone (2005), a true partnership between the producer (the environment, the local culture and the people), the supplier (the tourism industry) and the consumer (the tourist) is critical for integrating community needs with the sustainable use of the environment while providing profits to the stakeholders involved. It is through partnerships that organizations, government and communities are able to collectively address concerns and determine mutually agreed upon objectives that will benefit all stakeholders involved, thus embarking on a more sustainable approach to tourism development. The purpose of a partnership is to eventually produce consensus and harmony that will lead to new opportunities and innovative solutions. Partnerships must include the views of all stakeholders within a destination and identify various roles and responsibilities for each stakeholder so that they can contribute to the overarching goal of moving the destination toward a more sustainable management of tourism. The key elements of a partnership are that all

- stakeholders are interdependent;
- solutions emerge by dealing constructively with difference;
- joint ownership of decisions is involved;
- stakeholders assume collective responsibility for the future direction of the domain; and
- partnerships remain a dynamic, emergent process (Gray 1989: 11 in Selin 1999: 262).

These key elements are the underlying principles for a multi-stakeholder partnership, which provides a cohesive environmental vision, enabling the tourism destination to focus resources, share information, increase environmental and social action in the destination, learn from the leaders and ultimately protect the resources that sustain the destination. Collaboration leads to the sharing and implementing of ideas as well as creative methods to deal with solutions.

Gray (1996: 61–65) outlined a three-phase framework for the collaboration process. The first phase, for problem setting, requires that multiple stakeholders agree on what the problem is, and that the problem is important enough to work with others to find a solution. In addition, this phase must ensure that all stakeholders are included to fully understand the process. If key stakeholders are excluded from this phase, Gray argues that this could cause technical or political problems during the implementation phase of collaboration (Gray 1989; Medeiros de Araujo & Bramwell 2002; Jamal & Stronza 2009). The second phase, of direction setting, focuses on establishing rules, groups and agreements between the stakeholders. In addition, phase two requires the exploration of options through discussing the interests and values of each group, then finally reaching an agreement to proceed with a particular course of action (Medeiros de Araujo & Bramwell 2002; Jamal & Stronza 2009). The last phase of collaboration sees the implementation of the chosen course of action, requiring support and structure, including monitoring for compliance (Medeiros de Araujo & Bramwell 2002; Jamal & Stronza 2009).

Although collaboration theory has many potential advantages, there are some important difficulties and obstacles involved. Collaboration requires frequent and regular meetings involving discussion and decision-making with various individuals or organizations (Medeiros de Araujo & Bramwell 2002). This type of demanding schedule can be problematic for many who wish to be involved. It is possible that financial and time constraints can be difficult to overcome, creating a barrier to participation in regular meetings (Medeiros de Araujo & Bramwell 2002). Therefore, certain groups may dislike or refuse to work together thereby hindering the collaboration process (Medeiros de Araujo & Bramwell 2002; Jamal & Stronza 2009).

The application of collaboration theory in tourism planning, management and development has become very prevalent over the past decade to help manage emerging environmental issues: climate change, biodiversity loss, resource depletion and impacts from globalization (Selin 1999; Plummer *et al.* 2006; Jamal & Stronza 2009). Since tourism is a complex industry that impacts several groups (Hardy & Beeton 2001; Medeiros de Araujo & Bramwell 2002; Jamal & Stronza 2009), this poses a challenge in terms of implementing collaboration (Medeiros de Araujo & Bramwell 2002). Specifically in tourism, each group will differ in terms of their interests at a local, regional or national scale as well as their influence over decision-making (Jamal & Stronza 2009).

Selin and Chavez (1995) developed a model of the evolution of tourism partnerships based on Gray's seminal work. They proposed that tourism partnerships progress through five stages: antecedents, problem setting, direction setting, structuring and outcomes (Selin & Chavez 1995; Plummer *et al.* 2006). Figure 1 outlines Selin and Chavez (1995) tourism partnership model.

Selin and Chavez's (1995) model begins with an antecedent that causes the partnership to be initiated. Crisis, such as serious marine biodiversity loss in a dive tourism destination, is frequently an antecedent that initiates tourism partnerships. In addition to a crisis, a broker or convener may initiate the process. From this environmental context, partnerships evolve through problem setting, direction setting and structuring, resulting in the outcomes of the partnership (Selin & Chavez 1995). Throughout this model, it is evident that a common vision among stakeholders is an important

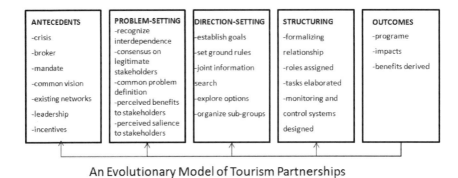

Figure 1. Tourism partnership model. *Source:* Selin and Chavez 1995: 848.

aspect of tourism partnership formation. Existing professional or social networks helps naturally develop relationships and expand their past or present work toward the goals of the partnership (Selin & Chavez 1995). A strong-willed, enthusiastic leader is often the catalyst for partnership development in tourism, as are incentives (including grants) and the vested interest of stakeholders (Selin & Chavez 1995). Areas that are likely to experience successful partnership development have a strong sense of community, which helps motivate participation in the partnership (Selin & Chavez 1995). Small islands are thought to be ideal settings for partnership collaboration as they commonly have a strong sense of community, along with existing networks.

Collaboration through partnership development involves initiating dialogue and creating relationships between stakeholders in order to tackle a common issue. Each stakeholder brings forth individual strengths such as knowledge, expertise and capital, and is more effective as part of a joint effort rather than an individual one. By working together, stakeholders can exchange information, learn from one another, develop innovative policies, adapt successfully to a changing environment and channel energy toward a collective good (Carr *et al.* 1998; Kernel 2005).

This paper utilizes Gray's (1989) collaboration theory and Selin and Chavez's (1995) model to examine collaboration in tourism development on the island of Gili Trawangan, Indonesia. On this island, they have utilized stakeholder engagement and planning to develop a multi-stakeholder partnership aimed at addressing sustainability, resulting in success with the implementation of several innovative initiatives.

Study Area

Gili Trawangan is a small island located among the Gili Islands, off the coast of Lombok in Indonesia, in a designated marine protected area, the West Nusa Dua

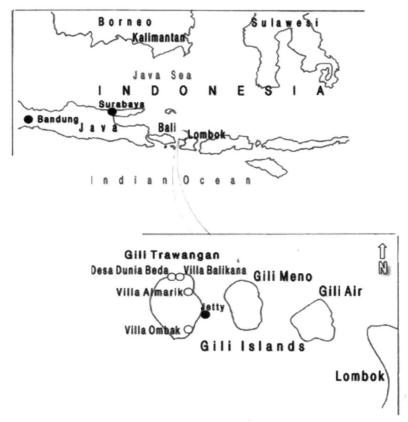

Figure 2. Map of Gili Trawangan, Indonesia. *Source:* Graci and Dodds 2010: 122.

Marine Park. Figure 2 identifies the location of Gili Trawangan in relation to other islands in Indonesia.

Gili Trawangan is approximately three by two kilometers in area, has low-lying topography with a small hill to the south, rising to 72 meters above sea level (Hampton 1998). Gili Trawangan is the most developed of all three Gili Islands (the other two islands being the newly developed Gili Air and the mostly undeveloped Gili Meno). Gili Trawangan has an approximate population of 474 families, composed of roughly 1,900 local people, along with numerous expatriates living on the island (Graci 2007). The majority of land use on the island is related to tourism, with the remainder being coconut plantation and small fields of agricultural crops and livestock. In recent years, however, the majority of undeveloped land is quickly being sold and developed, drastically increasing the amount of people who live and visit the island. Gili Trawangan is a sun, sand and sea destination, with tourism being the dominant

31

economic activity on the island, as more than 80% of the families on Gili Trawangan are employed by tourism in some form (Graci 2007). The main tourism season is June–September with smaller peaks in December, January and February (Hampton 1998; Graci 2007). Gili Trawangan is not a very developed tourism destination in terms of mass tourism resorts, infrastructure or services. The main tourists on Gili Trawangan are backpackers and dive tourists, but as the island is rapidly developing and more accommodations are being built, this is changing. Previously there were only two high-end resorts and few mid-level accommodations on the island, but as of 2010, several new mid- and high-end small-scale accommodations were being built. Island transportation consists of non-motorized sources such as bicycles and cidomos (horse drawn carts), with mostly unsealed dirt roads and few paved roads. The island has limited fresh water shipped in barrels from the mainland on a daily basis. Only the high-end resorts, mid-level accommodations and restaurants use fresh water (Hampton 1998; Graci 2007). The island's energy source is based on a generator and there are many power outages throughout the course of a day. In the last few years, there has been an increase in the number of daily boats bringing tourists to the island, with direct transport from Bali. This has changed the nature of tourism on the island, as a more diverse clientele has begun to visit. Numerous accommodations have pools, there is horseback riding offered on the island and several high-end and culturally diverse dining establishments have opened catering to more of the mass tourist culture. These recent changes have resulted in the island beginning to move from the development stage to the consolidation stage of the tourism lifecycle.

Methodology

This paper is based upon fieldwork that was conducted in Gili Trawangan, Indonesia, over three visits in May–July 2005, October–November 2005 and December 2007. Research was also conducted in the summer of 2010 but focused on specific aspects of waste management and sea turtle conservation. A case study approach was undertaken for this study that consisted of an in-depth investigation of the issues surrounding tourism development and sustainability in Gili Trawangan. The case study approach presented the opportunity to apply a multi-method approach to a unique setting (Sommer & Sommer 1992). The first phase of this research consisted of undertaking an environmental impact assessment in 2005 to determine the environmental and social impacts occurring through tourism development on the island. In addition, 45 in-depth, semi-structured key informant interviews were conducted with a cross section of stakeholders including the local community, local government, western businesses, local businesses, employees and tourists. The interviews identified the barriers to implementing sustainable tourism initiatives on the island, the history of development and sought to investigate innovative ways to move the sustainability agenda forward. The environmental impact assessment and interviews formed the basis for a sustainable tourism strategy for the island. The strategy recommended the development of a multi-stakeholder partnership and subsequent actions that needed to be addressed. The sustainable tourism strategy was released in February 2006 and formed the basis for the actions that have been implemented on the island. In 2007, follow-up interviews were conducted with 20 of the original stakeholders interviewed in 2005 in addition to 20 interviews with stakeholders that were new to the island but showed an interest in the development of sustainability initiatives. These interviews sought to determine the cause for the slow progression of the implementation of the sustainable tourism strategy and to identify further strategies to ensure ease of implementation. New issues that have developed on the island were discussed. A snowball sampling method was used to recruit key informants for the interviews. This technique is used in social science research for developing a research sample where existing study subjects recruit future subjects from among their acquaintances. This research technique works well as a breadth of key stakeholders can be identified (Sommer & Sommer 1992). Through the various phases of research conducted on the island using multiple methods, a multi-stakeholder partnership was developed and sustainability initiatives were implemented.

Results

This study sought to determine the success of the multi-stakeholder partnership that was developed on Gili Trawangan to guide the implementation of sustainability initiatives. The stakeholders involved prior to and during the implementation of this partnership included representatives from the expatriate and local tourism businesses, local government, and community which includes expatriates living on the island as well as local Indonesians, tourists and employees.

An Evaluation of the Gili Trawangan Multi-Stakeholder Partnership

Challenges to Sustainable Tourism Development

Over the last number of years, Gili Trawangan has faced many challenges regarding sustainable development and maintaining the ecological integrity of the island. The main issues on the island have related to waste management, coral reef degradation, beach erosion, unplanned or unauthorized development, illegal fishing and tension between the westerners living on the island and the locals. It is also riddled with an unresponsive provincial government that does not provide any financial assistance to the island and a corrupt local government that is appointed through a feudal system of ownership versus a democratic election. Many of the locals on the island live in poverty.

In 2002, the Gili Ecotrust was organized by a number of the dive shops on the island. The purpose of the Ecotrust was to collect and manage a dive tax (initially at US$3 per diver and US$1 per snorkeler) which was used to pay local fisherman to stop detrimental fishing practices and to hire a patrol boat for the area. When the Ecotrust was first developed, despite the numerous ideas for how to increase sustainability in Gili Trawangan, and a common belief by a number of business owners that current practices were inadequate, there was a lack of momentum to move forward and implement initiatives. The lack of momentum was a result of the 'pass the buck' mentality, where everyone believed that they were too busy to contribute to the development and implementation of initiatives. Despite the concern that the environment on the island was degraded, several business owners did not want to take responsibility for implementation, especially when it involved time and money. It was evident that several of the business owners on the island had numerous complaints about the management of the environment, yet it was difficult to rally support in terms of volunteer time to manage the systems on the island. For example, only one business owner in conjunction with the local government managed the eco-tax funds to pay the fishermen, a practice that was not looked upon favorably as a sustainable solution by many of the business owners; however, no other solutions were put forth. The business owners felt that it was an ineffective method, as one patrol boat was unable to guard all areas around the island and this did not deter fisherman from the neighboring islands of Bali and Lombok. The payment did not encourage education on the reasons not to fish or skills training for the fisherman, rather just supported inaction.

Another challenge with the Ecotrust was that one person managed the funds and day-to-day workings of the Ecotrust, in addition to running their own successful dive business. It was not plausible for one person to voluntarily in his/her minimal spare time to manage the organization effectively. Despite the ideas and enthusiasm from other stakeholders on the island, no one was willing to take responsibility. This lack of responsibility was evident with the organization of a beach clean-up team that was funded by the Gili Ecotrust. The beach clean-up team was supported by all businesses participating in the Ecotrust; however, without any management, direction or motivation on how to proceed with the clean-up on a regular basis, it quickly ceased (Graci 2007).

Another challenge to sustainability on the island is due to corruption of the local government. On the local level, corruption occurred through the random pricing structure that government-appointed businesses charge in terms of waste collection. Expatriate businesses are charged an inflated rate over local businesses, despite the success or size of the business. These fees are based on personal relationships so that one expatriate business owner can pay up to triple the amount for the same services as another, who has a good relationship with the waste collection agency (Graci 2007). This has led to businesses on the island not wanting to participate in the waste management system. The disparity of policies on the island is dependent upon personal relationships, bribes and government corruption. This has led to the frustration of the stakeholders, particularly in terms of volunteering time and money to implement sustainable tourism initiatives. Many initiatives have been funded independently and several stakeholders felt powerless to oppose the current structure for fear of making their own lives difficult and negatively affecting their business. Physical attributes such as infrastructure, or lack thereof, are also an impediment. Gili Trawangan currently ships in barrels of fresh water on a daily basis to the island. Structures such as sewage treatment plants (sewage is currently either disposed of in homemade septic tanks, to the sea or open pits on the side of the road in the village) cannot be built, as salt water will degrade the infrastructure. In addition, technology continues to be a challenge. Even if initiatives such as solar power or a sewage treatment plant were installed, it would be difficult to fix or adjust technologies due to the remoteness of the island and lack of skill and cost. Space is also an issue on the island, as many businesses would like to install composters to dispose of their own organic waste, but do not have the space available (Graci 2007). Despite the fact that several of the tourists on Gili Trawangan supported a sustainability strategy and have no issue contributing to the eco-tax while diving or snorkeling, many tourists were not necessarily aware of the environmental issues, nor do they factor this into their motivations for visiting this destination. Tourists on Gili Trawangan are party tourists and divers. The majority of tourists are young (18–24 years old) backpackers and due to the inexpensive nature of their experience on this island, do not demand a higher quality of sustainability (Dodds *et al.* 2010). Therefore, the tourists will contribute their one-time fee of US$6 if they are diving or US$1 if they are snorkeling, but will not pay higher premiums for sustainability initiatives nor factor this into their decision when choosing an establishment to eat or stay. They are also satisfied with the status quo and despite attempts at banishing water bottles on the island, still consume water in bottles and contribute to the ever-growing waste problem on the island. This is due to the disconnection of the tourists with the rest of the island, as tourists on Gili Trawangan are not usually exposed to the village or are unaware of any of the issues. As with many paradise islands, tourists are only exposed to the beach, bars, restaurants and diving; however in the recent years, the loss of several of the beaches has led to massive overcrowding on the one beach that is left on the island. Tourists have commented that the island is becoming overcrowded and displeased with the state of the beach. They have also commented on the rubbish on the island, which many times is littered in public areas.

Overcoming Challenges: The Implementation of a Multi-Stakeholder Partnership

Despite the number of challenges that this island is facing, they have moved forward and have implemented a number of innovative initiatives driven by the implementation of a multi-stakeholder partnership.

The Antecedent Stage

In the island of Gili Trawangan, the antecedent to this partnership was the concern among the local community and businesses that the degradation of the environment would lead to the eventual demise of this tourism destination. Due to the crisis that arose because of coral bombing and other detrimental fishing practices, stakeholders joined together to formally manage the crisis. The Ecotrust formally began to monitor illegal fishing through providing financial incentives to fisherman to stop illegal fishing practices and hiring a patrol boat for the area.

Partnerships are also championed by a strong leader whose energy and vision mobilized others to participate (Selin & Chavez 1995). It was due to the vision of one dive shop owner that the Ecotrust was born and continued to gain momentum. As this dive shop owner had a good working relationship with the other stakeholders (such as the locals, other businesses and government), she took charge to manage the Ecotrust in the early years. She managed the collection of funds, holding of meetings, managing complaints and implementing the initiatives until 2007 when an environmental coordinator was hired.

In addition, as it is a very small island, there was a common vision among all stakeholders to protect the resources of the island, as it is their livelihood and home. Partnerships can also be encouraged by providing incentives to potential partners. In order to collaborate on protecting the marine environment, incentives were provided to the fisherman to stop illegal fishing and cease with harmful coral bombing practices as well as to the dive shop owners to participate in order to protect their business investment. As well, the existing networks of the island that result due to living in a small communal space with little development for many years encouraged collaboration.

The Problem-Setting Stage

In the problem-setting stage, consensus is reached on who has a legitimate stake in an issue. Stakeholders start to appreciate the interdependencies that exist among them and realize that problem resolution will require collective action. The participants begin to mutually acknowledge the issue that brings them together. The goal of this stage is to have stakeholders communicate about the issue and eventually act upon it. Having stakeholder involvement ensures that they will remain committed to the process of partnership development.

The problem-setting stage becomes an avenue for dialogue and collaboration among stakeholders, which in the case of Gili Trawangan included the local community, local businesses, expatriate businesses, employees, tourists and local government. Consultation was conducted with all stakeholders to identify the major issues on the island. Communicating about their concerns, stakeholders were able to brainstorm innovative methods to deal with the issues on the island. The consultation identified that waste management, coral reef degradation, beach erosion, health impacts through burning of waste and lack of local community involvement to participate in decisions regarding the island and the tourism industry were some major issues. Rapid and unsound developments such as building on the beach were also major areas of concern to the stakeholders. The consultation was used as the basis for a sustainability strategy that was developed for the island to prioritize initiatives and identify a form of collaboration to manage the implementation of the strategy.

The Direction-Setting Stage

In the direction-setting stage, collaboration evolves into a direction-setting stage where participants begin to identify a common purpose and shared interpretations of the future emerge as stakeholders identify commonly held beliefs and vision (Selin & Chavez 1995). This process is facilitated by the setting of goals and ground rules and by organizing subgroups to examine specific issues.

After the consultation occurred in the previous stage, a sustainability strategy was developed that focused on setting a mission statement to provide a clear direction toward achieving the common goal of sustainability. It incorporated best practices of sustainable tourism development worldwide and identified initiatives that can be implemented on the island.

The underlying principle of the sustainability strategy was to protect the environment by implementing a series of goals and objectives. It was also to ensure that there was dialogue and transparency occurring among the stakeholders to facilitate the buy-in and motivation to implement the initiatives. The need for a multi-stakeholder partnership to increase accountability and manage the implementation of projects was also recommended. The partnership was structured with the use of sub groups to explore options and gather support to accomplish the goals and objectives identified in the strategy.

The Structuring Stage

The purpose of the partnership, which has been incorporated into the structure of the Gili Ecotrust, was to be the avenue to initiate dialogue among all stakeholders and to create a plan for the island that everyone can adhere to. The formalization of the partnership mirrors phase four of Selin and Chavez's (1995) model which is the structuring phase. This phase formalizes the collaboration and its relationships, elaborates on the tasks necessary to achieve the goals and develops the systems for implementation. Stakeholders involved in the partnership were designated various roles and responsibilities for an environmental coordinator and the stakeholders involved in the sub-groups. Formalizing the partnership enables the stakeholders to focus resources, share information, increase environmental action and learn from the leaders. At this stage, it was identified that the role of the Gili Ecotrust was to

- make decisions and oversee the implementation of the sustainable tourism strategy;
- provide guidance and information to the community via community meetings and workshops;
- organize project teams to implement the sustainability initiatives;
- manage the eco-tax;
- provide accountability for finances and decisions made; and
- provide a mechanism for complaints on the management of the environment.

The formalized Ecotrust has been the avenue to ensure that the goals of the strategy are being achieved.

The Outcome Stage

At this stage, the programs that were developed by the collaboration are being implemented and the benefits derived from the collaboration. The Ecotrust, which is currently managed by an environmental coordinator, has succeeded in reaching this stage of the collaboration as it has implemented a number of initiatives garnering positive impacts on protecting the environment. It has also ensured collaboration through enabling stakeholders to voice their concerns while also becoming involved in major issues on the island. Monthly meetings with business owners, local governments and the community are held in order to work together to tackle the issues on the island.

The Gili Ecotrust now has the participation of numerous stakeholders on the island and has been responsible for working with the local community in order to monitor the surrounding area to ensure illegal fishing is not occurring. It is also working with the local school to educate children about waste disposal and how to protect the coral reefs, beginning dialogue on how to manage waste on the island, starting a waste separation program, organizing beach and coral clean-ups and ensuring that the horses that work the cidomo carts have constant access to freshwater and are treated humanely. Each dive shop has sponsored its own biorock in front of their properties. The biorocks provide low-level electrical current to a structure, which is placed under water and eventually grows into a coral reef balmy. This balmy attracts fish and leads to the regeneration of the coral reef. Plans for a waste management and green sea turtle conservation strategy were being explored in 2010. The environmental coordinator has now been hired full time and is currently learning the local language in order to negotiate contracts with waste management organizations and the government. Even if all the initiatives identified in the strategy are not implemented immediately, success is evident through the formation of a partnership that has brought together various stakeholders on the island to create dialogue and build relationships. This partnership will also lead to the sharing of information and best practices. By including locals in public consultation meetings, the local level of education is being raised and cultural exchange is occurring. This has, and will lead to new knowledge and overcoming challenges. Through the involvement of locals, empowerment has resulted. The partnership has led to increased accountability among the government, locals and westerners. This has also led to a cohesive environmental vision and language, where all who live on Gili Trawangan want to protect the resources that sustain the island and continue living in a clean environment.

Discussion

Despite efforts from a number of local businesses to further sustainability initiatives on the island of Gili Trawangan, challenges to sustainable tourism implementation still exist. The purpose of developing and implementing a collaborative partnership is to provide a holistic approach to sustainable tourism implementation that includes all stakeholders. This case study identifies that collaboration through multi-stakeholder partnerships can successfully lead to the implementation of programs and initiatives that can move a destination toward sustainability. In the beginning stages of collaboration, it is necessary to identify the challenges and work with all stakeholders to determine a collective vision. Increasing levels of local involvement and considering the views of all stakeholders are pertinent in achieving sustainable tourism measures, as they bring together a wider group of stakeholders with common interests (Farrell 1994; Middleton & Hawkins 1998; Tosun 2001; Puppim de Oliviera 2003). Further, residents are regarded as the rightful custodians of an area, and their needs should not be overridden by outside interests (Din 1993; Ruhanen 2008). Each stakeholder has a different view, and in order to achieve sustainable tourism, multiple stakeholders working together in collaboration to achieve goals, which benefit the greater good, is important. Collaboration and participation are needed in order to address the overall concept of the public good as well as environmental and social concerns in the context of development rather than solely market interests. It also must be mindful of the many other sectors – taxation, transportation, housing, social development, environmental conservation and protection and resource management. As these different industries all affect tourism, it cannot operate in isolation, and in order for successful island sustainable tourism to result, it must benefit more than just the business owners (Graci & Dodds 2010).

The case study of Gili Trawangan identifies that managing relationships with primary stakeholders can result in more than just continued participation. By developing long-term relationships with primary stakeholders, a set of value-creating exchanges happen that are relational rather than transactional since 'transactional interactions can be easily duplicated and thus offer little potential for competitive advantage' (Hillman & Keim 2001: 127). Collaboration and mutual trust leads to better cooperation and long-term viability, however this will only be successful if the process is open, consultative and aims to set objectives where each stakeholder will benefit. Effective stakeholder management will build trust and give stakeholders a sense of empowerment and ownership in the development process.

Once the problem is defined, it is necessary to establish goals as well as roles and responsibilities to achieve these goals. In Gili Trawangan, information was sought through consultation and conducting an environmental audit. This fed into a strategy that achieved buy-in from all stakeholders. The nature of the partnership was also one that fostered continuous dialogue and involvement as well as was financially stable through the collection of an eco-tax. The funds collected provided the ability to hire an environmental coordinator that was responsible for the day-to-day tasks related to the partnership. This also increased the level of success of the collaboration because this person acted as the link between all stakeholders. As it was the responsibility of the coordinator to ensure that tasks were completed and that communication did not break down, tasks were implemented to achieve the stated goals. In addition, monthly meetings and constant communication and consultation included all stakeholders in joint decision-making and ensured that the process was dynamic leading to its success. This case study has identified that momentum and good will are not enough, a collaborative effort toward sustainability is necessary for success.

It is recommended that this case study be taken as a good example of collaboration. Despite the number of challenges that this island has and currently is facing, due to collaboration, constant dialogue, a common vision and working together, challenges have and continue to be overcome. Selin and Chavez's (1995) tourism partnership model has identified the stages that a partnership can go through and this paper has used a case study to illustrate this. It is recommended that further tourism partnerships be analyzed to identify whether the challenges faced are similar and whether the partnership has followed the progressive stages as identified by Selin and Chavez (1995).

Conclusion

The multi-stakeholder partnership that developed as a result of collaboration in Gili Trawangan followed the five stages as identified by Selin and Chavez (1995) in their collaboration model. The island of Gili Trawangan went through the first phase when a crisis regarding illegal fishing and bombing developed and through leadership created the Gili Ecotrust to deal with these issues. This led to the problem-setting phase where a common vision and problem definition was identified, stakeholders consulted and collaboration began to occur. The third phase led to the goals being set, information sought out and options explored. Sub-groups to tackle certain initiatives were organized. The fourth phase consisted of formally structuring the partnership through hiring a full-time coordinator and assigning key roles and responsibilities to the stakeholders involved. The fifth stage led to the development of key outcomes such as the installation of a number of biorocks on the island, the beginning of a waste collection and management system, initiatives for turtle conservation and dialogue being created among stakeholders. Following Selin and Chavez's (1995) model which was built on the principles of Gray's collaboration theory, the multi-stakeholder partnership developed in Gili Trawangan can be considered successful and innovative in terms of sustainable tourism development.

References

Berresford, J. (2004) *Tourism in the Region*. Regional Review Hearing Report, pp. 1–11.

Bramwell, B. & Alletorp, L. (2001) Attitudes in the Danish tourism industry to the roles of business and government in sustainable tourism, *International Journal of Tourism Research*, 3, pp. 91–103.

Bramwell, B. & Lane, B. (2005) Sustainable tourism research and the importance of societal and social science trends, *Journal of Sustainable Tourism*, 13(1), pp. 1–3.

Carbone, M. (2005) Sustainable tourism in developing countries: Poverty alleviation, participatory planning and ethical issues, *The European Journal of Development Research*, 17(3), pp. 559–565.

Carr, D. S., Selin, S. W., & Schuett, M. A. (1998) Managing public forests: Understanding the role of collaborative planning, *Environmental Management*, 22(5), pp. 767–776.

Din, K. (1993) Dialogue with hosts: An educational strategy towards sustainable tourism, in: M. Hitchcock, V. King, & M. Parnwell (Eds) *Tourism in South-East Asia*, p. 32 (New York: Routledge).

Dodds, R., Graci, S., & Holmes, M. (2010) Does the tourist care? A comparison of visitors to Koh Phi Phi, Thailand and Gili Trawangan, Indonesia, *Journal of Sustainable Tourism*, 19(2), pp. 207–222.

Douglas, C. H. (2006) Small island states and territories: Sustainable development issues and strategies – Challenges for changing islands in a changing world, *Sustainable Development*, 14, pp. 75–80.

Fadeeva, Z. (2005) Translation of sustainability ideas in tourism networks: Some roles of cross-sectoral networks in change towards sustainable development, *Journal of Cleaner Production*, 13(2), pp. 175–189.

Farrell, B. (1994) Tourism as an element in sustainable development, in: V. Smith & W. Eadington (Eds) *Tourism Alternatives*, pp. 115–132 (Bognor Regis, UK: John Wiley).

Fennell, D. (2003) *Ecotourism, 2nd ed.* (London: Routledge).

Foggin, T. & Münster, D. O. (2003) Finding the middle ground between communities and tourism, *Africa Insight*, 33(1/2), pp. 18–22.

Goeldner, C. R. & Ritchie, J. R. (2006) *Tourism: Principles, Practices, Philosophies* (New Jersey: John Wiley).

Graci, S. (2007) Accommodating Green: Examining barriers to sustainable tourism development. Paper presented at the TTRA Canada conference, Montebello, Quebec.

Graci, S. & Dodds, R. (2010) *Sustainable Tourism in Island Destinations* (London: Earthscan).

Gray, B. (1989) *Collaborating* (San Francisco: Jossey-Bass).

Gray, B. (1996) Cross-sectoral partners: Collaborative alliances among business, government and communities, in: C. Huxham (Eds) *Creating Collaborative Advantage* (London: Sage).

Gray, B. & Wood, D. (1991) Collaborative alliances: Moving from practice to theory, *Journal of Applied Behavioral Science*, 27(1), pp. 3–22.

Halme, M. (2001) Learning for Sustainable Development in Tourism Networks, in: *Ninth International Conference on Sustainability at the Millennium: Globalization, Competitiveness and the Public Trust* (Bangkok: Greening of Industry Network).

Hampton, M. P. (1998) Backpacker tourism and economic development, *Annals of Tourism Research*, 25, pp. 639–660.

Hardy, A. & Beeton, R. (2001) Sustainable tourism or maintainable tourism: Managing resources for more than average outcomes, *Journal of Sustainable Tourism*, 9(3), pp. 168–192.

Hashimoto, A. (2002) Tourism and sociocultural development issues, in: R. Sharpley & D. J. Telfer (Eds) *Tourism and Development: Concepts and Issues*, pp. 202–230 (Clevedon: Channel View Publications).

Hillman, A. J. & Keim, G. D. (2001) Shareholder value, stakeholder management and social issues: What's the bottom line? *Strategic Management Journal*, 22, pp. 125–139.

Jamal, T. & Stronza, A. (2009) Collaboration theory and tourism practice in protected areas: Stakeholders, structuring and sustainability, *Journal of Sustainable Tourism*, 17(2), pp. 169–189.

Kernel, P. (2005) Creating and implementing a model for sustainable development in tourism enterprises, *Journal of Cleaner Production*, 13, pp. 151–164.

Kerr, S. A. (2005) What is small island sustainable development about? *Ocean & Coastal Management*, 48, pp. 503–524.

Medeiros de Araujo, L. & Bramwell, B. (2002) Partnership and regional tourism in Brazil, *Annals of Tourism Research*, 29(4), pp. 1138–1164.

Middleton, V. & Hawkins, R. (1998) *Sustainable Tourism: A Marketing Perspective* (Oxford: Butterworth-Heinemann).

Plummer, R., Telfer, D., & Hashimoto, A. (2006) The rise and fall of the Waterloo-Wellington Ale Trail: A study of collaboration within the tourism industry, *Current Issues in Tourism*, 9(3), pp. 191–205.

Puppim de Oliviera, J. A. (2003) Government responses to tourism development: Three Brazilian case studies, *Tourism Management*, 24(1), pp. 97–110.

Ruhanen, L. (2008) Stakeholder participation in tourism destination planning, *Tourism Recreation Research*, 34(3), pp. 283–294.

Scheyvens, R. & Momsen, J. H. (2008) Tourism and poverty reduction: Issues for small island states, *Tourism Geographies*, 10(1), pp. 22–41.

Scheyvens, R. & Russell, M. (2012) Tourism, land tenure and poverty alleviation in Fiji, *Tourism Geographies*, 14(1), pp. 1–25.

Selin, S. (1999) Developing a typology of sustainable tourism partnership, *Journal of Sustainable Tourism*, 7(3&4), pp. 260–273.

Selin, S. & Chavez, D. (1995) Developing a collaborative model for environmental planning and management, *Environmental Management*, 19(2), pp. 189–195.

Sommer, B. & Sommer, R. (1992) *A Practical Guide to Behavioural Research. Tools and Techniques* (New York: Oxford University Press).

Tearfund. (2002) *A Call to Responsible Global Tourism*, Report, UK. Available at http://www.tearfund.org (accessed 21 February 2010).

Tosun, C. (2001) Challenges of sustainable tourism development in the developing world: The case of Turkey, *Tourism Management*, 22, pp. 289–303.

Weaver, D. (2001) Mass tourism and alternative tourism in the Caribbean, in: D. Harrison (Eds) *Tourism and the Less Developed World: Issues and Case Studies*, pp. 161–174 (Wallingford, UK: CABI).

World Travel and Tourism Council (WTTC). (1995) *Agenda 21 for the Travel & Tourism Industry – Towards Environmentally Sustainable Development* (London: WTTC).

World Travel and Tourism Council (WTTC). (1999) *Travel & Tourism – Millennium Vision* (London: WTTC).

United Nations World Tourism Organization (UNWTO). (2005) *Definition of Sustainable Tourism*. Available at http://www.worldtourism.org (accessed 17 June 2007).

United Nations World Tourism Organization (UNWTO). (2006) *Tourism Barometer*. Available at http://www.world-tourism.org/facts/menu.html (accessed 15 February 2007).

Notes on Contributor

Dr. Sonya Graci is an Assistant Professor of the Ted Rogers School of Hospitality and Tourism at Ryerson University in Toronto, Canada. She is also the co-founder of the Icarus Foundation, a not-for–profit organization that focuses on the sustainability of tourism, and the Director of Accommodating Green, a sustainability consultancy.

Resilience and Non-Linear Change in Island Tourism

AMRAN HAMZAH[*] & MARK P. HAMPTON[**]

[*]Faculty of Built Environment, Universiti Teknologi Malaysia, Johor Bahru, Malaysia
[**]Kent Business School, University of Kent, Canterbury, UK

ABSTRACT *Perhentian Kecil, located off the east coast of peninsular Malaysia, is predominantly a small-scale tourism destination, specifically for backpackers and independent travellers. Against the context of an aggressive drive by the state government to remove small-scale tourism development in favour of formal and high-end resorts, this paper examines the local responses to the exogenous factors that had threatened the equilibrium, and hence sustainability, of the tourism systems on the island. The paper draws upon a longitudinal study with multiple visits over an extended period since the mid-1990s. Using insights from Resilience Theory, the paper argues that this island destination is an example of non-linear change rather than conventional resort evolution. The paper also discusses how the authors – as researchers – had to realign their research framework and approach to take into consideration the growing complexities of tourism development in small island destinations.*

Introduction

For many small islands, tourism is economically significant as a source of income and employment. In some insular areas such as the Caribbean, tourism accounts for over 75% of some countries' GDP (Graci & Dodds 2010). Islands, especially small islands, continue to fascinate and attract tourists (Royle 2001), and for tropical less-developed countries (LDCs) such as Malaysia with many offshore islands, developers and government planners see the potential to develop resorts. However, what of small islands that already host international tourism, albeit at a small scale and catering for backpackers? What issues and tensions might emerge as these small island destinations face significant change?

The Perhentian islands, off the east coast of peninsular Malaysia, have been a tourism destination since the late 1980s when backpacker tourists 'discovered' these islands. The two main islands, Perhentian Besar ('large Perhentian island') and Perhentian Kecil ('small Perhentian'), have experienced differing forms of tourism development. This paper focuses on Perhentian Kecil, which has remained broadly a small-scale tourism destination, specifically for backpackers and independent travellers. Against the backdrop of an aggressive drive by the Terengganu state government to get rid of small-scale tourism development in favour of formal and high-end resorts, this paper examines the local responses to the exogenous factors that had threatened the equilibrium, and hence sustainability, of the tourism systems on the island. In addition, this paper documents how the authors had to realign their research framework and approach to take into consideration the growing complexities of tourism development in small island destinations.

Modelling the Evolution of Tourism in Small Islands

Island tourism has a growing literature since the seminal work of Hills and Lundgren (1977) in the Caribbean, and Archer's (1977) work on economic impacts. The well-cited and highly influential model developed by Butler (1980) of the Tourist Area Life Cycle (TALC) suggested a stages approach to understanding resort evolution and proposed that resorts moved through 'exploration', 'involvement', 'development', 'consolidation' and, finally, 'stagnation'. For many destinations, the post-stagnation stages are the most crucial (or even problematic) since the model suggests that resorts may experience rejuvenation or may continue to decline. Since the 1980s, authors have applied Butler's TALC to islands (Weaver 1990; Choy 1992), and many others have researched environmental impacts and sustainability (Wilkinson 1989; de Albuquerque & McElroy 1992; Briguglio et al. 1996; Bardolet 2001; Gössling 2001). Research has also examined other geographical aspects such as the links between island ecotourism and economic development (Klak & Flynn 2008) and, most recently, small-scale tourism as a possible form of 'soft growth' for islands (Timms & Conway 2011). Much of the literature though concerns large resorts or mass tourism in islands, so small-scale tourism, particularly backpackers and independent travellers, has a smaller literature, with the main research located in South-East Asia, the predominant backpacker region (Cohen 1982; Wall 1996; Hampton 1998; Spreitzhofer 1998; Fallon 2001; Hampton & Hampton 2009; Hamzah 1995, 1997, 2007).

Spatial temporal or evolutionary models have largely been used to analyse the evolution of small-scale tourism (Butler 1980; Oppermann 1993; Agarwal 1997; Dodds & McElroy 2008). There have also been criticisms of the model (Choy 1992; Getz 1992), but its simplicity makes it an attractive tool to explain the evolution of resort destinations, especially those that started from an 'involvement stage' initiated by the local community.

Lately, researchers have argued that the TALC's linear narrative is unable to rigorously analyse the complexity of the interactions and forces shaping destination areas

(McKercher 1999; Farrell & Twining-Ward 2004, 2005; Cochrane 2010). These are the proponents of Resilience Theory, a model that was initially developed by Holling (1973) for the field of ecology, but has lately been applied to other disciplines, including tourism. The main difference between the four phases of Resilience Theory and the TALC is that the former describes the evolution of tourism systems in a destination area as a cycle or a loop instead of a linear progression. The four phases are 'reorganisation', 'exploitation', 'conservation' and 'release' (Holling 2001). *Reorganisation* represents the rapid change that usually takes place after a 'destabilising event', which is often manifested in the form of the regeneration of societal structures. *Exploitation* explains the creation of new systems or institutions accompanied by new cultural, political and social relationships. *Conservation* refers to the formation of a stable but rigid state through newly formed and interconnected structures and capital. Finally, the *release* phase occurs when the disturbance event(s) destabilises the existing rigid structures to produce rapid changes (Holling 2001: 394).

The use of Resilience Theory in tourism studies has been rather limited. Among the few attempts to use the model in the context of tourism development, Calgaro and Cochrane (2009) applied Resilience Theory to develop strategies to strengthen the tourism systems in Thailand and Sri Lanka after the 2004 Tsunami. Schianetz and Kavanagh (2008) developed tourism indicators based on Resilience Theory, and Nguru (2010) applied the model to explain the resilience of the tourism system in Kampung Cherating Lama, the pioneer 'drifter enclave' in Malaysia. According to Resilience Theory, local knowledge is important for resource management, which is often generated via a process of 'learning by doing' (Folke *et al.* 2005). This explains why local communities had been able to develop environmentally friendly 'drifter enclaves' by applying their knowledge and expertise in sustainable vernacular development (Nguru 2010). Nonetheless, Resilience Theory also does not deny that cultural knowledge should be complemented by scientific knowledge (Folke *et al.* 2005), which is crucial in moving up small-scale tourism development along the value chain.

In the context of tourism development, Cochrane (2010) suggested that Resilience Theory could be used to describe the four phases that a tourism system goes through in its development path. The 'release' phase is considered to be the equal of TALC's 'rejuvenation' stage, but prior to this phase, a 'destabilising event' usually occurs (such as tsunamis, bird flu etc.) that may result in the destination going through a temporary decline. This happens before the destination is then revitalised through the community's resilient actions, such as innovation and adaptation to changing market forces and strong leadership, which would ensure that the destination will not succumb to permanent decline but reinvent itself. In the same light, the revitalisation that occurred in Kampung Cherating Lama, according to Nguru (2010), was due to the fact that practical business knowledge was accumulated and exchanged, and this helped the local community in understanding the market forces and tourist demand despite their lack of formal education.

The Research

This paper is based on a longitudinal study that began in the mid-1990s, with later visits in July 2006, July 2008, May 2009 and June 2010. The initial fieldwork commenced in 1994 in the form of a series of preliminary visits to the island, and one of the authors stayed with the local residents at Kampung Pasir Hantu. The participant-observer approach was adopted as part of the researcher's overall methodology in understanding the dynamics of small-scale tourism development for their doctoral work. The aim of the initial fieldwork was to establish contact and gain the trust of the local community who were directly involved in the development and operation of small-scale tourism development in Perhentian Kecil. These visits provided valuable insights into the local response towards the advent of tourism on the island, which included the dynamics of their business operation, empowerment process and relationships with policy-makers and tourists.

During the mid-1990s, small-scale tourism development was confined to Pasir Panjang (Long Beach) on the east coast, and one author identified the forces that were shaping the entrepreneurial capacity of the local community, given their lack of education and capital. In addition, it was a timely opportunity to closely examine the dynamics of local community involvement in the early stage of tourism development in Perhentian Kecil. This coincided with the 'involvement stage' of Butler's TALC (1980), and the participant-observer approach adopted allowed an examination of the phenomenon from the perspective of the local population by gaining their trust through regular stays with the local community at Kampung Pasir Hantu.

From 2000 to 2005, both authors had separately visited Perhentian Kecil several times and had observed the gradual evolution in its physical development from basic A-frame huts to more comfortable chalets with better facilities. Informal interviews with key informants from the local communities revealed that investors from the mainland were either taking over some of the 'mini resorts' that used to be operated by the local people or were becoming business partners. In addition, small-scale tourism development had expanded to Coral Bay, on the opposite coast of Perhentian Kecil. The authors then got to know each other through their participation in international tourism conferences. Recognising that they were working on common subject matters within the same geographical area, the authors decided to embark on a joint longitudinal study to examine the economic, social and ecological dimensions of small-scale tourism development in Perhentian Kecil. Having established a good relationship with the local community at Kampung Pasir Hantu and the local operators at Pasir Panjang, it was decided to focus on the evolution of the small-scale tourism development on the island from the perspective of the local stakeholders.

The first field visit of the joint research was carried out in 2006 with the aim of establishing baseline data on the small-scale tourism development and operation both at Pasir Panjang (Long Beach) and Coral Bay. As noted earlier, the island at that time had been attracting investors from outside, which corresponded with the

TALC's 'development stage'. The methodology used was a blend of semi-structured interviews, site mapping, participant observation and formal questionnaires. The scope of the 2006 fieldwork mainly covered the operators' business profile, such as the nature of business, source of capital, human resource development, partnerships between local operators and outsiders, relationship with local authorities, future planning etc.

Due to financial constraints, field visits could not be carried out in 2007. After securing new funding, fieldwork was resumed in 2008 and two experienced local research assistants (RAs) were employed to help with logistics and to undertake some interviews and translate others. The RAs were qualified to Master's level in tourism and both had worked with the authors on previous projects. Prior to visiting the island, training was held to induct the RAs into the project, pilot the questionnaires and discuss the semi-structured interviews.

The 2008 fieldwork took a new dimension because the new state government had managed to 'introduce' a formal resort (Bubu Resort) that was supposed to pave the way for the transformation of Perhentian Kecil into a high-end resort destination (*The New Straits Times* 2006). Coupled with the development of a two-storey shopping arcade on Long Beach, these new developments were receiving negative response from the local community as well as tourists (especially through blogs). At this juncture, the authors were presented with the opportunity to examine whether strong exogenous factors would lead to a possible demise of the small-scale tourism development to make way for formal resorts ('decline stage' followed by 'revitalisation stage' according to Butler's TALC). Much to the surprise of the authors, the 2009 field visit revealed that the anticipated demise of the informal sector, though buy-outs did not occur. Instead, the small-scale operators showed great resilience and flexibility to adapt to the new development scenario that was taking place on the island without losing their market share.

At this stage, the authors decided to revisit the appropriateness and limitations of evolutionary models as well as seek alternative theories to explain the new phenomenon that was shaping up in Perhentian Kecil, created by the tensions between powerful exogenous forces and the resilience of the local tourism systems. Based on the literature, the authors were attracted to the potential application of Resilience Theory, having noted how it was successfully used by Nguru (2010) in the case of Kampung Cherating Lama, which had gone through a similar development path as Perhentian Kecil. Having started the longitudinal research with the aim of plotting the spatial temporal evolution of small-scale tourism development in Perhentian Kecil in a linear progression (as in Butler's TALC), the authors later realised that the complexities of the phenomenon implied that the original research questions had to be revisited and readjusted.

Resilience Theory presented the authors a tool to comprehensively examine the counter-reactions towards the exogenous factors that occurred from 2004 onwards. There were two exogenous factors, namely the state government's directive to remove budget accommodation and the relaxation of affirmative policies to protect *Bumiputra* (Malay) entrepreneurship. In addition, there was an endogenous factor in the form of negative media reports on the deteriorating state of the coral reefs around Malaysia's islands (*The Star Online* 2010). Although Perhentian Kecil performed better than the other islands in terms of coral condition, the poor sewage treatment system employed by the small-scale operators was identified as one of the main contributors towards water pollution and possible coral depletion (Reef Check Malaysia 2008). These exogenous factors, in tandem with the endogenous factor, could be interpreted as being 'destabilising events' with the potential of upsetting the equilibrium (and the fundamental sustainability) of the tourism systems in Perhentian Kecil.

To reflect the changing conceptual framework of this longitudinal study, the research questions had also been reviewed and realigned from those that were initially concerned with understanding the dynamics of small-scale tourism development/operation within an enclavic type of development to those that investigated their evolving role within an inter-connected tourist system shared with other key stakeholders, such as government agencies, formal resorts, tourism marketers, new investors and environmental NGOs (see Table 1).

Throughout the longitudinal study, the qualitative method was used in the form of participant observation and semi-structured interviews, with key respondents selected from chalet/resort operators, restaurant and shop owners, dive schools, transport operators, environmental NGOs, tourists and local government officials. In addition, respondents were asked to recommend who else might be interviewed on the island using the 'snowballing' technique to gain further entry to a given population of potential respondents.

Tourism Development in Perhentian Kecil

Within the emerging South-East Asia backpacker trail, the Perhentian islands are one of the 'honeypot' sites in northern peninsular Malaysia, along with Penang and the Cameron Highlands. Typically, backpackers enter Malaysia from southern Thailand (or travel north from Singapore) and then journey in a circuit between Penang via the Cameron Highlands and then to the east coast specifically to visit the Perhentian islands. Backpackers often stay on islands or at other beach resorts as mini 'holidays', as a break from harder travelling within their larger trips around the region (Hampton 1998). Backpacker enclaves have been discussed elsewhere (Lloyd 2003; Brenner & Fricke 2007), and spatial flows of backpackers are beginning to be analysed (Rogerson 2007).

The Perhentian archipelago lies about 20 km off the coast of peninsular Malaysia in Terengganu state. The island group consists of two main islands, Perhentian Besar (Big Island) and Perhentian Kecil (Small Island), plus some small uninhabited islets. The Perhentian islands are located in a marine park and visitors pay a small entrance

Table 1. Evolution of conceptual framework during longitudinal study

Year	Physical development	Research questions	Model used in conceptual framework
1995–2005	Organic growth of small-scale tourism development at 'drifter enclaves'	• How did the local community respond to the advent of tourism? • What was the role of related government agencies to nurture *Bumiputra* entrepreneurs? • How did the local operators develop their business skills and business knowledge to cater for changing tourist demand?	Evolutionary models (Butler 1980; Oppermann 1993) to explain 'involvement' stage
2006	Outsiders taking over 'mini resorts' but maintaining physical form/setting up business partnerships with locals	• What percentage of tourism development was in the control of the local community? • Without access to capital, was establishing partnerships with outsiders the only option? Who were the outsiders in terms of their relationship with the local community?	• Evolutionary models (TALC) to describe 'development stage'
2008	Introduction of formal resort (Bubu Resort) and construction of two-storey shopping arcade at Long Beach	• How did the local operators initially respond to the introduction of formal resorts and tourism facilities? • Were the local operators ready to compete against the new operators with sophisticated business models?	TALC in combination with basic principles of Resilience Theory (McKercher 1999; Farrell & Twining-Ward 2004, 2005)

(Continued on next page)

Table 1. Evolution of conceptual framework during longitudinal study *(Continued)*

Year	Physical development	Research questions	Model used in conceptual framework
2009	Development of two new resorts along Coral Bay (Senja and Shari-La)	• Did the introduction of the pioneer formal resort resulted in a comprehensive takeover of the small-scale tourism operators? • Did the small-scale tourism operators upgrade their facilities and services to compete against the formal resort? • What role did 'local champions' and community organisations play in protecting the local operators' market share?	Adaptation of Resilience Theory in tourism destination management (Cochrane 2010; Nguru 2010)
2010	Upscaling of business operation by small-scale operators and commitment to physical upgrading	• Did the local operators embrace modern technology to enhance their business operation and marketing? • What were the roles of local knowledge and kinship in harnessing the resilience of the local operators? • Was there a desire from the local stakeholders to work together to enhance the economic competitiveness and ecological sustainability of Perhentian Kecil?	Model development based on Resilience Theory (McKercher 1999; Farrell & Twining-Ward 2004, 2005) (Cochrane 2010; Nguru 2010)

fee of RM5 (approximately US $1.50). There is one main *kampung* (village), Kampung Pasir Hantu, on Perhentian Kecil with a resident population of around 1500 (Figure 1). By virtue of its inclusion in the *Lonely Planet* guidebooks, Perhentian Kecil is well known to international tourists, especially backpackers. It is the most visited backpacker destination in Malaysia and has the highest per capita expenditure, which can be mainly attributed to their expenditure on scuba diving (MOTOUR 2007). Ironically, few tourists are aware of the geographical location of Perhentian Kecil within Terengganu state, much to the chagrin of the state government. In 2010, 287,149 international tourists visited Terengganu, of whom 90% purposely went to the Perhentians and Redang Island without visiting any other attractions in the state (MOTOUR Terengganu 2011).

The two main Perhentian islands appear to have experienced quite different forms of tourism development. Perhentian Besar now has more upmarket resorts with both international and domestic tourism accommodation, whereas Perhentian Kecil has mainly backpacker tourists/small-scale tourism accommodation and presently only three mid-range resorts. Perhentian Kecil has two main beaches: Pasir Panjang or Long Beach (east coast) and Coral Bay (west coast). Different forms of accommodation, restaurants, dive operators and other tourist infrastructure exist on both beaches, but interestingly, differences between the two beaches are now beginning to appear. Long Beach is larger, has more facilities and many bars, and attracts younger tourists, being seen as the 'party beach'. Coral Bay is quieter and attracts slightly older tourists and more families. The tourist accommodation is generally small scale and low cost, consisting of simple wooden chalets or A-frame buildings, sometimes built on a concrete base. Local materials are used both for construction and for fitting-out. The budget prices are typically $10–25 per night. Coral Bay had one larger resort, although it is still a mid-market type of accommodation, but in 2008, another mid-market place opened with 100 rooms, mainly targeting domestic groups. Not surprisingly, given the basic facilities, backpackers and independent travellers are the main market segments (Hamzah 1995). At present, there are no booking systems for most island accommodation, so they rely entirely on 'walk-in' trade. Consequently, during peak season, tourists arriving later in the day may find that all the accommodations have been filled by arrivals from earlier boats, and commonly they either have to sleep the first night on the beach or return to the mainland (Hamzah 2007). However, the newer resorts use online bookings or have agents on the mainland.

There is a lack of official data on tourist arrivals, but Kaur (2007) provided an interesting comparison between the number of accommodation units on Perhentian Kecil and those in other destinations in Terengganu, revealing that for a small area of 15 km^2, there were 47 chalets on Perhentian Kecil offering 1140 beds. In comparison with other popular tourism destinations in Terengganu, only the capital city of Kuala Terengganu surpassed this, having 41 hotels/chalets offering 1747 beds, but covering a much bigger area of 605 km^2. In high season, the accommodation units at Perhentian

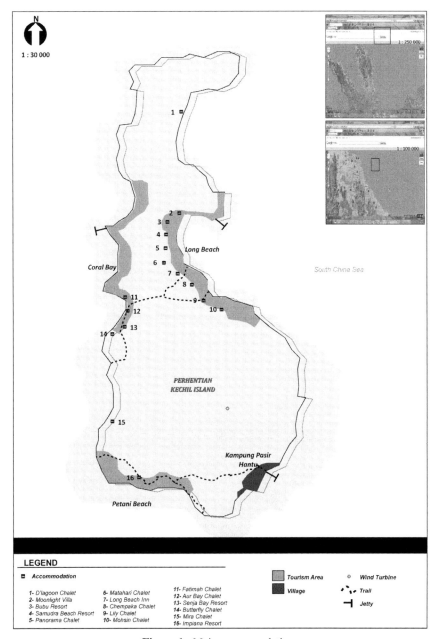

Figure 1. Main accommodation.

Kecil have a 100% occupancy rate. This raises a major question on the carrying capacity of the island. Carrying capacity threshold limits for Perhentian Kecil had been recommended by a study on coastal and island development commissioned by the Terengganu state government but they were not enforced (Sea Resources Management 2006). As noted above, the facilities are limited and somewhat basic. Rooms tend to have an attached toilet and simple shower. Some have air-conditioning, but most rooms just have a fan. There is some electricity, and chalet operators have their own generators, which run for limited hours during the evening. The more recent mid-range resorts offer better facilities and higher levels of comfort and service quality (Table 2).

The tourist infrastructure is basic, consisting of simple cafes and bars, limited – and relatively expensive – Internet facilities and some small shops. The island does not have any bank or automatic telling machine and has limited credit card facilities. The main tourist activities are scuba diving and snorkelling on the coral reefs and boat trips. The Bubu Resort offers parasailing, banana boat rides, kayaking and water skiing (Table 3).

Table 2. List of tourist accommodations on Perhentian Kecil

No	Accommodation	Number of units	No. of beds[a]	Location
1.	Rock Garden	32	64	Long Beach
2.	Bubu Long Beach Resort	39	78	Long Beach
3.	Chempaka Chalets	20	40	Long Beach
4.	Lemon Grass	20	40	Long Beach
5.	Simfony Chalets	28	56	Long Beach
6.	Matahari Chalets	30	60	Long Beach
7.	Moonlight Beach	28	56	Long Beach
8.	Panorama Chalets	31	62	Long Beach
9.	Lily Chalets	13	26	Long Beach
10	Mohsin Chalets	64	128	Long Beach
11	D'lagoon	64	128	Long Beach
12	Rajawali Coral	64	128	Coral Bay
13	Fatimah Chalet	11	22	Coral Bay
14	Aur Bay	10	20	Coral Bay
15	Butterfly Chalet	10	20	Coral Bay
16	Maya Beach Resort	12	24	Coral Bay
17	Senja Bay Resort	50	100	Coral Bay
18	Mira Chalet	8	16	Coral Bay
19	Shari-La Island Resort	71	142	Coral Bay
20	Petani Beach	5	10	Petani Beach
21	Impiani Resort	23	46	Petani Beach
	Totals:	562	1, 124	

[a]Estimated average two beds/room in each accommodation.
Source: Fieldwork notes.

Table 3. Tourist facilities on Perhentian Kecil

| No. | Facility | Numbers of units: | |
		Long Beach	Coral Bay
1.	Restaurant	7	6
2.	Multi-purpose shop	5	2
3.	Scuba diving shop	7	2
4.	Souvenir shop	3	1
5.	Batik/painting shop	1	—
6.	Mini shop	1	2
7.	Massage	1	—
8.	Bookshop	2	1
9.	Water taxi service	7	2
10	Snorkelling rental shop	5	2

Source: MOTOUR/UTM 2007.

The islands are accessed by speedboats from Kuala Besut harbour. Perhentian Besar has several wooden jetties, whereas until as recently as 2008, Kecil did not and so relied on small water taxis to transfer tourists from the speedboats to the shore. Interviews with water taxi boatmen showed that a circuit had emerged where the boatmen also worked in the Southern Thai islands in the Perhentians' 'off' (monsoon) season between October and February. However, with the completion of the two large concrete jetties on either beach (funded by the Ministry of Tourism Malaysia), the water taxi business disappeared and their services became redundant. Some had been forced to leave the island to look for alternative work elsewhere, while others had diversified into taking snorkelling trips for tourists or intra-island ferry trips.

Most of the food and drink required by the tourists were imported from the mainland. The islands do have some potable water supply from wells, but tourists prefer to drink bottled water. There are minimal medical facilities, and the only clinic is located at the local village, Kampung Pasir Hantu, and staffed by a paramedic and a midwife. There are no tourist police, and the newly constructed police station complex only has two regular policemen on duty. The state government has recently started preliminary work on the construction of a centralised water supply system for the island, and for sewerage, most accommodation units have septic tanks, which are emptied into the sea during the monsoon period. Solid waste and general garbage are regularly collected and shipped to the mainland by barge; however, this has been criticised, given that the large garbage bags often fall into the sea while being transported to the mainland. One resort operator commented that 'the private contractor has never bothered to reprimand his men for allowing some of the bags to fall off the barge. We suspect it is being done intentionally'. Since 2007, two wind powered turbines provide electricity to the villagers in the *kampung*, and the tourist operators still rely on their own diesel generators for electricity.

Analysis and Findings

Spatial Temporal Evolution of Tourism Development in Perhentian Kecil

Based on the longitudinal study that started from the mid-1990s, the evolution of tourism development in Perhentian Kecil was synthesised and initially described using Butler's TALC (1980) as the conceptual framework. Essentially, Perhentian Kecil has undergone three distinct stages of development: Stage 1: early 1990s until the mid-1990s, Stage 2: mid-1990s to early 2000s (until around 2003), and Stage 3: from around 2004 to date.

Stage 1: Early 1990s till Mid-1990s

This stage was characterised by the local response to the demand from tourism. The form of development was broadly 'organic', small-scale and unplanned. Arguably, the close-knit fishing community at Kampung Pasir Hantu, with little knowledge of the tourism business, became small-scale tourism entrepreneurs almost overnight. Perhentian Kecil was a relatively late starter and benefited from the exodus of back-packers from Cherating once domestic tourists began to overwhelm the 'drifter en-clave' there (Hamzah 1997). Due to the remote location of the island, there was no government intervention, and the new operators provided their own capital, thus ensuring complete local ownership and control. All the pioneer operators were from the local *kampung* (village) and were mostly related to each other. Due to the lack of capital, the initial development was mostly in the form of A-frame huts.

Although the *kampung* had a formal headman, the actual leadership was assumed by a colourful village elder, Pak 'A'. Despite not holding any official post, Pak 'A' was instrumental in setting up a boat cooperative at Kuala Besut harbour to transport tourists to Perhentian Kecil. He also represented the villagers in meetings organised by the District Office and provided strong moral support for the villagers who wanted to venture into the tourism business.

During this stage, the fieldwork revealed that it was common for the foreign tourists to go about topless and many were engaged in 'hedonistic' practices such as excessive drinking, which is common in much international tourism. Despite being located in a conservative Islamic state, the local operators had surprisingly developed a high tolerance level to such practices as they were becoming increasingly dependent on tourism as their main source of livelihood. According to a pioneer operator, 'we regard the topless bathing and drunkenness as occupational hazards as long as they are carried out at Long Beach' (Long Beach is separated from the *kampung* by a rocky cliff). Even in the early days, the local operators were fast learners in terms of understanding tourist demand, behaviour and expectations. At the same time, the operators were also very protective of the traditional values in the *kampung*, and as much as 'hedonistic' behaviour was tolerated at their 'work place' (Long Beach), participant observation showed that most of the locals were outraged whenever a foreign tourist(s) strayed into their *kampung* to take photographs. As their 'local champion' and moral guardian, Pak 'A' made sure that none of the beach boys who flocked to Long Beach were from the *kampung* and this form of 'territorial coexistence' survived throughout the 'involvement stage'.

In essence, the 'involvement stage' was a steep learning curve for the local community, during which they were observed to be continuously learning new skills, such as foreign languages, culinary skills and bookkeeping etc. Interestingly, their culinary skills were mostly learned from backpackers, especially the art of making banana pancakes, which are still considered as being the now-iconic food for many backpackers. More importantly, they were comfortable adjusting to a new system brought about by the advent of tourism, without sacrificing their traditional values.

Stage 2: Mid-1990s to Early 2000s

In this stage, outsiders started to form partnerships with the locals, but the semi-structured interviews revealed that these 'outsiders' were mainly *Bumiputras* residing in the nearby mainland towns/cities of Kuala Besut, Kota Bahru and Kuala Terengganu. They often had family ties with the islanders and maintained the small-scale and low-density development as well as employed locals as the workforce. Rooms and other facilities were improved but were still basic and low cost. Many of these new operators also supplied in-house restaurants/cafes and dive shops. One group of investors said: 'We do not need new development here such as the Berjaya resort type [a large scale resort group in Malaysia], no need for concrete jetties, tourists here want to relax and enjoy the natural beauty of the island and they could go to Kuala Lumpur if they want to see modern resorts and development'.

The lack of access to micro-credit facilities was one of the main reasons why locals sought partners from outside the island. Although Malaysia has both a Special Tourism Fund and a Tourism Infrastructure Fund created by the Ministry of Tourism, these were mainly exploited by mainland developers. According to an official from the commercial bank appointed to handle these funds, islanders 'do not know how to write business plans and do not have the collateral' (land is often owned by many family members). Without access to micro-credit, they turned to outsiders, with the local headman sometimes acting as the land broker.

This stage could be interpreted as the beginning of TALC's 'development stage', but the pace of development slowed from 1999 to 2004, which coincided with the period when the conservative Islamic political party, Parti Islam SeMalaysia (PAS), took control of the state government of Terengganu. In fact, there was a lull in Perhentian Kecil during this period, given that PAS was not supportive of tourism, and directives to hotels/resorts to provide separate swimming pools for male and female guests scared away investors. During this stage too, the local operators had become confident businesspeople in their own right and started to educate guests on the need for proper behaviour. This was surprisingly effective since topless bathing practically ceased almost overnight and 'full moon parties' had to go underground.

Stage 3: 2004 Until Present Day

In 2004, the Barisan Nasional (National Front) won back the control of the Terengganu state government and tourism was again regarded as a major economic driver. This period also marked the arrival of Bubu Resort, a formal and Malaysian Chinese-owned resort – the first of its kind in Perhentian Kecil. Bubu Resort also introduced a new 'business model' that differed significantly from the unpackaged stays of most backpackers. The new model is typically a package of three days, two nights full board, boat transfer plus snorkelling trip for RM 299 (US $93). Following the model of the Laguna and Berjaya Resorts on Redang Island, as favoured by the state government, 'this new business model for the islands will set a new benchmark for resort operators to follow, we do not want chalets that are charging RM30/night' ($9.30) (a state tourism official).

Unlike other backpacker areas such as Bali or coastal Mexico, until this period, the island had not experienced foreign ownership, including the so-called 'developer-tourists' (Brenner & Fricke 2007). Bubu Resort is fundamentally different, being more capital intensive. It consists of three-storey, permanent concrete buildings and has Chinese-Malaysian owners. In addition, the entire workforce was sourced from established hotels in Kuala Lumpur and 'translocated' to the island. It also caters for the mass package market of East Asian tourists (Chinese, Taiwanese and Hong Kong people). An interview with a Terengganu state tourism official (pers. comm., 2009) revealed his preference for the business model introduced by Bubu Resort, which he claimed 'should trigger a new trend in resort operations on Perhentian Kecil, which the local operators have no choice but to follow'. The new business model is said to be similar to that practiced in Redang Island, which has succeeded in attracting an influx of East Asian visitors (ECERDC 2010).

Once Bubu Resort opened for business, there were intense initial reactions from the local operators on the island. One operator lamented: 'What can we do, they have strong political connections, even though they are not *Bumiputras* [literally: 'son of the soil' that is Malay]' (Chalet owner A). Another said: 'Now it is a free-for-all!' (a landowner). A pioneer operator added 'too much development and concrete, [the] government should control it' (Chalet owner B).

From the findings of fieldwork between 2008 and 2009, it could be surmised that the arrival of Bubu Resort was initially regarded by the local operators as a threat to their survival. On the other hand, the policy-makers in the Terengganu state government welcomed Bubu Resort and its 'new' business model as the right catalyst to transform Perhentian Kecil into a high-yield tourism destination. These conflicting aspirations therefore created tensions which were about to upset the balance of power and tourist systems that had gradually evolved in Perhentian Kecil and had been mainly created by the local response to unsophisticated tourist demand.

Exogenous Factors and Their Destabilising Effects

Ever since the Barisan Nasional (National Front) won back control of Terengganu from the opposition PAS in 2004, the state government has been aggressively promoting the redevelopment of the formerly neglected Terengganu islands into a high-end resort destination. In this light, the state government has also been making strongly worded statements in the local media against backpacker tourism on Perhentian Kecil, such as: 'We want to get rid of backpackers from Perhentian Kecil as they destroy the coral reefs. Instead we encourage the development of high end resorts which generate greater economic impact to the local economy' (*The New Straits Times* 2006).

In essence, the advent of Bubu Resort plus two other formal resorts at Coral Bay could be interpreted as a 'destabilising event' that could trigger the 'relapse' stage according to Resilience Theory (Cochrane 2010). Once the rhetoric that greeted the arrival of Bubu Resort had simmered down, the local operators went through a denial stage. When asked whether she would upgrade her establishment and level of service to compete against Bubu Resort, a pioneer operator was adamant: 'Why should I change? My children are well provided for and my loyal customers keep coming back?' Repeating the same question to the pioneer operator a year after the interview, a change of heart was detected when she admitted that 'we would like to upgrade and increase the number of chalets using our own money, in fact I have already paid someone to come up with architectural drawings a few years ago but he just vanished' (Chalet owner C).

During the 2008 and 2009 field visits, the authors heard many tourist complaints regarding the archaic 'first-come-first-served' system still being used by the local operators. The common response was succinctly given by a local operator: 'I'm not in favour of telephone or online booking, it's a hassle and tourists can always book through the dive shops which offer the service'. A year later, she simply said: 'I'm interested in setting up an online booking system' (Chalet owner D).

In 2006, the local authority started building a new two-storey concrete shopping arcade on Long Beach to the anger of the chalet owners, who mounted a substantial local protest. In terms of the TALC, this shopping arcade development, combined with the new Bubu Resort and state government's overall policy for the island, could be seen as perhaps being the beginning of a 'consolidation' stage. However, the construction went on despite attracting an inspection by the then Chief Minister of Terengganu. The main complaint against the shopping arcade was that it would significantly block the view to the sea, given its location on the beach reserve. A long-established operator said: 'We were not consulted over the construction of the shopping arcade, it's not that we are against it but it should not be located along the beach where it would block the open view to the sea'. The shopping arcade opened in 2009, but has significantly changed the visual quality of Long Beach, given that the concrete building did not conform to the human scale of the surrounding mini resorts as well as blocked the surrounding chalets' view of the sea. Despite this, the field visit in 2010 revealed that the adult children of the pioneer operators have since set up internet cafes and tourist information kiosks within the shopping arcade and were handling the online booking for their parents' mini resorts. Suffice to say that while in terms of Resilience Theory, the exogenous factors did create a 'destabilising effect' on the tourist systems in Perhentian Kecil, the local tourism industry managed to quickly adjust their operation to accommodate the recent changes without using a confrontational approach.

To facilitate the development of Bubu Resort in Perhentian Kecil – given its Chinese-Malaysian owner – the Terengganu state government had to take the radical step of exploiting loopholes in the National Land Code (GOM 1965), which stipulates that only *Bumiputras* (Malays) are allowed to own and develop Malay reserve land. Most coastal areas and islands in Malaysia are located on Malay reserve land, including Perhentian Kecil. It should be highlighted that this kind of affirmative protection gave rise to the organic growth of small-scale tourist development within the fishing communities along the east coast of peninsular Malaysia.

Although the whole of Perhentian Kecil is gazetted as Malay reserve land, the law cannot stop non-Malays/*Bumiputras* from getting involved in development, provided that it is carried out in the form of a joint venture or partnership with a local landowner. More often than not, the island landowners are paid a nominal fee to act as sleeping partners, or what is locally known as the 'Ali Baba' syndrome. Although this practice is rife on uninhabited islands, such as Redang, Lang Tengah and Tenggol, it has yet (until Bubu Resort) to penetrate Perhentian Kecil due to the presence of a sizeable (and proud) local Malay community on the island. Despite this, interviews with the operators revealed that 65% of the resorts are currently operated in the form of partnerships with outsiders from the mainland (Table 4). However as mentioned earlier, many of these partners are related to the locals. Bubu Resort was supposed to be a 'guinea pig', with the blessing of the state government to test the reaction (and resolve) of the local operators (pers. comm., a state tourism official, 2008). At the height of the Bubu Resort controversy, the local champion, Pak 'A', suffered poor health and eventually passed away in 2009. His demise left a vacuum in terms of leadership and organisation because until today, there is no formal organisation representing the local operators: 'We don't need one – the other operators are our brothers, sisters and sons. We are family and that is stronger than any formal organisation' (Chalet owner C). Participant observation revealed that the community reaction to the arrival of Bubu Resort was that it brought them closer together and sibling rivalries were put aside. They agreed to accept and accommodate Bubu Resort but pledged that they would not be part of any collaboration with non-Malays that could result in the proliferation of such resorts in the future.

Table 4. Ownership status of mini resorts on Perhentian Kecil

No.	Accommodation	Local	Besut local	Outsider
1.	Rock Garden		√	
2.	Bubu Long Beach resort			√
3.	Chempaka chalets	√		
4.	Lemon grass	√		
5.	Simfony chalets			√
6.	Matahari chalets	√		
7.	Moonlight beach			√
8.	Panorama chalets	√		
9.	Lily chalets			√
10.	Mohsin chalets			√
11.	D'lagoon			√
12.	Rajawali coral			√
13.	Fatimah chalet	√		
14.	Aur Bay			√
15.	Butterfly chalet	√		
16.	Maya beach resort			√
17.	Senja Bay Resort			√
18.	Mira Chalet			√
19.	Petani Beach			√
20.	Impiani resort			√

Source: Fieldwork notes (2007).

Deteriorating Condition of Coral Reefs and the Resulting Change in Attitude

Besides the exogenous factors described earlier, there was also an endogenous factor that could have had a 'destabilising effect' on Perhentian Kecil, which is the deteriorating condition of the coral reefs around the island. Immediately after capturing back Terengganu from the opposition party in 2004, the newly installed Chief Minister instructed that the Terengganu islands should encourage the development of high-end resorts that are certified by Green Globe or the like so that tourists will pay premium rates to enjoy a world-class tourism experience (pers. comm., UPEN Terengganu, 2005). This sentiment was echoed in one of the tourism policies contained in the Terengganu state Structure Plan, which recommended 'the sustainability certification of resorts on the Terengganu Islands so as to attract Green and discerning tourists' (JPBD 2005).

Against this backdrop, media reports and reef monitoring studies carried out by environmental NGOs such as Reef Check Malaysia showed that the quality of coral reefs around Malaysian islands was deteriorating. Coral bleaching was also happening at an alarming rate, to the extent that several dive and snorkelling sites had to be temporarily closed by the Department of Marine Parks (*The Star Online* 2010). Prior to this, the Terengganu state government had been making bold press statements that blamed the deteriorating quality of coral reefs around Perhentian Kecil due to the budget establishments: 'We want to get rid of backpackers from Perhentian Kecil as they destroy the coral reefs ... ' (*The New Straits Times* 2006). The reef monitoring report published by Reef Check Malaysia (2008) vindicated the small-scale operators by concluding that the status of the reefs around Perhentian Kecil was better than that of reefs around the other islands, such as Redang and Tioman (larger-scale developments). However, the report also recommended that the poorly treated sewage problem from the chalets, using septic tanks, had to be addressed. During the 2008–2009 field visits, it was observed that these environmental NGOs were starting to work with the local operators in coming up with strategies and action plans to minimise negative impacts on the coral reefs. At the same time, the foreign tourists going to Perhentian Kecil were becoming more discerning and concerned about environmental sustainability.

During the earlier part of the longitudinal study, the local operators did not feel that their basic sewage treatment was causing water pollution and there had been no attempt to upgrade the existing system, although the government was introducing a centralised treatment system for the village. The 2010 field visit added questions on the willingness of the local operators to adhere to sustainability certification. The majority (92%) said that they were willing to participate in any sustainability certification exercise but could only afford to pay RM 1000 ($313) per resort. The majority also felt that the government should take the lead and subsidise the bulk of the cost, and suggested that the enforcement should be in the form of self-regulation by their local organisation, despite the fact that they had yet to set up a formal association.

Discussions and Conclusions

This paper raises a fundamental question: Is the island now reaching a 'tipping point'? In other words, has Perhentian Kecil reached the moment that could be identified as being when the destination changes from small-scale backpacker tourism to a very different form of tourism development? In essence, the 'tipping point' would also imply the transfer of local ownership and control to outsiders, which could lead to the marginalisation of the local community and potentially negative impacts on the fragile island environment due to overdevelopment. In terms of Butler's (1980) evolutionary TALC model, the findings of the longitudinal study have shown that tourism development in Perhentian Kecil had moved into the 'development' stage, with some characteristics starting to appear from the 'consolidation' stage.

The question can also be raised whether the path along Butler's S-shaped curve is inevitable or are local operators, as the weaker stakeholders – or 'prey' according to Cochrane (2010) – resilient enough to accommodate the changes to the tourist systems brought about by government policy and the arrival of 'predators' such as Bubu Resort?

The organic growth of small-scale tourism development on Perhentian Kecil mirrors the conceptualisation by Oppermann (1993), who identified the primary role of the informal tourism sector in establishing 'drifter' enclaves along the coastal areas of LDCs. Oppermann (1993) also argued that as such enclaves move along the TALC (Butler 1980), they are neither overwhelmed nor displaced by the formal sector but continue to exist alongside the latter. This parallel yet separate existence was originally postulated by Cohen (1982), but Oppermann (1993) suggested that as a competitive, attractive and strategically located enclave evolves into a major destination or hub with heavy investment from the formal sector, the informal sector also moves out of its enclavic nature to become part of mainstream tourism, albeit without losing its distinct informal features. This evolution process appears to be similar to the early stages of many other backpacker destinations in the region, such as Gili Trawangan in Lombok, Indonesia, in the early 1990s (Hampton 1998) or the Southern Thai islands in the early 1980s (Cohen 1982).

The earlier part of the longitudinal study presented the authors with the opportunity to closely examine the dynamics of small-scale tourism development as it gradually moved from Butler's 'involvement stage' to the 'development stage'. One interesting finding concerned the 'learning-by-doing' process (Folke *et al.* 2005), which the local operators went through to compensate for their lack of formal education and training. Ahmad (2005) discovered that the same process was adopted by most fishing communities along the coastal areas of Malaysia, and that the practical knowledge accumulated through this process was shared between the chalet operators within the community.

The arrival of Bubu Resort appeared to bring significant change to the existing tourism system in Perhentian Kecil. Previously, the island seemed to have a fairly uncomplicated tourism system where local family members met the young backpackers' basic needs and this demand was manifested in the form of small-scale, low density development that also had minimal environmental impacts. However, the arrival of Bubu Resort had initially threatened to upset this equilibrium. For the paper's authors, the research problem and questions became more complex at this stage. This then called for the linear narrative based on Butler's TALC (1980) to be revisited. Despite its limited application in tourism studies, Resilience Theory would be able to complement TALC to better understand the complexities of the scenario brought about by the advent of Bubu Resort, and more so, the forces behind it. At this stage, Perhentian Kecil exhibited outward signals of tourism systems that were trapped in transition, in the form of antagonistic reactions from the local community and foreign tourists, as well as 'trial by media' arguably mainly driven by the state government.

Explicitly, both the federal and the state government were trying to scale up coastal and island tourism development along the value chain, as exemplified by the high-value/high-yield tourism rhetoric in various tourism plans and policies that included Perhentian Kecil (e.g., see JPBD 2004; Sea Resources Management 2006;

ECERDC 2007; JPBD 2008; PEMANDU 2010). As a consequence, affirmative policies to protect *Bumiputra* ownership and control, as embedded in the country's New Economic Policy, are being compromised to make coastal and island tourism more competitive and lucrative. In the same light, protectionist measures created by the local planning authority are under pressure of being removed, and to be replaced by a forced commitment to sustainability certification with the view that eco-labelling will increase the island's competitive edge (ECERDC 2007).

It remains to be seen whether the small-scale, locally owned accommodation at Perhentian Kecil will withstand government intervention and new market forces to maintain their identity and market share. Interestingly, since the arrival of Bubu Resort in 2004, the anticipated wave of takeovers, similar to what had happened in neighbouring Redang Island once a large-scale resort (Berjaya Resort) was introduced, has yet to materialise at Perhentian Kecil. It should be pointed out that Redang Island was uninhabited before the advent of tourism, whereas Perhentian Kecil had a sizeable and resilient community.

The situation in Perhentian Kecil resembles the development path that Kampung Cherating Lama experienced, when the arrival of two formal resorts in the late 1980s (Butler's 'development stage') signalled an inevitable transformation of Malaysia's pioneer 'drifter enclave' into a formal resort destination. In applying Resilience Theory to the case of Kampung Cherating Lama, Nguru (2010) discovered that the local operators' ability to adapt to changing market demand and 'kinship support' rather than government intervention were instrumental to their survival once their main market segment, which were the backpackers, left *en masse* for Marang and, subsequently, Perhentian Kecil.

The study findings also support the contention by Dahles (2000) that small-scale tourism operations are more flexible and respond better and swiftly to changes in the marketplace. By using Resilience Theory to describe the impact created by Bubu Resort, it could be said the 'old tourism systems' that had been in place since the advent of tourism had been destroyed. In retrospect, the 'old tourism systems' were already showing signs of becoming irrelevant to current tourist demand, such as the archaic 'first-come-first-served' system and the conviction that small-scale tourism development does not contribute towards environmental degradation. Bubu Resort set a higher standard of service and a business operation that optimises the use of information technology. After an initial reluctance, the local operators too embraced modern technology by getting their adult children to set up Internet cafes and handle online bookings, thus fulfilling the changing expectations of modern-day backpackers (Hampton 2010). Their commitment to responsible tourism principles is now evident in their willingness for their establishments to obtain sustainability certification.

Instead of being taken over and marginalised by large, corporate resorts, the local operators are making a significant contribution towards the creation of a new tourist system in Perhentian Kecil. Community leadership that used to be provided by a 'local champion' has now been assumed by an informal community organisation with the desire to represent and move up the small-scale establishments along the value chain. It is anticipated that a formal tourism association may soon be established, with Bubu Resort as a member.

With better organisation and a sustainable business model, the relationship with government agencies should also improve, which should pave the way for strong multi-stakeholder partnerships to be formed. In turn, this will also enhance access to MOTOUR's Special Tourism Fund as a way of incentivising local operators to move up the value chain. To surmise, the tourist systems in Perhentian Kecil are in the process of being reinvented, having recovered from the shock created by the forces behind Bubu Resort, which should lead to a more sustainable development path.

Perhentian Kecil has many lessons for other LDCs that have embraced island tourism as a catalyst for development. The evolution and life cycle of similar enclavic tourism developments have been deconstructed in the past mainly using spatial temporal models, of which Butler's TALC (1980) had provided a practical framework. While writers such as Choy (1992), Getz (1992) and Agarwal (1997) have criticised the application of Butler's TALC, proponents of Resilience Theory (McKercher 1999; Farrell & Twinning-Ward 2005; Lepp 2008) concur that even though the TALC is considered too linear to analyse the complexity of tourism destinations, its six stages provides a symbiotic interface with the four phases or loops that are considered to be more effective and realistic in analysing this complexity.

By incorporating Resilience Theory towards the end of the longitudinal study, another dimension could be added to the research by capturing not only the physical evolution but also the social construction of the tourist space in Perhentian Kecil (Phillimore & Goodson 2004). There had been the risk that by applying TALC throughout the longitudinal study, the research might have become stuck in a 'comfort zone' without questioning the appropriateness of using a positivist line of enquiry throughout. A mechanistic attempt to equate the evolution of tourism development with the various stages of Butler's TALC would have been a futile exercise once the dynamics of small-scale tourism development on the island had been comprehensively investigated, although approaches are still common (see Graci & Dodds 2010). In the final analysis, the longitudinal study not only produced a new perspective of the evolution of small-scale tourism development but also became a form of rite of passage for the authors as researchers.

Acknowledgements

The research on which this paper reports is associated with two projects, one funded by the Ministry of Tourism, Malaysia, and the other by the British Council (PMI2 Project funded by the UK Department of Business, Innovation and Skills [BIS]) for the benefit of the Malaysian Higher Education Sector and the UK Higher Education Sector. The authors are grateful for the Ministry's assistance, particularly Dr Junaida Lee Abdullah, but the views expressed here are not necessarily those of the Ministry,

BIS or British Council. We would also like to thank Che Wan, JD, Joern, Lngesh and Shima for their assistance with fieldwork, as well as the interview respondents who generously gave their time. The usual disclaimers apply.

References

Agarwal, S. (1997) The resort cycle and seaside tourism: An assessment of its applicability and validity, *Tourism Management*, 18(2), pp. 65–73.

Ahmad, G. (2005) Small firms network in tourism and hospitality: Chalet firms and its owner-managers network, unpublished doctoral dissertation, University of Strathclyde, Glasgow, 2005.

Archer, B. (1977) *Tourism, Multipliers: The State of the Art* (Cardiff: University of Wales Press).

Bardolet, E. (2001) The path towards sustainability in the Balearic Islands. in: D. Ioannides, Y. Apostolopoulos, & S. Sonmez (Eds) *Mediterranean Islands and Sustainable Tourism Development*, pp.193–213 (London: Continuum).

Brenner, L. & Fricke, J. (2007) The evolution of backpacker destinations: The case of Zipolite, Mexico, *International Journal of Tourism Research*, 9(3), pp. 217–230.

Briguglio, L., Butler, R., Harrison, D., & Filho, W. (Eds) (1996) *Sustainable Tourism in Islands and Small States: Case Studies* (London: Pinter).

Butler, R. (1980) The concept of a tourist area cycle of evolution: Implications for management of resources, *Canadian Geographer*, 24, pp. 5–12.

Calgaro, E. & Cochrane, J. (2009) *Comparative Destination Vulnerability Assessment for Thailand and Sri Lanka* (Stockholm: Stockholm Environment Institute).

Choy, D. (1992) Life cycle models for Pacific island destinations, *Journal of Travel Research*, 3, pp. 26–31.

Cochrane, J. (2010) The sphere of tourism resilience, *Tourism Recreation Research*, 35(2), pp. 173–185.

Cohen, E. (1982) Marginal paradises: Bungalow tourism on the islands of Southern Thailand, *Annals of Tourism Research*, 9, pp. 189–228.

Dahles, H. (2000) Tourism, small enterprises and community development. in: G. Richards & D. Hall (Eds) *Tourism and Sustainable Community Development*, pp. 154–169 (London: Routledge).

de Albuquerque, K. & McElroy, J. (1992) Caribbean small island tourism styles and sustainable strategies, *Environmental Management*, 16, pp. 619–632.

Dodds, R. & McElroy, J. (2008) St Kitts at a crossroads, *ARA Journal of Travel Research*, 1(2), pp. 1–10.

ECERDC (East Coast Economic Region Development Council) (2007) *East Coast Economic Region (ECER) Master Plan* (Kuala Lumpur: ECERDC).

ECERDC (East Coast Economic Region Development Council) (2010) *Development Plan for Kampung Penarik Mainland Coastal Tourism Development and Setiu Wetlands State Park, Merang Setiu Terengganu* (Kuala Lumpur: ECERDC).

Fallon, F. (2001) Conflict, power and tourism on Lombok, *Current Issues in Tourism*, 4(6), pp. 481–502.

Farrell, B. H. & Twining-Ward, L. (2004) Reconceptualising tourism, *Annals of Tourism Research*, 31(2), pp. 274–295.

Farrell, B. H. & Twining-Ward, L. (2005) Seven steps towards sustainability: Tourism in the context of new knowledge, *Journal of Sustainable Tourism*, 31(2), pp. 109–122.

Folke, C., Hahn, T., Olsson, P. & Norberg, J. (2005) Adaptive governance of social-ecological systems, *Annual Review of Environment and Resources*, 30, pp. 441–473.

Getz, D. (1992) Tourism planning and destination life cycle, *Annals of Tourism Research*, 19, pp. 752–770.

GOM (Government of Malaysia) (1965) *National Land Code (Act 56)* (Kuala Lumpur: Government of Malaysia).

Gössling, S. (2001) Tourism, economic transition and ecosystem degradation, *Tourism Geographies*, 3, pp. 430–453.

Graci, S. & Dodds, R. (2010) (Eds) *Sustainable Tourism in Island Destinations* (London: Earthscan).

Hampton, J. M. & Hampton, M. P. (2009) Is the beach party over? Tourism and the environment in small islands: A case study of Gili Trawangan, Lombok, Indonesia. in: M. Hitchcock, V. T. King & M. Parnwell (Eds) *Tourism in South East Asia Revisited*, pp. 206–308 (Copenhagen: NIAS Press).

Hampton, M. P. (1998) Backpacker tourism and economic development, *Annals of Tourism Research*, 25(3), pp. 639–660.

Hampton, M. P. (2010) Not such a rough or lonely planet? Backpacker tourism: An academic journey. in: K. Hannam & A. Diekmann (Eds) *Beyond Backpacker Tourism: Mobilities and experiences*, pp. 8–20 (Clevedon: Channel View Publications).

Hamzah, A. (1995) The changing tourist motivation and its implications on the sustainability of small-scale tourism development in Malaysia. Paper presented at the World Conference on Sustainable Tourism, Lanzarote, Spain, April 24–29.

Hamzah, A. (1997) The evolution of small-scale tourism in Malaysia: Problems, opportunities, and implications for sustainability. in: M. J. Stabler (Ed) *Tourism and Sustainability: Principles and Practice*, pp. 199–217 (Wallingford: CAB International).

Hamzah, A. (2007) ICT for tourism SMEs: A partnership building approach. Paper presented at the UNCTAD Asia-Pacific e-Tourism Conference, Kota Kinabalu, Malaysia, March 13–14.

Hills, T. & Lundgren, J. (1977) The impact of tourism in the Caribbean: A methodological study, *Annals of Tourism Research*, 4, pp. 248–267.

Holling, C. S. (1973) Resilience and stability of ecological systems, *Annual Review of Ecology and Systematic*, 4, pp. 1–23.

Holling, C. S. (2001) Understanding the complexity of economic, ecological and social systems, *Ecosystems*, 4, pp. 390–405.

JPBD (Jabatan Perancangan Bandar dan Desa Semenanjung Malaysia) (2004) *Rancangan Tempatan Daerah Kuantan 2004–2015* (Kuala Lumpur: JPBD).

JPBD (Jabatan Perancangan Bandar dan Desa Semenanjung Malaysia) (2005) *Rancangan Struktur Negeri Terengganu 2005–2015* (Kuala Lumpur: JPBD).

JPBD (Jabatan Perancangan Bandar dan Desa Semenanjung Malaysia) (2008) *Rancangan Tempatan Daerah Besut 2008–2020* (Kuala Lumpur: JPBD).

Kaur, C. R. (2007) Ecotourism in Malaysia's marine parks: Principles, issues and the effects of 'green washing' practices. Paper presented at the 5th Asia Pacific Ecotourism Conference (APECO) – Marine Ecotourism: Emerging Best Sustainable Practices and Success Stories, Merang, Malaysia, October 27–28.

Klak, T. & Flynn, R. (2008) Sustainable development and ecotourism: An Eastern Caribbean case study. in: E. L. Jackiewicz & F. J. Bosco (Eds) *Placing Latin America: Contemporary Themes in Human Geography*, pp. 115–136 (Lanham, MD: Rowman & Littlefield).

Lepp, A. (2008) Attitudes towards initial tourism development in a community with no prior tourism experience: The case of Bigodi, Uganda, *Journal of Sustainable Tourism*, 16(1), pp. 5–22.

Lloyd, K. (2003) Contesting control in transitional Vietnam: The development and regulation of traveller cafes in Hanoi and Ho Chi Minh City, *Tourism Geographies*, 5(3), pp. 350–366.

Mckercher, B. (1999) A chaos approach to tourism, *Tourism Management*, 20(4), pp. 425–434.

Ministry of Tourism (MOTOUR) (2007) *About Malaysia*. Available at http://www.virtualmalaysia.com/visit_malaysia/index.cfm?sec=1 (accessed 16 August 2010).

Ministry of Tourism (MOTOUR) & Universiti Teknologi Malaysia (UTM) (2007) *Study on the Contribution and Potential of Backpacker Tourism in Malaysia* (Kuala Lumpur: MOTOUR Kuala Lumpur).

MOTOUR Terengganu (Ministry of Tourism Malaysia Terengganu Office) (2011) *Terengganu Tourism Statistics 2010* (Kuala Terengganu: MOTOUR Terengganu).

Nguru, A. I. (2010) Resilience in tourism business: A case study of Cherating Lama Village, Pahang, unpublished Master's Tourism Planning thesis, Universiti Teknologi Malaysia, Skudai.

Oppermann, M. (1993) Tourism space in developing countries, *Annals of Tourism Research*, 20(3), pp. 535–556.

PEMANDU (Performance Management and Delivery Unit) (2010) *Economic Transformation Programme (ETP): A Roadmap for Malaysia* (Kuala Lumpur: Prime Minister's Department).

Phillimore, J. & Goodson, L. (2004) (Eds) *Qualitative Research In Tourism: Ontologies, Epistemologies and Methodologies* (London: Routledge).

Reef Check Malaysia (2008) *Coral Reef Monitoring Report* (Malaysia: Reef Check Malaysia Bhd.).

Rogerson, C. (2007) Backpacker tourism in South Africa: Challenges and strategic opportunities, *South African Geographical Journal*, 89(2), pp. 161–171.

Royle, S. (2001) *A Geography of Islands: Small Island Insularity* (London: Routledge).

Schianetz, K. & Kavanagh, L. (2008) Sustainability indicators for tourism destinations: A complex adaptive systems approach using systemic indicator systems, *Journal of Sustainable Tourism*, 16(6), pp. 601–628.

Sea Resources Management (2006) *Terengganu Coastal and Islands Study* (Petalaying Jaya: Sea Resources Management).

Spreitzhofer, G. (1998) Backpacking tourism in South-East Asia, *Annals of Tourism Research*, 20(4), pp. 979–983.

The New Straits Times (2006, October 2) Perhentian shifting focus to high end tourists, p. 25.

The Star Online (2010, April 10) *Tourism Ministry Give the Thumbs Up on High End Redang*. Available at http://thestar.com.my/news/story.asp?sec=nation&file=/2010/4/10/nation/6028886 (accessed 10 April 2010).

Timms, B. & Conway, D. (2011) Slow tourism at the Caribbean's geographical margins, *Tourism Geographies*. doi: 10.1080/14616688.2011.610112.

Wall, G. (1996) One name: Two destinations: Planned and unplanned coastal resorts in Indonesia. in: L. Harrison & W. Husbands (Eds) *Issues in Tourism: Case studies in Planning, Development and Marketing*, pp. 41–57 (Chichester: Wiley).

Weaver, D. (1990) Grand Cayman Island and the resort cycle model, *Journal of Travel Research*, 2, pp. 4–15.

Wilkinson, P. (1989) Strategies for tourism in island microstates, *Annals of Tourism Research*, 16, pp. 153–177.

Notes on Contributors

Amran Hamzah is Professor of Tourism Planning in the Faculty of Built Environment, Universiti Teknologi Malaysia. His interests include sustainable tourism planning, small-scale tourism and local communities.

Mark P. Hampton is Senior Lecturer in Tourism Management at Kent Business School, University of Kent. His research interests include small-scale tourism development in South-East Asia, and coastal, island and marine tourism.

Cruise Passengers in a Homeport: A Market Analysis

JUAN GABRIEL BRIDA[*], MANUELA PULINA[**], EUGENIA RIAÑO[*]
& SANDRA ZAPATA AGUIRRE[†]
[*]Competence Centre in Tourism Management and Tourism Economics (TOMTE), School of Economics and Management, Free University of Bolzano, Italy
[**]Economics Department (DiSEA) & CRENoS, University of Sassari, Italy
[†]Institucion Universitaria Colegio Mayor de Antioquia (Medellin, Colombia)

ABSTRACT *The aim of this study is to examine cruise passengers' characteristics, preferences and their overall experience in a port of call. Based on 1,361 survey data collected from passengers in the port of call of Cartagena, during the third quarter of 2009, a three-step multivariate market segment analysis is employed. First, a correspondence analysis is run to reveal the underlying factors in the data; second, based on the correspondence analysis, a hierarchical cluster investigation is performed to segment the sample into homogeneous groups; third, a decision tree is computed to characterise each group. The cluster analysis identifies six distinct market segments differentiated by nationality, satisfaction, safety perception and expenditure. The findings imply several policy directions. In particular, institutions should enhance the perception of safety in Cartagena to guarantee repeated visits, an ad hoc marketing policy may encourage revisit by young South Americans, and managers should extend the inland visiting time that is likely to produce local multiplier effects.*

Introduction

With a forecast of approximately 15 million cruise passengers worldwide in 2010 (Florida-Caribbean Cruise Association [FCCA] 2011; see also Douglas 2011), the cruise industry experiences a remarkable growth. Like the worldwide market trend, cruise tourism in Cartagena de Indias has been rapidly growing and has become a significant element of the local economy. Located in the northern coast of Colombia, Cartagena is a UNESCO World Heritage Site for its majestic walled city and fortresses. This historic heritage, together with its modern infrastructure, has helped this port to become a strategic destination for the main cruise companies. Being also a part of the most preferred region for cruising (the Caribbean), this port of call has been recently included in the worldwide cruises' itineraries.

The number of cruise ship docks in Cartagena has experienced a significant change in the last years. In fact, the port now hosts 80% of the total cruise passengers arriving to Colombia, according to the data provided by the Ministry of Tourism (2010). Since the '90s, cruise ships periodically visited the port. According to the data provided by the Sociedad Portuaria Regional de Cartagena, 246,951 cruise passengers arrived aboard cruise ships during the 2008/2009 cruise year (i.e. the 12 months beginning in May 2008 and ending in April 2009). These included 242,144 passengers spending a day in the port city and 4,807 passengers embarking on their cruise in Cartagena. Amongst the former, an estimated 205,822 passengers (85%) disembarked and visited Cartagena.

During their short visit (on average 6 hours), cruisers have the opportunity to visit the main attractions of the destination, to experience the local culture and purchase goods and services, which are likely to produce multiplier effects within the local economy. This implies that each dollar spent by a visitor on land will generate a direct, indirect and induced effect on several sectors of the local economy. These activities have recently aroused the interest of policy makers and researchers in studying the different impacts generated by this niche of tourism (Klein 2003; Dowling 2006; Organización Mundial del Turismo 2008; Brida & Zapata Aguirre 2010).

Cruise activity generates different economic benefits. These effects are generated not only by cruise passengers but also by crew members and the cruise ship itself. It is also important to take into account that passengers' expenditure is limited by the length of time that the ship spends at a port. According to McKee (1998), if the cruise line could be persuaded to stay longer at a port of call, it would be possible to have an increase in consumers' spending. Added time at a destination translates into more employment and revenues for tourist-related services and multiplier effects for the whole destination economy.

So far, several studies related to cruise passengers' economic impact have been conducted for different destinations, employing various empirical techniques (e.g. Braun *et al.* 2002; Chase & Alon 2002; Chase & McKee 2003; Seidl *et al.* 2006, 2007; Pratt & Blake 2009). Overall, the findings are relatively heterogeneous and depend on the destination analysed. However, by examining different ports of call, in various geographical areas, it may be possible to detect common factors affecting cruiser segments behaviour. Such findings provide useful information for destination managers and policy makers for understanding cruisers' characteristics and motivations for choosing a specific destination, their expenditure pattern and level of satisfaction whilst visiting a destination, the likelihood to return as land tourists and recommend the visited port. Besides, competitiveness issues amongst destinations can also be addressed. In this respect, market segmentation is a key strategy for tourism stakeholders to deal with diversity within a market and focus their products and communication towards each segment more efficiently (Prebensen 2005).

To the authors' best knowledge, the current literature features no empirical studies on cruise passengers' expenditure behaviour in a port of call. Hence, the empirical analysis, based on a high-quality, original database collected from passenger surveys conducted during the third quarter of 2009, aims to provide an in-depth investigation on passengers' behaviour when visiting the port of Cartagena de Indias (Colombia). The sample of the survey consists of 1,361 interviews of cruise passengers before their return to the cruise ship. Specifically, the objective is to assess cruisers' characteristics, preferences and perceptions and to segment the overall cruiser population into homogeneous groups. The approach consists of three methodological enhancements. First, a correspondence analysis is applied to find the underlying factors in the data. Second, a hierarchical cluster analysis and two stopping rules allow identifying a set of homogeneous groups, within which individuals are characterised by similar demographic features, expenditure pattern and overall perception on their experience in Cartagena. Finally, a classification and regression tree is used to identify which variables are better predictors for classifying individuals in the different clusters. The empirical findings provided in this paper give destination managers, local government and policy makers valuable information to formulate private and public development and marketing strategies for tourists' repeat land visits.

The paper is organised as follows. In Section 2, a literature review is provided on cruise passengers' experience on a port of call whilst visiting the destination. In Section 3, an overview of the cruise industry in Cartagena is given. Section 4 provides a description of the data, methodology and empirical findings emerging from the factor-cluster investigation. Concluding remarks are given in the last section.

The Destination

At least three different Colombian ports have been accessed by international cruise ships in the last few years, including Santa Marta, San Andrés and Cartagena de Indias. The city of Cartagena lies on the northern Caribbean shore of Colombia (South America). The port of Cartagena is some 640 kilometres northwest of the country's capital, Bogota, and about 150 kilometres southwest of the town of Santa Marta. Cartagena de Indias was a major centre of colonial Spanish settlement in the Americas. This city is the capital of the department of Bolivar, with a population of 812,595 persons (1997 estimate).

Cartagena de Indias continues to be an economic hub as well as a very popular tourist destination. It is a UNESCO World Heritage site and many of Cartagena's Spanish Colonial buildings and fortifications still stand. Many colonial buildings can be found in the Old City, including the Palace of the Inquisition, a cathedral and a Jesuit college. The port of Cartagena is Colombia's largest port on the Caribbean Sea and lies on the northern shores of Cartagena Bay. This Port is one of the most modern in South America and one of the busiest in Colombia. The cruise ship terminal of the port of Cartagena is located on Manga Island, adjacent to the industrial dock area and is approximately 3 kilometres away from the Old Town.

Cruise tourism is an increasingly important sector of the tourism industry in Cartagena de Indias. Very recently, the city has emerged as a very popular port of call on Caribbean cruise itineraries. When cruise passengers arrive at the port, they can choose to stay on board or to join a guided excursion or tour; they can explore the city on their own, or hire a taxi for sightseeing. The most popular sites for cruisers in Cartagena are the Old City, the San Felipe castle, the Pierino Gallo shopping area and the Heredia Theatre. However, little is known about cruise tourism development in this destination. As described in Table 1, the number of cruise ship visits to Cartagena has increased from 38 in 2006 (including 42,000 passengers and 18,000 crews) to 168 visits in 2009 (270,000 passengers and 120,000 crews).

Table 2 shows the distribution of cruise arrivals at the destination during 2009. Note that cruise ships typically arrive between October and April, at an average of one cruise ship per day.

A Review on Cruisers' Experience in a Port of Call

Research on cruise tourism has become more popular since the beginning of this decade (e.g. Braun *et al.* 2002; Dwyer *et al.* 2004; Dowling 2006; Andriotis & Agiomirgianakis 2010). A vast literature review on economic, sociocultural and environmental effects deriving from cruise activity is provided by Brida & Zapata Aguirre (2010). In this paper, the objective is to provide an in-depth literature review on passengers' perception when visiting a port of call. Destinations, or ports of call, can be regarded as one of the main reasons why travellers choose specific cruises (Henthorne 2000). This should be an argument for encouraging destination managers to identify their cruise passengers market and enhance those factors that can motivate visitors to consider the same destination for a future land vacation. Most cruise industry studies have focused on quality, motivation, satisfaction and intention to repurchase a cruise trip (e.g. Qu & Ping 1999; Wilkinson 1999; Petrick 2004a, 2004b, 2005; Petrick *et al.* 2006, 2007; Petrick & Sirakaya 2004; Duman & Mattila 2005; Weaver 2005; De la Viña & Ford 2001). But, to the best of our knowledge, just a few papers have concentrated on analysing the different characteristics, behaviour and onshore experience of cruise passengers whilst visiting a port of call.

For the United States, Gabe *et al.* (2006) carry out a logit regression model to identify the factors that influence a cruise passenger's intention to return to the port of Bar Harbor. The study was conducted during the 2002 cruise season. Their results indicate that factors such as the total number of visits and the length of stay in port have a positive effect on the stated likelihood to revisit the destination, whilst the distance between respondents' place of residence and Bar Harbor has a negative effect. The authors also conclude that household income does not play a significant role on cruisers' stated intention to return to Bar Harbor.

Table 1. Cruise ship arrivals in Cartagena de Indias, 1998–2009

Year	Ships	Passengers	Crews	Year	Ships	Passengers	Crews	Year	Ships	Passengers	Crews
1998	161	148,733	76,343	2002	71	85,880	39,299	2006	38	42,024	18,626
1999	162	178,586	86,616	2003	32	31,063	14,335	2007	76	108,892	49,775
2000	117	147,511	73,874	2004	43	38,946	18,312	2008	137	206,691	95,514
2001	127	168,855	80,391	2005	35	41,542	17,993	2009	168	270,257	120,420

Source: Sociedad Portuaria Regional de Cartagena.

Table 2. Cruise ship arrivals in Cartagena de Indias in 2009: seasonal variation

Month	Ships	Passengers	Month	Ships	Passengers	Month	Ships	Passengers
January	26	37,076	May	1	1,240	September	1	1,913
February	24	40,412	June	0	0	October	19	27,838
March	23	38,363	July	0	0	November	20	32,853
April	24	42,784	August	1	1,931	December	29	45,847

Source: Sociedad Portuaria Regional de Cartagena.

Using data obtained from a survey conducted on cruise passengers who visited an ecotourism area located close to the Panama Canal, Thurau *et al.* (2007) apply a factor analysis to identify the travel preferences of passengers visiting the area. They employ a cluster analysis to determine the different market segments of the respondents and a chi-square analysis to develop the different profiles of each segment by identifying the statically significant variables. They show that the different clusters are related to different activities at the destination, that is culture, adventure and natural attractions.

Following Gabe *et al.* (2006), similar objectives are defined by Silvestre *et al.* (2008). In order to analyse the main factors of attractiveness of the Azores to cruise passengers and determine which of them influences their intention regarding repurchasing the trip and recommending this cruise to friends and relatives, the authors conducted a survey during the 2004 cruise ship season with a total sample of 973 respondents. Results of the structural equation model performed show that factors such as the city's attractions and the overall visit experience are the most important determinants of the intention to return to the Azores and to recommend the islands to friends and relatives. Hence, these researchers suggest the need to implement policy measures aimed at improving these aspects. Other factors such as safety, hospitality of the locals and cleanliness of the environment are recognised as less relevant. Though satisfaction with the local population and services positively and significantly influence value for money, their influence on behavioural intentions is not found to be statistically significant.

From a survey conducted by the Curaçao Tourism Development Bureau (CTDB) in cooperation with the Curaçao Institute for Social and Economic Studies (CURISES) during the 2005–2006 cruise season, Miriela and Lennie (2010) examine the factors that motivate cruise passengers to return to Curaçao for a land-based vacation. Empirically, a logit analysis is applied. Their findings reveal that the following variables have a positive impact on cruise passengers' intention to return to the island: the number of hours spent in Curaçao, being employed, and being a repeat cruise passenger. Cruise tourists who received information onshore and with a higher level of education are also more likely to return. By contrast, high-income cruise tourists and cruise tourists who had taken the overall sightseeing excursion are not inclined to come back as land tourists.

Andriotis and Agiomirgianakis (2010) study cruise ship passengers' motivation, satisfaction and likelihood of return to the port of Heraklion (Crete, Greece) using a factor analysis. The findings suggest that 'exploration' and 'escape' are amongst the main motivations of visitors, and 'product and services' as well as 'tour pace' are significant dimensions in shaping overall satisfaction levels. Researchers point out to destination managers of Heraklion that they may direct their efforts in extending the amount of time that passengers spend offshore.

Though several studies refer to the experience of cruisers within the ship, to the best of the authors' knowledge, only a few studies exist on cruisers' experience in a port of call (e.g. Fanning & James 2006; Silvestre *et al.* 2008; Andriotis & Agiomirgianakis 2010). Nevertheless, some stylised facts can be drawn. Whatever the approach used, length of stay and overall experience, in terms of culture and attractions provided in the destination, are the main factors that positively influence cruisers' perception and their intention to repeat their visit to the same destination either as cruisers or land tourists. The present paper, via a cluster and a classification tree analysis, aims at expanding this strand of research, providing new evidence on the main factors characterising customers' preferences and motivations.

Methodology and Data

The aim of this study is to understand cruise passengers' characteristics, preferences and perceptions. As a further objective, unique groups of visitors are identified to examine how they differ in their behaviour and socio-demographics characteristics. To achieve the proposed objectives, a quantitative analysis, organised in three parts, is conducted. In the first part, a correspondence analysis is applied to reveal the underlying factors (or dimensions) in the data. This technique is a special case of factor analysis, where the input variables are qualitative. This procedure is carried out with the survey items in order to guarantee the absence of correlations between factorial scores.

In the second part, based on the correspondence analysis results, a hierarchical cluster analysis is introduced to find homogeneous groups. Cluster analysis consists of grouping similar objects according to their degree of similarity. Objects within each cluster are more closely related to one another than objects assigned to different clusters, and each cluster can be distinguished from the others (Brida *et al.* 2010).

Finally, in the third part, a Decision Tree is constructed (Breiman *et al.* 1984) to characterise and describe the grouping. This is a standard machine learning technique that has been used for a wide range of applications. This non-parametric procedure allows one to create a classification algorithm without any assumption on the involved distribution. The procedure is robust against outliers and is a valid tool independently of the nature of the explanatory variables, which can be continuous, binary nominal or ordinal.

To this aim, data were collected by means of face-to-face interviews with cruise passengers in Cartagena. Based on the literature review and discussions with Cartagena cruise stakeholders (including port managers, tour operators and local and national government tourism offices), a survey was designed. The questionnaire was submitted by trained personnel to onshore visitors soon after they finished visiting the city and prior to returning on board during the months of October and November 2009. It consists of 23 questions that were compiled in four sections. The first section collects demographic information. The second section assembles information on the trip, such as the main reason for choosing it and how the cruise trip was purchased. The third section contains questions on visitors' expenditure behaviour. Finally, in the fourth section, tourists were asked to indicate their satisfaction with the port of call around 20 different items, with a five-point Likert scale, ranging from 'very dissatisfied' to 'very satisfied'. Moreover, their perception of security was assessed

Table 3. Characteristics of cruisers to Cartagena de Indias

Residence	(%)	Age	% in category
USA	56.6	56	64.4
Europe	8.8	46–55	16.5
Canada	9.3	26–45	16.8
Venezuela	16.7	16–25	1.6
Other Latin-American countries	5.0	<15	0.7
Education	(%)	Income	% in category
Below high school	2.16	<$25,000	8.4
High school	18.07	$26,000–$50,000	14.5
College/degree	56.57	$51,000–$75,000	16.2
Postgraduate	23.20	$76,000–$100,000	10.4
First cruise (% yes)	25.1	$101,000–$150,000	8.0
First visit (% yes)	87.8	$150,000	7.5
Marital Status (% married)	75.4	Do not know/no answer	34.9
Intend to return (% yes)	46.3	Recommend (% yes)	59.2

through a four-point Likert scale, ranging from 'very unsafe' to 'very safe'. The questionnaire was administered into two languages: Spanish and English. The population of this study consists of passengers older than 18 years of age who disembarked from the cruise ship to the city of Cartagena between September 27 and November 14, 2009. During this period, 28 cruise ships arrived in the port with 42,936 passengers. The questionnaire was submitted to 1,451 visitors, and after a revision, 1,213 were retained as valid and complete.

In Table 3, a summary of the descriptive statistics of the sample is presented. The great majority of the respondents were from the United States (56.6%), followed by Venezuelan visitors (16.7%). More than 70% of the sample was married. More than half of the cruise visitors were over 56 years of age and had either a college level of education or a college degree. Their income was almost equally spread between 26 and 75 thousand US$. Almost one third (25.1%) were first-time cruisers, and the vast majority (87.8%) were first-time visitors in Cartagena.

Results from Correspondence Analysis

From the application of the correspondence analysis to over 53 items, five factors arise that explain 83.1% of the total data variance according to the Benzecrí's index (Escofier & Pages 1988). The interpretation and denomination results from the values of their loadings are reported in Table 4.

The first factor, 'High satisfaction with human and physical capital', is connected with the satisfaction variables. Table 4 shows this factor to be predominant, representing 38.1% of the total data variance. By construction, it also discriminates the cruisers

Table 4. Factor analysis

Factors	Loadings	% inertia	% accumulated inertia
Factor 1: High satisfaction with human and physical capital		38.11	38.11
Initial shore side welcome	8.85		
Harbour facilities and services	9.57		
Time for the visit of Cartagena	8.22		
Variety of attractions	8.59		
The historic centre	8.53		
Tourism information	8.03		
Friendliness of residents	8.48		
Factor 2: Repeated cruise travellers		18.27	56.38
Age	10.06		
Is this your first cruise ship?	10.96		
Nationality	12.73		
Number of previous trips	10.32		
Probability of return	8.08		
Factor 3: Perception on safety		12.2	68.58
Safety in port	19.51		
Safety in streets and roads	20.01		
Safety in taxis	19.45		
Safety in tours	18.81		
Factor 4: Purchases ashore		8.19	76.77
Tour guide services	8.82		
Souvenirs	9.4		
Total expenditure	15.9		
Factor 5: Compliance with human and physical capital		6.31	83.08
Initial shore side welcome	8.35		
Harbour facilities and services	8.78		
Variety of attractions	10.03		
The historic centre	11.5		
Tourism information	11.06		

Note: The most important variables for each factor are presented. The percentage of inertia shows which factors are those that mostly explain the variability of the original data.

who have a high level of satisfaction against the others. The second factor, 'Repeated cruise travellers', identifies the cruise passengers who have travelled before, and are older than 56 years. The variable with the highest loading is 'nationality', that relates to the fact that Americans are the oldest customers. The third factor, 'Perception of safety', identifies the degree of perceived security in the port, in streets and roads, taxis and tours. It separates a safety perception from an unsafe perception of the destination. The fourth factor, 'Purchases ashore', includes souvenirs, tour guides and total expenditure that accounts for the highest loadings. It discriminates individuals who actually did purchase something against those who did not purchase any item or service. The fifth factor, 'Compliance with human and physical capital', includes the initial welcome, tourism information, variety of attractions, harbour facilities and services, the historic centre. It separates cruisers who are satisfied against those who are not satisfied with their holiday experience.

Results from Cluster Analysis

The cluster analysis, carried out using a hierarchical classification method with the factorial scores of the five factors obtained below, identifies six groups of cruisers. The stopping rules used are the Pseudo-F (Calinski & Harabasz 1974) and the Pseudo-t test (Duda & Hart 1973). Both tests indicate that the optimal number of clusters is six. The general results from the cluster analysis are provided in Table 5.

- *Cluster 1*: Cruisers with a positive perception on safety and the lowest expenditure pattern. This group contains 307 respondents (22.6% of the sample) and identifies those tourists who have a positive perception on safety. They belong to the oldest population with an average age above 56 years. These types of consumers do not spend much during their offshore shopping trip. The total expenditure pro capita is just above 70 US$. Hence, they do not contribute much to the multiplier effects on the local economy.

Table 5. Cluster analysis

	Cluster 1	Cluster 2	Cluster 3	Cluster 4	Cluster 5	Cluster 6
First cruise trip	23.5%	30.1%	15.8%	20.9%	26.5%	30.0%
North Americans	74.6%	66.3%	74.5%	64.2%	58.8%	41.7%
South Americans	17.9%	23.6%	10.9%	18.9%	24.8%	27.8%
Europeans	5.9%	8.7%	11.5%	12.2%	11.8%	19.3%
More than 4 hours out of the port	34.2%	35.5%	32.7%	42.6%	42.4%	40.3%
Visit more than five places	28.9%	32.9%	30.3%	35.8%	36.1%	36.8%
Purchase an organised tour	59.3%	70.3%	75.2%	70.3%	77.3%	58.7%
Guide tour expenditure	31,7	27,8	48,1	54,5	39,0	35,6
Food expenditure	11,5	19,8	11,4	25,6	21,3	16,4
Souvenirs expenditure	23,7	29,7	37,9	28,2	25,1	37,8
Jewellery expenditure	117,8	159,1	142,9	94,8	87,7	139,7
Total expenditure per capita	73,3	93,4	105,6	95,5	73,6	93,1
Likely to return to Cartagena	38.7%	43.5%	35.7%	45.9%	47.9%	52.0%
Likely recommend Cartagena as a destination	52.7%	55.0%	49.1%	60.1%	58.8%	66.8%

Note: For some significant statements in the questionnaire, the table shows the percentage of members of each cluster that gives a positive answer and the average expenditure in US$.

- *Cluster 2*: Satisfied cruisers with a positive perception on safety and with a high expenditure pattern. This group contains 276 cruisers (20.3% of the sample) and identifies those tourists who are satisfied with their vacation experience, have a positive perception on safety in Cartagena and have a relatively high expenditure pattern (93 US$); 60.4% of the individuals had purchased food, with an average expenditure of 19 US$, whilst average expenditure on souvenirs was 29 US$. Amongst all the clusters, they have the highest average expenditure for jewellery, particularly emeralds, hence producing important multiplier effect within the local economy (159 US$). They belong to the oldest population group and less than half expects to revisit the destination, but 55.5% would recommend the trip.

- *Cluster 3*: Repeat cruisers with an overall negative perception on the visit experience and the highest expenditure pattern. This group consists of 166 members (12.2%) and identifies those visitors who would not particularly recommend the destination to friends and family (only 49.1%). They belong to the oldest population group, and they do not regard Cartagena as a safe destination. These types of consumers have the highest average expenditure pro capita of approximately 105.6 US$. Hence, they produce economic benefits to the local economy, creating important multiplier effects. The activity of the members of this cluster during the visit to Cartagena consists mostly of shopping, and their high expenditure is a consequence of buying jewellery and handicrafts. As their motivation to visit the destination is shopping rather than sightseeing, they stay at the destination less time than the average passenger. These passengers perceive the destination as not safe, but they still choose to buy emeralds and other type of jewellery and handicrafts. In sum, the apparent contradiction of high expenditure and negative perception of the visit can be explained as a consequence of the fact that they just visit Cartagena to buy some special goods.

- *Cluster 4*: Cruisers with a negative perception on safety. This group consists of 149 individuals (10.9%). It identifies those visitors who may be repeat cruisers and have a negative perception on the safety of Cartagena, though they are generally satisfied with their tourism experience. They belong to the oldest population group. In economics terms, this cluster has an average expenditure above 95 US$; 60.4% of the individuals has purchased jewellery with an average expenditure of 95 US$. Besides, their average expenditure during land tours in general is the highest with respect to the other groups (54 US$). Hence, this group of consumers has a particular role within the local economy.

- *Cluster 5*: Highly satisfied cruisers with a good perception of safety. This group consists of 239 members (17.5%) and identifies those visitors who are highly satisfied with their visit experience in Cartagena and have a good perception of the destination's safety. More than half of them state that they would come back as land tourists in Cartagena (47.9%), whilst 58.8% is likely to recommend the destination to friends and family. Their average expenditure per capita is 74 US$.

- *Cluster 6*: Young first cruisers with an overall good perception. This group consists of 234 members (16.5%). It is characterised by young individuals – 57.0% are between 26 and 45 years old – with a high level of education – 67.0% has a Bachelor education; 30.0% of individuals has experienced a cruise holidays for the first time and the great majority bought the cruise package from a travel agency (62.8%). They are likely to revisit Cartagena as land tourists (52.0%) and to recommend it to friends and family (66.8%). Overall their holiday experience has been positive. This type of consumers can be regarded as risk takers. They prefer visiting several locations in Cartagena on their own rather than being supported by a tour guide; 91.5% visited San Felipe Castle, 76.0% visited Las Bovedas and 64.1% visited the emerald shops.

Classification Tree

The basic idea behind the decision tree is to first identify prediction rules from the data and then illustrate them as a binary tree where each terminal node (leaf) corresponds to a class, whilst all the intermediate nodes represent measured variables. From a practitioner's point of view, this methodology enables one to provide clearer policy and marketing implications. In this case, the model will be used as a form of discriminating analysis. The aim is to identify which variables are better predictors for the classification of individuals in the different clusters obtained through the previous analysis. The response variable has six categories, corresponding to the segmentation obtained in the previous section. The predictors are the same variables used for the cluster analysis. The algorithm begins with the whole sample, and the splitting is performed based on two main criteria: first, a criterion to evaluate the homogeneity of the nodes obtained in the splitting: the function of impurity. This measure is in relation to classes; a pure node is one that is composed of individuals of the same cluster or class. In this case, the algorithm uses the Gini's Index as a measure of impurity. Second, a criterion to determine the best split in each step, which is the deviance criterion. When the impurity function reaches a minimum value defined a priori, the splitting stops.

Figure 1 shows the classification tree. Only 5 of the original 53 variables are represented in the CART (Classification and Regression Tree). The most discriminating variables are 'opinion about safety and security in the port', 'nationality', 'satisfaction with the harbour facilities and services', 'satisfaction with the historical centre' and 'satisfaction with the variety of attractions'.

For example, following the first path, individuals who consider the port of Cartagena as unsafe are included in Cluster 4. However, if individuals regard the port of call as safe, then one discriminates them with respect to their nationality. Hence, if the cruisers are from South America, they are included in Cluster 6, if they are from North America, Europe and other countries, they are classified otherwise, and so on.

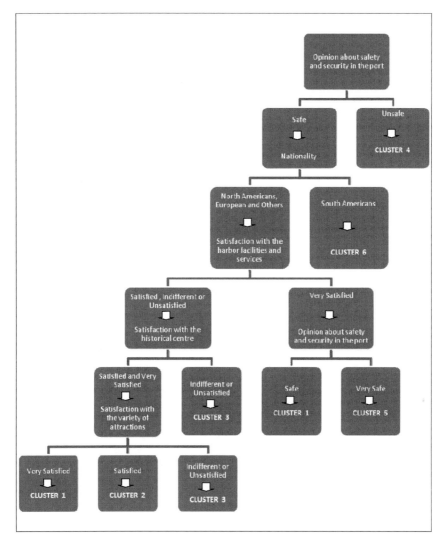

Figure 1. Classification tree obtained as a result of using the product of the cluster analysis as response variable. *Note*: the terminal nodes of the tree are classified into one of the six groups obtained from the cluster analysis. The paths to terminal nodes indicate which variables discriminate between groups.

Table 6 compares the response variables, with six clusters, with the prediction of the model obtained. Note that the model has a relatively strong predictive power, with approximately 68% of correct classified cases. Clusters 4 and 6 have the best predictions (94.6% and 86.1%, respectively), and in fact, these clusters are terminal

Table 6. Misclassification table

Observed	Cluster 1	Cluster 2	Cluster 3	Cluster 4	Cluster 5	Cluster 6	Total	percentage
			Predicted					
Cluster 1	151	86	8	12	34	17	308	49.2
Cluster 2	28	211	11	2	8	17	277	76.4
Cluster 3	20	43	79	10	2	12	166	47.9
Cluster 4	2	5	1	141	0	0	149	94.6
Cluster 5	43	20	0	4	145	26	238	60.9
Cluster 6	19	9	0	1	2	192	223	86.1
Total	263	374	99	170	191	264	1361	67.6

Notes: The table shows observed versus predicted values for the response variable. The misclassification error is represented out of the diagonal, where are the cases in which the model prediction is different to the real classification of the individuals allocated.

nodes at the beginning of the tree. This means that a good prediction can be obtained by just considering either one or two key variables.

Overall, these findings give important indications to economic agents that can use relatively straightforward information to analyse and discriminate amongst clusters of consumers, knowing the variables that most affect their perceptions on the destination. For example, Cluster 1 is composed of very heterogeneous individuals, which makes it more difficult to predict the key variables affecting their perception, whereas Cluster 4 can be considered as the most predictable group.

Discussion and Conclusions

Though the cruise sector has been experiencing a remarkable growth in recent years, to the best of the authors' knowledge, few papers investigate cruise passengers' experience within a port of call. The present study has contributed to this strand of literature, by investigating cruisers' characteristics, preferences and perceptions. To this aim, microeconomic data were collected via a survey of cruise ship passengers who stopped in Cartagena de Indias (Colombia) during the third semester of 2009. The contribution of this paper has consisted in a methodological enhancement based on a high quality and an original database. First, the use of a hierarchical cluster analysis has identified a set of clusters, within which individuals are characterised by similar demographic features, expenditure pattern and overall perception on their holiday experience in Cartagena. Second, a CART has been used to identify which variables are better predictors for classifying individuals in the different clusters.

Specifically, the factor analysis performed in this study has identified five factors that explain 83% of the total data variance. These factors are as follows: (a) high satisfaction with human and physical capital, (b) repeated cruise travellers, (c) perception of safety, (d) purchases ashore and (e) compliance with human and physical capital.

By identifying coherent groups of individuals with common sets of perception on the overall visit experience, expenditure pattern and safety of the destination, the cluster analysis has offered a more carefully targeted approach to the segmentation of cruisers. It must be noted that (as is usual in other studies) some demographic variables, such as gender, do not discriminate other variables. However, a distinct cluster including young people has been identified that distinguishes such a group of individuals with respect to older customers.

The classification tree analysis has provided a valid and practical tool to identify the variables and factors that most affect each cluster. Turning to the highly predictable and reliable groups, it has emerged that Cluster 4 (Cruisers with a negative perception on safety) is only influenced by the negative perception of safety in the harbour. This implies that Cartagena policy makers should promote and build an imagine of safety for these visitors who, on the one hand, are repeat cruise tourists and, on the other hand, have a high overall expenditure pattern, especially for guide tours, hence representing profitable customers for businesses. Notably, this finding is in contrast with Silvestre *et al.*'s (2008) study, for the Azores, where safety is not recognised to be an important factor in customers' intention to repurchase the trip and recommend it. It is worthwhile noticing that with respect to the expenditure in guided tours, there is no difference in the tour guides' revenues whether the passenger purchases the tour from the cruise line or directly from the operator. However, the consumer incurs in a greater expenditure in the former type of purchase. Normally, the tour operator charges 50 US$ for a tour, whereas a passenger buying a tour before arriving to the destination pays approximately 100 US$. It is surprising that 63.4% of the interviewed sample declared to have purchased the tour from the cruise line. Nevertheless, this higher price pays for a higher perception of security and reputation of the cruise line.

Cluster 6 (Young first time cruisers with an overall good perception) has also turned out to have a high prediction reliability. The demographic profile and attitude towards the trip in this cluster is very distinct with respect to all the other clusters. These are not repeat travellers but have a good expenditure pattern especially on jewellery and souvenirs. Hence, ad hoc marketing campaigns and special offers may encourage young Latin Americans to revisit Cartagena as land tourists. As a matter of fact, distance has been found to be a critical determinant for repeated visits (Gabe *et al.* 2006). For the members of this cluster, the relatively short distance between their country of origin and Cartagena may encourage their return to the destination. Notably, this finding is consistent with the recent survey run by Cruise Lines International Association (CLIA; see Dowling 2006), where it is emphasised that if, on the one hand, full-time retirees are declining and family cruisers are increasing, then, on the other hand, passengers are becoming more youthful and demand more active itineraries.

Cluster 3, though having a low reliability, is composed of repeat cruisers with an overall negative perception on the visit experience. Nevertheless, on the one hand, they have also shown the highest expenditure pattern, especially in jewellery and guide tours; on the other hand, on average they only spent 4 hours visiting Cartagena. Hence, as shown by other empirical studies for Bar Harbour (Gabe *et al.* 2006), Curaçao (Miriela & Lennie 2010) and Heraklion in Crete (Andriotis & Agiomirgianakis 2010), destination managers should direct their efforts to extending the length of stay in Cartagena. This policy may be able to establish more economic, social and cultural benefits to the residents.

Overall, the empirical findings provided in this paper can give destination managers, local government and policy makers valuable information to formulate private and public development and marketing strategies for repeat tourism visits in Cartagena. Specifically, it would be possible to enhance a marketing plan directed to members of Cluster 6, mainly young South American customers. This policy may be implemented with specific campaigns (e.g. brochures, special holiday packages) that are likely to be economically feasible and effective. Moreover, for the particular segment of the market, characterised by high spenders, repeat visitors who also have a negative perception of safety (Cluster 4), local institutions and managers should promote international campaigns in order to change visitors and tourists' perception of safety and develop a positive image of the destination. This cluster needs to be targeted by specific marketing policies, as it is composed of high spenders who are important for the local economy.

Future research will involve the repetition of the survey and analysis for a different period of time (such as the low season) and other port of call destinations. It would be also of interest to compare cruisers' behaviour with that of stay-over tourists in Cartagena. However, no data are available at this stage.

Acknowledgements

This study is part of a larger research project funded by the Colombian Tourism Board – Proexport Project: "El impacto del turismo de cruceros. Análisis empírico para el caso del Caribe Colombiano", the Autonomous Province of Bolzano, Project "Tourism, growth, development and sustainability. The case of the South Tyrolean region" and by the Free University of Bolzano, Project "L'impatto del turismo di crociere. Analisi empirico per il caso del Caraibi Colombiano". They played no active role in the design, analysis or publication of this research.

References

Andriotis, K. & Agiomirgianakis, G. (2010) Cruise visitors' experience in a Mediterranean port of call, *International Journal of Tourism Research*, 12, pp. 390–404.

Braun, B. M., Xander, J. A., & White, K. R. (2002) The impact of the cruise industry on a region's economy: A case study of Port Canaveral Florida, *Tourism Economics*, 8(3), pp. 281–288.

Breiman, L., Friedman, J., Stone, C. J., & Olshen, R. A. (1984) *Classification and Regression Trees* (New York: Chapman and Hall).

Brida, J. G., Such, M. J., Parte Esteban, L., & Risso, W. A. (2010) The international hotel industry in Spain: Its hierarchical structure, *Tourism Management*, 31(1), pp. 57–73.

Brida, J. G. & Zapata Aguirre, S. (2010) Cruise tourism: Economic, socio-cultural and environmental impacts, *International Journal of Leisure and Tourism Marketing*, 1(3), pp. 205–226.

Calinski, R. B. & Harabasz, J. A. (1974) Dendrite method for cluster analysis, *Communications in Statistics – Theory and Methods*, 3(1), pp. 1–27.

Chase, G. & Alon, I. (2002) Evaluating the economic impact of cruise tourism: A case study of Barbados, *Anatolia: An International Journal of Tourism and Hospitality Research*, 13(1), pp. 5–18.

Chase, G. L. & McKee, D. L. (2003) The economic impact of cruise tourism on Jamaica, *Journal of Tourism Studies*, 14(2), pp. 16–22.

De la Viña, L. & Ford, J. (2001) Logistic regression analysis of cruise vacation market potential: Demographic and trip attribute perception factors, *Journal of Travel Research*, 39, pp. 406–410.

Dowling, R. K. (2006) *Cruise Ship Tourism* (London: CABI).

Duda, R. O. & Hart, P. E. (1973) *Pattern Classification and Scene Analysis* (London: Wiley).

Douglas, W. (2011) *Berlitz Guide to Cruising & Cruise Ships*. Available at http://www.berlizpublishing.com (accessed 10 January 2011).

Duman, T. & Mattila, A. S. (2005) The role of affective factors on perceived cruise vacation value, *Tourism Management*, 26(3), pp. 311–323.

Dwyer, L., Douglas, N., & Livaic, Z. (2004) Estimating the economic contribution of a cruise ship visit, *Tourism in Marine Environments*, 1(1), pp. 5–16.

Escofier, B. & Pages, J. (1988) *Analyses Factorielles Simples et Multiples* [Multiple and Simple Factor Analysis] (Paris: Dunod).

Fanning, C. & James, J. (2006) When one size doesn't fit all, in: R. K. Dowling (Ed) *Cruise Ship Tourism* (London: CABI).

Florida-Caribbean Cruise Association (FCCA). (2011) *Florida-Caribbean Cruise Association. Cruise Industry Overview 2011*. Available at http://www.f-cca.com/research.html (accessed 18 October 2010).

Gabe, T., Collen, L., & McConnon, J. (2006) Likelihood of cruise ship passenger return to a visited Port: The case of Bar Harbor, Maine, *Journal of Travel Research*, 44, pp. 281–287.

Henthorne, T. L. (2000) An analysis of expenditures by cruise ship passengers in Jamaica, *Journal of Travel Research*, 38(3), pp. 246–250.

Klein, R. A. (2003) *Cruising Out of Control: The Cruise Industry, the Environment, Workers, and Maritimes. Canadian Center for Policy Alternatives – Nova Scotia*. Available at http://www.policyalternativies.ca (accessed 20 November 2008).

McKee, D. L. (1998) Cruise tourism: Assessing its structural and environmental costs, *Caribbean Affairs*, 8(1), pp. 135–147.

Ministry of Tourism. (2010) *Tourism 2010: Cruise ships and passengers arrivals to Colombia*. Available at https://www.mincomercio.gov.co/publicaciones.php?id=16590 (Accessed 3 November 2010).

Miriela, C. G. L. & Lennie, P. (2010) *Cruise Tourists Returning to Curaçao for a Land-Based Vacation: A Logit Model*, BNA.WP/10/1 (Research Department of the Central Bank of the Netherlands Antilles). Available at http://sta.uwi.edu/conferences/09/salises/documents/L.%20Pau.pdf (accessed 25 October 2011).

Organización Mundial del Turismo. (2008) *Turismo de cruceros. Situación actual y tendencias* [Cruise Tourism. Current situation and trends]. (Madrid: Primera edición).

Petrick, J. F. (2004a) First timers' and repeaters' perceived value, *Journal of Travel Research*, 43(1), pp. 29–38.

Petrick, J. F. (2004b) The roles of quality, value, and satisfaction in predicting cruise passengers' behavioral intentions, *Journal of Travel Research*, 42(4), pp. 397–407.

Petrick, J. F. (2005) Segmenting cruise passengers with price sensitivity, *Tourism Management*, 26, pp. 753–762.

Petrick, J. F., Li, X., & Park, S.-Y. (2007) Cruise passengers' decision-making processes, *Journal of Travel & Tourism Marketing*, 23(1), pp. 1–14.

Petrick, J. F. & Sirakaya, E. (2004) Segmenting cruisers by loyalty, *Annals of Tourism Research*, 31(2), pp. 172–173.

Petrick, J. F., Tonner, C., & Quinn, C. (2006) The utilization of critical incident technique to examine cruise passengers' repurchase intentions, *Journal of Travel Research*, 44(3), pp. 273–280

Pratt, S. & Blake, A. (2009) The economic impact of Hawaii's cruise industry, *Tourism Analysis*, 14(3), pp. 337–351.

Prebensen, N. (2005) Segmenting the group tourist heading for warmer weather: A Norwegian example, *Journal of Travel & Tourism Marketing*, 19(4), pp. 27–40.

Qu, H. & Ping, E. W. Y. (1999) A service performance model of Hong Kong cruise travelers' motivation factors and satisfaction, *Tourism Management*, 20, pp. 237–244.

Seidl, A., Guillano, F., & Pratt, L. (2007) Cruising for colones: Cruise tourism economics in Costa Rica, *Tourism Economics*, 13(1), pp. 67–85.

Seidl, A., Guillano, F., & Pratt, P. (2006) Cruise tourism and community economic development in Central America and the Caribbean: The case of Costa Rica, *Pasos Online*, 4(2), pp. 213–224.

Silvestre, A., Santos, C. M., & Ramalho, C. (2008) Satisfaction and behavioral intentions of cruise passengers visiting the Azores, *Tourism Economics*, 14(1), pp. 169–184.

Thurau, B., Carver, A., Mangun, J., Basman, C., & Bauer, G. (2007) A market segmentation analysis of cruise ship tourists visiting the Panama Canal Watershed: Opportunities for ecotourism development, *Journal of Ecotourism*, 6(1), pp. 1–18.

Weaver, A. (2005) Spaces of containment and revenue capture: 'Super-sized' cruise ships as mobile tourism enclaves, *Tourism Geographies*, 7(2), pp. 165–184.

Wilkinson, P. (1999) Caribbean cruise tourism: Delusion? Illusion? *Tourism Geographies*, 1(3), pp. 261–282.

Notes on Contributors

Juan Gabriel Brida is Associate Professor of Economics at the School of Economics and Management, Free University of Bolzano. His research interests and expertise are in the areas of tourism economics and economic growth. He has a degree in Mathematics from the Universidad de la República (Uruguay) and a PhD in Economics from the University of Siena.

Manuela Pulina holds a PhD in Applied Economics, University of Southampton (UK). She is a Lecturer at the Economics Department (DiSEA), University of Sassari & CRENoS, Italy. Her main research interests are tourism economics, crime economics, heritage economics and applied econometrics.

Eugenia Riaño holds a degree in Statistics. She was Research Assistant at the Free University of Bozen and currently she is Research Assistant at the Institute of Statistics – UdelaR, Uruguay. Her research area is sampling theory and multivariate analysis.

Sandra Zapata Aguirre holds a degree in Tourism Management. She was Research Assistant at the Free University of Bozen and is currently a member of the research group Grupo de Investigación Empresarial y de Turismo (GIET) at the Faculty of Management – Institución Universitaria Colegio Mayor de Antioquia (Medellin, Colombia). Her research interests and expertise are in the areas of tourism management and planning.

The Power of Place: Tourism Development in Costa Rica

ERIC NOST

Department of Geography, University of Kentucky, Lexington, USA

ABSTRACT *In this paper, I question how representations of tourist destinations color and are colored by development. Presenting the results of ethnographic fieldwork conducted on the southern Caribbean coast of Costa Rica, I find that the authenticity of portrayals of place is important not for its veracity, but for the social work it performs. Authenticity is not merely socially constructed but expressive of social relations which value people and places. Tourist perceptions of the* caribe sur *as genuinely underdeveloped—gauged by an analysis of photos and guidebooks as well as surveys—produce an approach to resource use within the community that is limiting. Because the value of the place is its underdevelopment, development itself constrains the possibility of sustaining further growth. Ultimately, reading development via place can be a guide for critically appreciating contemporary patterns of tourism and sustainable development in the* caribe sur *and elsewhere.*

Bar Brawls and Big Marinas: Tourism Development in *Caribe Sur*

In this paper, I question how representations of place color and are colored by development on the southern Carribbean coast of Costa Rica (Figure 1). The economic life of that region – the *caribe sur* – depends upon tourism. To differing extents, the region's diverse population of English-speaking Afro-Caribbeans, nearly half of Costa Rica's indigenous population, Hispanic-Costa Ricans, and expatriate North Americans and Europeans participate in the tourism trade all make up ... Yet in spite of tourism, and the region's extensive history of community resource management and development (Gump 2001; Frantz 2003), Talamanca (which includes the coastal *caribe sur* as well as nearby mountainous areas) remains the most impoverished of the Costa Rica's 81 *cantones*. Recent events there have brought to the fore the connections between tourism, these development strategies, and representations of the region as a place.

In the early morning hours of April 19, 2008, a resident of Cahuita – a small, relatively dispersed settlement of about 1,000 on the coast – was shot and killed at

Figure 1. The *caribe sur*. *Source*: Author.

Coco's Bar, a popular hangout for tourists as well as locals. Although the reporting was relatively benign, the town has received critical attention in recent years for gruesome violence in a place that tourists and locals alike typically consider *tranquilo*. This type of negative press coverage is lamented by local business owners for scaring away potential tourists and damaging the local economy (Kelly 2004).

A few days later at the University of Costa Rica (UCR), students draped a large banner that read "Long live Puerto Viejo – Without the Marina" over the campus's main library. The university newspaper, *Semanario Universitario*, had recently published a front-page story on a proposed marina complex to be sited in Puerto Viejo de Talamanca, a town about 15 kilometers south of Cahuita. The story articulated several of the potential ecological and social effects that the large-scale development might engender, such as damage to nearby coral reef systems and crime (Chacón 2008). In a similar report, a female US tourist explained, "I'm a tourist and if this is constructed I won't come here anymore. I like the simplicity and naturalness of Puerto Viejo that would be lost with this (Plaza & Carvajal 2008)."

The shooting incident raises some appealing questions. How does the image of a place motivate or daunt tourists and to what end for local economic development? The remark of the U.S. tourist, poses the reverse. It hints at a tension between development and the reasons travelers visit the region, suggesting that states of development inspire travel. She will only continue to travel to Puerto Viejo if the marina project, which would generate substantial revenue but ruin the town's "simplicity and naturalness," is scrapped. But what is the true character of the town? Is such an essential definition even available?

My answer is that in the *caribe sur*, depictions of place in brochures and text produce and sustain a dialectical communication between tourists and promoters about the place, in which its perceived authenticity emerges as the central selling point. Yet what travelers interpret as genuine is a lack of development – indeed, an historic underdevelopment. Such judgments of the place are central to conflicts over regional growth and management of natural resources. At the core of these contests, tourists, locals, and foreign residents all attempt to define the *caribe sur*. While tourism is heralded as a means to achieve development – and indeed, as the only road to development for poor peoples (UNWTO 2005 in Schellhorn 2010) – I argue that the negotiated results of such rhetorical maneuvering reveal a limited promise of sustainable development.

Authenticity as Social Relation

Place, authenticity, and development each lay claim to their own literature within tourism studies. Place is conceived of as a locus that defines where tourism activities occur, as in a tourist destination (Crang 2006; Hernández-Lobato *et al.* 2006). But beyond geographical coordinates, the term bears notions of meaning. The representation of places inspires travel (Hernández-Lobato *et al.* 2006; Su 2010) as tourists decide where to visit after reading or hearing about a place (Urry 1990; Young 1999). But here crucial questions spring forth: how are these places imagined and by whom? Should places be understood more in terms of their performance (what is done in place) or their representation (what is portrayed of place)?

Places are best understood as constructed socially. They are the product of dynamic attempts at definition by various actors who operate and express themselves within capitalist, colonial, patriarchal, and other such structures. This meaning of place, moreover, is not static. It is continuously reworked through "agency, struggle, and resistance," (Tucker 2007, p. 142) be it by tourists (D'Hauteserre 2006; Tucker 2007), development interest groups (Schollmann *et al.* 2001), or locals (Su & Teo 2008). Related, place is not simply "out there"; rather, it is made and remade by specific agents (Crouch 2000).

However, within this constructionist view, the epistemology of place meaning is contested. Some consider place as knowable through its depiction in images, texts, and maps. Places can thus be read semiotically (Knudsen *et al.* 2007; Metro-Roland 2009). This perspective has the advantage of treating language and the "demarcat[ion of] social reality" (Schollmann *et al.* 2001) as powerful. However, a reliance upon existing imagery and text runs the risk of obscuring struggles at the heart of the creation of places, as images can be passively read (Crouch 2000). Instead, it is argued, place ought to be known by the ways people perform it (Crouch 2000, 2010;

Hanna *et al.* 2004; Minca 2007). The meaning of place, then, is linked with what people do on the ground, in place, as part of a process.

The representation and performance of place are not mutually exclusive. In this study, I approach place in a manner similar to Hanna *et al.* (2004) and Crouch (2010) in considering representation as a sort of performative work that is done by tourists, locals, and others – all those who weigh in on the matter and meaning of place. Images are not final products but contain a social history and a contemporaneous currency.

The performance of place may emphasize how individuals are disciplined and how that discipline is contested (Crouch 2000; Tucker 2007), but such a perspective misses out on important "powers" of place stemming from "wider economic and political relations of power" (Bianchi 2009, p. 490). The display of place is performed by multiple constituents in a matrix of power relations. Del Casino & Hanna (2000) suggest that representations in maps and guides struggle continuously to "fix" identities by delineating what is appropriate for a given bounded space (see also Harvey 1990). The social production of space via this intertextual illustration is not essentializing. Rather, representations permit space for ambiguity, allowing for manifold disputes of meaning and it is this contestation which makes place identity in constant flux (Harvey 1990; Del Casino & Hanna 2000; Schollman *et al.* 2001; Lacy 2002; Sundberg 2003; Cresswell 2004; Davis 2005; Su 2010). Thus, a critique of representations can, when their creation and what work they perform is kept in mind, illustrate overlooked power in place.

Authenticity

Authenticity has a contentious history as a concept in tourism studies (Wang 1999; Reisinger & Steiner 2006; Lau 2010). The questions of how authenticity is made to matter – if at all – and to what end have been dealt with diversely. Authenticity variously refers to verifiable cultural traits (MacCannell 1976), is negotiated (Cohen 1988), is socially constituted (May 1996; DeLyser 1999; West & Carrier 2004), or is simply unimportant (Reisinger & Steiner 2006).

Dydia DeLyser (1999) has written persuasively on authenticity. She suggests that authenticity is constructed at multiple scales; the validity of information about other cultures is filtered at an individual level, yet such filters are in many ways defined by broader trends in society. A tourist at a western U.S. ghost town may express their amusement at the anachronism of an authentic artifact, but such authenticity becomes "a vehicle through which the narratives of the mythic West, of progress, and American virtues, are made tangible and believable to visitors" (DeLyser 1999, p. 624). Authenticity is thus elicited in things, but is not a thing to be measured per se. Authenticity is a "vehicle," a means to an end. Notions of the authentic perform and the reason they can be valuable to researchers (cf. Wang 1999; Reisinger & Steiner 2006; Lau 2010) is because of the work they do to enroll people in social projects.

In this sense, authenticity is a social relation enacted between people. West and Carrier (2004, p. 485) approach this sort of conceptualization in building the salient claim that what ecotourists consider authentic is not derived from conservationists or any other informed individual or group, but "that it is the framework of Nature and the frontier" through which tourists judge authenticity. Importantly, this authenticity is inseparable from ecotourism, which they brand as a project of promoting markets in social goods. The convention that a particular nature is authentic enables an eco-friendly tourism to function as the neoliberal form of sustainable development.

Davis (2005) elaborates on how landscapes are thus transformed by conceptions of the world. Place representations discursively "legitimize certain uses and prohibits others" and in performing so produce the material landscapes of place (Davis 2005, p. 609). Authenticity as such a vision of place is a social relation reproduced by tourists and locals. West and Carrier (2004) demonstrate this concept in Jamaican ecotourism. Discourse concerning authentic nature becomes, in dialectical fashion, actually existing material reality as tourists successfully make their claim to authorities to have fishing boats removed from areas around a beach. Authenticity becomes a social relation – valuing, ordering, and reorganizing people, places, and resources.

This authenticity cannot be engaged without considering the representation of place. Britton (1991) urged geographers to critique what he deemed "markers of tourism space" – representations like maps, brochure images, guidebooks of travel areas. While Urry (1990) has been important in this regard, others have added valuable contributions to the conversation (Edensor 1998; Del Casino & Hanna 2000; Davis 2005). In particular, Catherine Lutz and Jane Collins's (1993) deconstruction of image meaning in the *National Geographic* magazine is useful. Lutz and Collins nullify the idea of the magazine as an unbiased scientific source by presenting how its printed images actually encode messages and value impositions about its subjects. The magazine projects cultures and places as harmoniously associated with nature and essential qualities of human existence, yet this view contrasts with the dynamism of change that cultures and places readily experience. As in *National Geographic* photography, notions of authenticity are expressed through and embodied in displays of place. Moreover, such notions are more projections of social desires than realities (Wang 1999).

Development

If authenticity is indeed a social relation, how does it operate? How do ideas of place actually "find ground" and create social and material reality? In the Bikini Atoll, for instance, the might of U.S. military and media is a transformative power (Davis 2005). Yet the many means by which places are made visible are typically bracketed from questions of economic development.

As social relation, authenticity of place is inseparable from development – the interrelated social (e.g., income and well-being) and material (e.g., physical infrastructure like roads and resorts as well as environmental impact) aspects of economic

92

growth. The uneven global development that sustainable development seeks to rectify is driven in part by forces of homogenization and differentiation in the capitalist economy (Smith 1990; Sywngedouw 1997). Capitalism tends toward equalizing the rate of profit across space and in place as it achieves greater economies of scale while it simultaneously seeks niches that yield comparatively high rates of profit. It is a commonplace that globalization standardizes places so that they become like everywhere else. However, Harvey (1990) has noted that in a globalized world, capital moves freely but locale remains fixed. In order to attract residents, businesses, or, in this case, visitors, places work to distinguish themselves from other, often homogenized, areas. Capital serves to augment the assembly of place and place-identity (Harvey 1993; O'Hare 1997; Sywngedouw 1997; Kneafsey 1998). As such, tourism may be "destroying" places, but at the same time it is creating others.

Place, authenticity, and development can be analytically united. Sustainable development studies in particular tend to treat place as a *mise-en-scène* which enframes sets of peoples and resources whose interaction could be made more sustainable (D'Hauteserre 2005; Lu & Nepal 2009; Wearing *et al.* 2010) Thus, much of the work on tourism development focuses on how to manage destinations for growth (Young 1999; Landorf 2009). Related, such studies chart the trajectory of destinations' development (Saarinen & Kask 2008), as opposed to the processes that make such development contingent (Young 1999; D'Hauteserre 2005). In this vein, there is scant attention paid to explaining destination success or failure in terms of the way place identity is framed (cf. Hernández-Lobato *et al.* 2006).

O'Hare (1997), however, posits a dialectical relation between place and tourism development on Australia's east coast. A "narrative of landscape" that historically depicted the area as relaxing informs development discourses. Decision-makers have codified the village's low-key atmosphere by enforcing building codes that restrict high-rise projects. Yet the result of tourists' demand is not always a given; place ideas are often disputed. Saarinen (1998) emphasizes the power relationships between groups offering competing notions of development and place by describing how the transformation of a tourism region, in this case the Finnish Lapland, is dependent upon negotiated notions of development. Who gets to choose how local resources are managed? The answer regularly relies on a complex interaction of power. Bianchi (2003) proposes that, "tourism spaces, therefore, reflect the contest over the meaning and 'appropriate' use to which particular places should be devoted" (Bianchi 2003, 27).

Place-meaning is therefore constituted by multiple parties within webs of power. Tourist promoters aim to ascribe an identity to place, as do locals, and authenticity is one key frame in which these identities are articulated. It is socially written at multiple layers from the individual (DeLyser 1999) to the state (Bianchi 2003) to the ideological (May 1996) and its performance is as a social relation amongst people and places. As such, authenticity is inextricable from the material matters of development.

Figure 2. "The main street". A tourist view of Cahuita's main drag. The view from afar portrays the town as relatively empty and underwhelming. *Source*: marichica88 – Flickr, 2010 – http://www.flickr.com/photos/rachel_patterson/5687710645/.

Tourist Motivations for Visiting the *Caribe Sur*

The style, scale, and materiality of tourism encountered on the Pacific coast of Costa Rica contrasts sharply with that of the Caribbean. The Pacific specializes in providing beach access and mass excursions and is heavily reliant on large-scale investment (national and foreign). Tourism in the *caribe sur* tends to center around intimate experiences with nature and culture and is undertaken with a smaller degree of investment and physical infrastructure (Anuario de Turismo 2006).

Tourism has replaced banana production as the mainstay of the regional economy there. Increased access to the region, the arrival of electricity in 1976, the failure of the cacao crop in the late 1970s and early 80s, and the establishment of Cahuita National Park in 1978 are both popularly and scholarly deemed additional contributors to the formation of the tourism industry in Cahuita (Leary 1996) and elsewhere in the region (GreenCoast.com). In 1993, after the government proposed an entry fee increase at the national park, locals seized control of the park and started investing entry fees – now voluntary donations – in community projects (Frantz 2003). The period immediately following the takeover of park management, from the early to mid 1990s, is imagined by locals as the pinnacle of tourism in Cahuita (Figure 2). At some point in 1990s, main growth in the sector shifted to Puerto Viejo. The town lacks the immediate vicinity of a national park, but supplies a number of beaches that host excellent surfing conditions. In both places, tours to neighboring protected natural areas are popular.

Methods

Drawing upon original ethnographic study in the field in 2008, I assess text and image content analyses against what tourists themselves describe as motivations for visiting the *caribe sur*. A set of promoter (online and printed) and tourist photos was gathered for the image analysis. After an initial scan of the set for major themes and reoccurring objects, coding questions were produced as a means of determining frequency in the depiction of: location (Puerto Viejo area, Manzanillo, Cahuita, anywhere else in Talamanca, or indiscernible), environment (town, jungle, beach, inside), people (how many, what kind, and activity), and the presence of wildlife, palm trees, hammocks, empty boats, or mountains (Djafarova & Andersen 2010). One third of all images from each data set were randomly selected to craft a study sample (tourists, $n = 30$; online promoters, $n = 55$; and print promoters, $n = 26$), which was then coded.

Participant observation can be an effective way of gaining access to tourists and understanding their experiences on their own terms (Cook 1997; Graburn 2002; Pereiro 2010). In Cahuita, I regularly volunteered at the local national park and beach. As part of this strategy, I used short surveys to seek out both tourists' and locals' perceptions of the area. One hundred and one surveys were administered to visitors to Cahuita National Park along Playa Blanca and 38 visitors to Playa Cocles, located near Puerto Viejo. Interviewees were allowed to provide more than one answer. They were not asked to supply an overarching reply as to why they decided to visit or what they enjoyed the most. This approach entails methodological complications in that it is not entirely clear which motivations are primary, but provides richer qualitative data to work with and still generates basic quantitative results. Answers were distilled into a few main themes (Parfitt 1997). Forty nine short surveys were also collected from Cahuita residents. A fairly common tactic in tourism research (King *et al.* 1993; Chris Choi & Murray 2010), participants were asked about their favorite aspects of Cahuita, why tourists came to town, and the benefits and drawbacks of tourism there.

Additionally, several longer semi-structured interviews were conducted with contacts in the community. Interviewees were owners of either restaurants or *cabinas* in Cahuita. Conversations were intended to get a sense of Cahuita's experience of tourism, particularly how tourism there has developed historically and its effects. Interviews with members and directors of charity, environmental, and developmental organizations in Talamanca were also undertaken to assess tourism in a broader, regional context.

Images

Do promoters employ certain images as tools in selling the place and do tourists grasp and reproduce such rhetoric? While the Caribbean coast of Costa Rica is indeed populated by palm trees, for instance, the incidence of images depicting palm tree beaches in promotional material is likely exaggerated. This is interesting given that perhaps the most popular beach in all of Talamanca—Cahuita National Park – is lined with almond trees and relatively few palms. Promoters utilize the palm in a third of all photos, but it is featured significantly less in images grabbed by tourists. Palm trees are nearly 15 times more likely to appear in promoter pictures than in tourist pictures. The frequency of images displaying empty fishing boats is also exaggerated. Furthermore, there are only a handful of beaches in the region, yet beaches are heavily featured in both tourist and vendor images. However, online promoters are three times as apt to depict beach images as are tourists. Finally, there is an absence of crowds and other people from images of place. There are not as many people featured in tourist promotions as one would actually encounter in place regardless of the season.

The difference in the imagery produced by promoters and tourists denote a rhetoric that promoters employ and that tourists fail to reproduce. Promoters' imagery coalesces around a few elements like palm trees and empty boats, whereas tourists' imagery is less consistent. Standardized images become rhetorical devices through which promoters participate in the discourse of place. Tourists do not typically engage in and reproduce such rhetoric, as their aim is not to sell, but that is not to say that tourists do not internalize the promoter discourse. The meanings sustaining the rhetoric can still matter for tourists. Tim Edensor (1998, 13) explains that representations "are part of a technology of enframing sights which forms the epistemological apparatus through which tourists see and interpret difference." How do visitors to the *caribe sur* understand difference there?

Tourists' shots of a single building emphasize the West Indian architecture typical of the area. Broader takes of the town highlight greenery at the expense of the built environment. Related, there is an evident focus on depopulated spaces; very few images include people. Promoters stress that the *caribe sur* is a place with relatively few other tourists – a place where one could relax. Tourists agree; the only people within their photos are themselves. The use of palm tree beach imagery unites a larger ideal of the Caribbean as relaxing and natural in place at the scale of the Costa Rican *caribe sur*. The image of the palm has stereotypically signified a peaceful atmosphere and environment throughout the Caribbean (Daye 2005). Indeed, the gaze of both tourists and promoters is directed toward the (palm tree) beaches of the area. The vast majority of photos are taken either of the beach or on the beach, shunning the mountainous and indigenous interior. The *caribe sur*, at least in the tourist discourse, is distinctively a "sand and sun" place.

Guidebooks

Brochure images are not the only way travelers discover the area and are not the only way the *caribe sur* is made to matter for them. The frequent usage of guidebooks entails that information about the area is transmitted to would-be visitors through short, stylistic characterizations. In these texts, the *caribe sur* is again depicted as a place that is depopulated, natural, and relaxing.

I asked travelers to both Playa Blanca in Cahuita National Park (CNP) and to Playa Cocles, a 10 minutes walk from Puerto Viejo proper, how they first learned about either Cahuita or Puerto Viejo. The most common responses from visitors to

Figure 3. Empty boats are a common trope in guidebook depictions of the area, as in this representation of Puerto Viejo from *Frommer's Top Destinations 2011 – Puerto Viejo, Costa Rica* (Greenspan 2011).

the CNP were "Word of Mouth" ($n = 36$, 39%) or "Guidebooks" ($n = 34$, 37%). At Playa Cocles, "Word of Mouth" was overwhelmingly the most provided response. From the "Guidebooks" category, the one source that was specifically mentioned was *Lonely Planet* ($n = 16$, 17%). *Lonely Planet* describes Cahuita as having a "very laid-back vibe," "a decidedly Afro-Caribbean flavor" and as "breathtakingly beautiful" (Vorhees & Firestone 2006, 470). Descriptions of Cahuita encountered in other popular guidebooks like Fodor's all note an underwhelming physicality and lack of other tourists. Cahuita is "dusty," "laid-back," (Kelly 2004, 196) "offbeat," (Baker 1999, 383) comprised of "just two puddle-dotted, gravel-and-sand streets running parallel to the sea, intersected by a few cross-streets," (Kelly 2004, 196) and "a village [of] no more than two parallel dirt streets crossed by four rutted streets overgrown with grass, with ramshackle houses spread apart throughout" (Baker 1999, 383). Depictions of Puerto Viejo are analogous (Greenspan 2011), but reveal tensions between the town's economic growth and the tranquility that a historic lack of development has engendered. Puerto Viejo has a "laid-back attitude" and consists of "little more than one long paved road that follows the road," though it is also "touristy" (Vorhees & Firestone 2006, 480) (Figure 3). "The development is low density," but a "boom in tourism has taken place in the last few years, "creating a "plethora" of tourist-related activities in town (Kelly 2004, 199).

Surveys

What guidebooks intimate is that there exists a slight but substantial difference in attitudes toward Puerto Viejo and Cahuita. The reasons images and guidebook text propose tourists travel to the area are reinforced by tourists' stated purposes. First, results from short surveys of tourists buttress previous findings (Gump 2001) that nature is a primary reason for visiting Cahuita. However, the data do not maintain the conclusion that nature is *the* primary reason for visiting Cahuita. More visitors responded, "I came here for the beach" ($n = 27$, 27%) than "I came here the flora, fauna, vegetation or other similar aspect of nature (other than the beach)" ($n = 20$, 20%) and just as many answered, "I heard it was a nice/beautiful place" ($n = 20$, 20%). Visitors to Cahuita National Park traveled to Cahuita not just because of its natural resources, beauty, or park, but also because it is a tranquil place that is "not over touristy" ($n = 19$, 19%). To visitors, Cahuita is "a relaxed town" and a "low-key place."

Responses from visitors to Playa Cocles near Puerto Viejo differ from those at Cahuita National Park. Recommendations were tourists' principal motivation for traveling to Puerto Viejo ($n = 9$, 24%). Visitors remarked, "I heard it was nice from friends who had been here" or "it was recommended by two friends. They say you must absolutely go to Cahuita and Puerto Viejo." Many visitors ($n = 6$, 16%) answered that they traveled to Puerto Viejo randomly. Unlike Cahuita, natural surroundings are not a persuasive reason for visiting Puerto Viejo. Only a few respondents ($n = 2$, 5%) listed nature as a reason for traveling to the town.

The data on tourist motives demonstrate a distinction between the two places, which observation and informal conversations co-sponsor. There are few responses from the Playa Cocles surveys that fit the "Nature" category, unlike Cahuita, where one-fifth of respondents replied that they had visited to encounter nature. Furthermore, though visitors to both places list the atmosphere as a purpose for visiting, many clarified that Puerto Viejo was more "congested" and had more people and nightlife than Cahuita, an argument *Lonely Planet* puts forth as well. Both Cahuita and Puerto Viejo are tranquil and natural places, but each to its own degree.

Caribe Sur as Authentically Underdeveloped

The results of fieldwork narrate a common story. Images from promoters and text from guidebooks market the *caribe sur* as a relaxing, natural Caribbean getaway. At one level, tourists are merely seeking "sand and sun." Yet there are beaches elsewhere in the world, including many more on the Pacific coast (Costa Rica Tourism 2011). Why do people elect to travel specifically to the *caribe sur* and to what end?

The correlation between tourist motivations and the representation of place ought to be viewed as a dialectical process, one that operates at different geographical scales. The manner in which the display of place is manufactured, framed, exported, and acted upon is a continuous give-and-take between tourists and promoters. Silver (1993, p. 316) posits that it is local promoters who "contribute to how ideas of the other are imagined and conceptualized within Western consciousness." These promoters do indeed depict place and in many ways do so as they wish, without regard to tourists. However, those portraying place are not always local. Tourists regularly act on depictions provided by other travelers or media such as Lonely Planet. Moreover, visitors are rarely agenda-less and businesses have a real, fiscal incentive to appeal to what inspires travel. Thus, the rhetoric Talamancan promoters employ in images to gain customers is rooted in their understanding of tourists' desires. Empty boats and palm trees are entities encountered in the *caribe sur* that promoters feature because they can symbolize the experience promoters presume tourists will prefer. In this way, tourists' actions as bearers of place-ideas play a powerful role in fashioning general notions about – and as we will see, transforming – destinations.

Even more incisive analyses of the dialectic are achievable. Tourist motives and place-meaning operate at various scales (Vaccaro & Beltran 2007). Generally, tourists consider Costa Rica an alternative to destinations elsewhere in the Caribbean like Cancún. Within Costa Rica, tourists deem the Caribbean coast as different from the mass tourism ventures on the Pacific. Yet visitors formulate one further distinction that highlights the fickle nature of tourist motivations. Between Puerto Viejo and Cahuita, they consider the latter to be less "touristy." In this model of decision-making, different travelers funnel into the places appropriate to their expectations of place. Thus, the traveler encountered in Cahuita and in Puerto Viejo may be regarded as the embodiment of a type of tourist that covets sand and sun, values local culture, seeks a relaxing atmosphere, and dislikes the presence of other foreigners.

This kind of tourist seeks the authentic in desiring the "pristine" and the "tranquil," traits which take form in space in Talamanca, not North America or Western Europe, or even the beaches of the Costa Rican Pacific. It is the *caribe sur*'s beaches, diversity, and historic *under*development that enable promoters in Cahuita and Puerto Viejo to represent an authenticity of place. That visitors invent distinctions between Cahuita and Puerto Viejo because of their ostensibly different development environments – when in fact the places are quite similar (Nost 2008) – stresses the value tourists discover in discerning genuine landscapes of development.

This claim is significant because notions of the *caribe sur* as an underdeveloped place are situated problematically against locals' desired development of the place. What is crucial to this authenticity is not its veracity, but what work it achieves. As May (1996, p. 321) notes, "at issue is not so much which image or meaning is correct, but it is a question of the material politics articulated by each vision." The work that authenticity performs is to develop social relations of a certain political economic kind; the value of the people and resources in this place is their underdevelopment. Yet these social relations do not go uncontested. The notion of the *caribe sur* as undeveloped belies struggles for development. The *caribe sur* is a "space stemming from a variety of social processes that are often occluded by its symbolic representations" (Bartling 2006, p. 394).

Recent project proposals underscore tensions between locals and foreigners. In 2008, an international firm presented the town with plans to construct a significantly-sized marina within the harbor of Puerto Viejo (Plaza & Carvajal 2008) (Figure 4). Though the plan has since then been withdrawn (Barquero 2008), the firm's intentions triggered an acute controversy.

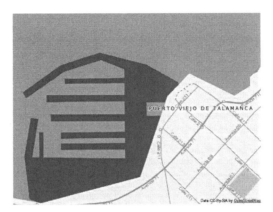

Figure 4. The planned marina in relation to Puerto Viejo. See Plaza y Carvajal 2008. Source: © OpenStreetMap contributors. Data: Open Database License. Cartography: CC BY-SA (OpenStreetMap.org/copyright). Figure: by Author.

Broadly, the project split both foreigners and locals. Ex-pats opposed the marina out of the fear that it would spoil the atmosphere and natural settings for which they had come to Puerto Viejo. Many actively participated in town hall councils on the issue. Individual tourists, always only an ephemeral presence in the area at any given time, likely did not weigh in very vocally (save the female tourist quoted earlier). But given the purposes for which tourists travel to the area they would have likely objected to the construction. Even other Costa Ricans, like the students who hung a banner at the UCR library, were concerned for the loss of the town's character. Some residents also adopted this stance, additionally rejecting the argument that such a plan would provide new jobs. However, other locals and foreigners either promoted the project or were indifferent. A few residents of Cahuita, for instance, noted in reference to not only the marina but also tourism writ large, that it was Puerto Viejo's prerogative to manage its resources as it preferred. Other residents of Cahuita and Puerto Viejo saw the marina as a providential source of capital and employment. Furthermore, many ex-pats viewed adopting any (public) stance on the project as an unwieldy and unethical interference in others' affairs. These ex-pats believed that as foreigners they had no right to tell locals how to develop when many were so impoverished.

These debates over development strategies were at the same time integral to the creation of place-meaning. Individuals and groups, especially the coalition against the marina, drew upon notions of place to formulate their claim. In some sense, local ideas of place jibe well with the meaning tourists glean from the place. When asked, "what is your favorite part of Cahuita?" locals responded only with the beach ($n = 21$, 39%), the tranquility ($n = 14$, 26%), nature ($n = 10$, 19%), and the people ($n = 9$, 17%). These answers correlate strongly with tourists' motivations for travel and expectations of the place as measured through images, guidebooks and surveys. What is principal, however, is the way that these facets of place are manipulated.

They are photographed, written about, or in any other way reduced and characterized so that the rhetoric and meaning that tourists receive is different than what locals experience in place. Images and guidebooks emphasize the beaches of the *caribe sur*, its tranquility, and the natural surroundings, but in a way that adds a certain sense of the place as underdeveloped, a meaning that does not play out in the way locals perceive and discuss place.

Indeed, in the debate over the marina, many of the meanings uncovered in the tourist discourse are subverted. A couple of videos made in opposition are emblematic. The author of one short video positions themself as outside of the community but aims to rally around the "danger" Puerto Viejo confronted (Salvemos Puerto Viejo Costa Rica 2008). Projected in front of images that could have been taken straight out of a brochure, the threat is made clear: "Goodbye to the surf, the tranquility, the local culture, the natural charm." The audience is encouraged to aid people who have "chosen to live at the rhythm of the Caribbean." The point here is straightforward: images can be put to different uses by different actors. The same authenticity is mobilized to sell tourism as it is to stop a marina. And yet a similar video from locals used typical imagery while making the argument that what it meant for residents to live in the *caribe sur* was not authenticity but a sense of pride in the community and the beneficial management of natural and cultural resources (¡No a la Marina! 2008).

Thus, even though the creators of these film shorts and most foreigners both opposed the marina, they did so for deviating purposes. The tourist rhetoric's depiction of the *caribe sur* as authentic is situated problematically against the locals' portrayal because it characterizes the place as unpopulated and underdeveloped. The fact that such a tension exists between two parties *critical* of the project strengthens the proposition that meanings of place are manifold.

Aporia of Tourism Development

The marina controversy was, on the surface, a referendum on development. In another sense it was centered on the meaning of place. It reveals how the portrayal of place in terms of authenticity creates social relations that are contested and reworked. The association between development and place meaning, then, is dialectical. The landscape enables tourism promoters to depict place as a function of development (Davis 2005). In the context of the *caribe sur*, the resulting discourse fixes an identity of "authentically underdeveloped" to the space that is the *caribe sur*, setting the stage for how further development will take form. Will development be led by substantial foreign investment or with local capital, input, and ownership?

The answers are negotiated within a framework of power and privilege. The restriction of certain kinds and numbers of tourists aids the interests of foreigners who, like the female tourist from the U.S. quoted earlier, travel or move to the area explicitly for the relaxing vibe. When questioned, "why would you live there? There is nothing down there," one ex-pat responded, "personally I like it the way it is as it has kept the development down to a minimum and the 'Disney set' out and tends to cater to a more 'down to earth traveler.' I think the rumors and myths have served many of us who have chosen to live here very well" (Puerto Viejo Satellite 2011). Foreigners deploy their influence in an endeavor to maintain the status quo.

Thus place is paramount to understanding development. Not because development *takes place* somewhere but because place encapsulates crucial social relations. A critical view of the discursive representation of place points to these relations. Notions of the *caribe sur* as authentic express a way of relating and ordering people, places, and resources (Crang 2006). Yet the goal is not to leave the analysis in the realm of representation, forgetting its "material" aspects (Bartling 2006; Bianchi 2009). Indeed, the illustration here of authenticity as social relation demonstrates how economic homogenization and differentiation find ground in place. Because the appropriate use value of this place has come to be its authentic underdevelopment, additional development erodes the possibility of further, sustainable growth.

But the tension between the need for further development, sustainable or not, and the tourist desire to visit an "undeveloped" space is real (see also Wainwright 2008). The traveler's desire for authentic difference does inherently constrict avenues for development; growth does not occur in a vacuum. Even relatively small-scale ventures like indigenous village visits bring in wealth and the resulting infrastructural changes turn-off many kinds of travelers, for whom the meaning of place no longer corresponds with their expectations (Young 1999).

So, how to work through this aporia (Wainwright 2008)? There is no easy answer, but at the very least advocates of sustainable development must explore place as the intersection of social relations, instead of attempting to managerially revalue people and resources while ignoring or leaving in intact the very relations which may well undermine such revaluing. As Cresswell (2004, p. 11) asserts, "place is a way of seeing, knowing, and understanding the world." Reading development in the *caribe sur* via place is a guide for critically appreciating contemporary patterns of tourism and development in both the *caribe sur* and elsewhere.

Acknowledgements

I am grateful for advice from Eric Carter, Kathy Kamp, and Marilyn Romero Vargas in preparing previous versions of this paper. The usual disclaimers apply.

References

Anuario de Turismo (2006) Available at http://www.visitcostarica.com/ict/backoffice/treeDoc/files/Anuario%20de%20Turismo%202006%20(VERSION%20FINAL).pdf (accessed 12 March 2011).

Baker, C. P. (1999) *Costa Rica Handbook* (Emeryville, CA: Avalon Travel Publishing).

Barquero, S. M. (2008) Plan de marina en Puerto Viejo se archiva, *La Nación*, p. 8.

Bartling, H. (2006) Tourism as everyday life: An inquiry into The Villages, Florida, *Tourism Geographies*, 8(4), pp. 380–402.

Bianchi, R. V. (2003) Place and power in tourism development: Tracing the complex articulations of community and locality, *Revista de Turismo y Patrimonio Cultural*, 1(1), pp. 13–32.

Bianchi, R. V. (2009) The 'critical turn' in tourism studies: A radical critique, *Tourism Geographies*, 11(4), pp. 484–504.

Britton, S. (1991) Tourism, capital, and place: Towards a critical geography of tourism, *Environment and Planning D: Society and Space*, 9(4), pp. 451–478.

Chacón, V. (2008) Proyecto de marina enfrenta fuerte oposición, *Semanario Universidad*.

Chris Choi, H. & Murray, I. (2010) Resident attitudes toward sustainable community tourism, *Journal of Sustainable Tourism*, 18(4), pp. 575–594.

Cohen, E. (1988) Authenticity and commoditization in tourism, *Annals of Tourism Research*, 15(3), pp. 371–386.

Cook, I. (1997) Participant observation, in: R. Flowerdew & D. Martin (Eds) *Methods in Human Geography*, pp. 127–150 (London: Longman).

Costa Rica Tourism (2011) *Costa Rican Beaches*. Available at http://www.tourism.co.cr/costa-rica-beaches/costa-rica-caribbean-beaches/index.html (accessed 12 March 2011).

Crang, M. (2006) Circulation and emplacement: The hollowed performance of tourism, in: C. Minca & T. Oakes (Eds) *Travels in Paradox: Remapping Tourism*, pp. 47–64 (Lanham, MD: Rowman Littlefield).

Cresswell, T. (2004) *Place: A Short Introduction* (Oxford: Blackwell).

Crouch, D. (2000) Places around us: Embodied lay geographies in leisure and tourism, *Leisure Studies*, 19, pp. 63–76.

Crouch, D. (2010) Flirting with space: Thinking landscape relationally, *Cultural Geographies*, 14(1), pp. 5–18.

D'Hauteserre, A.-M. (2005) Tourism, development, and sustainability in Monaco: Comparing discourses and practices, *Tourism Geographies*, 7(3), pp. 290–312.

D'Hauteserre, A.-M. (2006) A response to 'tracing the commodity chain of global tourism' by Dennis Judd, *Tourism Geographies*, 8(4), pp. 337–342.

Davis, J. S. (2005) Representing place: "Deserted Isles" and the reproduction of Bikini Atoll, *Annals of the Association of American Geographers*, 95(3), pp. 607–625.

Daye, M. (2005) Mediating tourism: An analysis of the Caribbean holiday experience in the UK national press, in: D. Crouch, R. Jackson, & F. Thompson (Eds) *The Media and the Tourist Imagination*, pp. 14–26 (London: Routledge).

Del Casino, V., Jr. & Hanna, S. (2000) Representations and identities in tourism map spaces, *Progress in Human Geography*, 24(1), pp. 23–46.

DeLyser, D. (1999) Authenticity on the ground: Engaging the past in a California Ghost Town, *Annals of the Association of American Geographers*, 89(4), pp. 602–632.

DeLyser, D. (2003) Ramona memories: Fiction, tourist practices, and placing the past in Southern California, *Annals of the Association of American Geographers*, 93(4), pp. 886–908.

Djafarova, E. & Andersen, H.-C. (2010) Visual images of metaphors in tourism advertising, in P. Burns, J.-A. Lester, & L. Bibbings (Eds) *Tourism and Visual Culture Volume 2: Methods and Cases*, pp. 35–43 (Wallingford: CABI).

Edensor, T. (1998) *Tourists at the Taj* (London: Routledge).

Frantz, L. (2003) Co-management of Cahuita National Park: A Recent History, Doctoral dissertation, Associated Colleges of the Midwest Tropical Field Research Program, San José, Costa Rica.

Graburn, N. H. H. (2002) The ethnographic tourist, in: G. M. S. Dann (Ed) *The Tourist as a Metaphor of the Social World*, pp. 19–40 (Wallingford: CABI).

GreenCoast.com (2011) *The Culture and History of the Puerto Viejo Area*. Available at http://www.greencoast.com/area-information/the-culture-history-of-the-puerto-viejo-area (accessed 12 March 2011).

Greenspan, E. (2011) *Frommer's Top Destinations 2011 – Puerto Viejo, Costa Rica.* Available at http://www.frommers.com/micro/2010/top-destinations-2011/puerto-viejo-costa-rica.html#; (accessed 1 October 2011).

Gump, C. (2001) Cahuita and its National Park: The Green Image and the Green Tourist, Thesis, Doctoral dissertation, Asscoiated Colleges of the Midwest Tropical Field Research Program, San José, Costa Rica.

Hanna, S. P., Del Casino, V., Jr., Selden, C. & Hite, B. (2004) Representation as work in 'America's most historic city', *Social and Cultural Geography*, 5(3), pp. 459–481.

Harvey, D. (1990) *The Condition of Postmodernity: An Enquiry into the Origins of Cultural Change* (Cambridge, MA: Blackwell).

Harvey, D. (1993) From space to place and back again: Reflections on the condition of postmodernity, in: J. Bird (Ed) *Mapping the Futures*, pp. 3–29 (London: Routledge).

Hernández-Lobato, L., Solis-Radilla, M. M., Moliner-Tena, M. A., & Sánchez-García, J. (2006) Tourism destination image, satisfaction, and loyalty: A study in Ixtapa-Zihuatanejo, Mexico, *Tourism Geographies*, 8(4), pp. 343–358.

Kelly, S. M. (2004) *Fodor's Costa Rica* (New York: Fodor's Travel Publications).

King, B., Pizam, A., & Milman, A. (1993) Social impacts of tourism: Host perceptions, *Annals of Tourism Research*, 20(4), pp. 650–665.

Kneafsey, M. (1998) Tourism and place-identity: A case-study in rural Ireland, *Irish geography*, 31(2), pp. 111–123.

Knudsen, D., Soper, A. & Metro-Roland, M. (2007) Commentary; gazing, performing, and reading: A landscape approach to understanding meaning in tourism theory, *Tourism Geographies*, 9(3), pp. 227–233.

Lacy, J. (2002) Beyond authenticity: The meanings and uses of cultural tourism, *Tourist Studies*, 2(1), pp. 5–21.

Landorf, C. (2009) Managing for sustainable tourism: A review of six cultural World Heritage Sites, *Journal of Sustainable Tourism*, 17(1), pp. 53–70.

Lau, R. W. K. (2010) Revisiting authenticity: A social realist approach, *Annals of Tourism Research*, 37(2), pp. 478–498.

Leary, K. (1996) A Recent History of Cahuita, Doctoral dissertation, Associated Colleges of the Midwest Tropical Field Research Program.

Lu, J. & Nepal, S. (2009) Sustainable tourism research: An analysis of papers published in the *Journal of Sustainable Tourism, Journal of Sustainable Tourism*, 17(1), 5–16.

Lutz, C. & Collins, J. (1993) *Reading National Geographic* (Chicago: University of Chicago).

MacCannell, D. (1976) *The Tourist: A New Theory of the Leisure Class* (New York: Schocken Books).

May, J. (1996) In search of authenticity off and on the beaten track, *Environment and Planning - Society and Space*, 14, 709–736.

Metro-Roland, M. (2009) Interpreting meaning: An application of Peircean semiotics to tourism, *Tourism Geographies*, 11(2), 270–279.

Minca, C. (2007) The tourist landscape paradox, *Social and Cultural Geography*, 8(3), 433–453.

¡No a la Marina de Puerto Viejo! (2008) *YouTube - ¡No a la Marina de Puerto Viejo!* Available at http://www.youtube.com/watch?v=NjH54jiktTg (accessed 26 April 2009).

Nost, E. (2008) Tourism, Conservation, and Development in the District of Cahuita, Costa Rica, Doctoral dissertation, Associated Colleges of the Midwest Tropical Field Research Program, San José, Costa Rica.

O'Hare, D. (1997) Interpreting the cultural landscape for tourism development, *Urban Design International*, 2(1), pp. 33–54.

Parfitt, J. (1997) Questionnaire design and sampling, in: R. Flowerdew & D. Martin (Eds) *Methods in Human Geography*, pp. 76–109 (London: Longman).

Pereiro, X. (2010) Ethnographic research on cultural tourism: An anthropological view, in: G. Richards & W. Munsters (Eds) *Cultural Tourism Research Methods*, pp. 173–187 (Wallingford: CABI).

Plaza, S. y Marvin Carvajal. (2008) Plan para construir marina crea controversia en Puerto Viejo, *La Nacion*, 5 April 2008.

Puerto Viejo Satellite (2011) *About Puerto Viejo, Costa Rica*. Available at http://puertoviejosatellite.com/about.php (accessed 12 March 2011).

Reisinger, Y. & Steiner, C. (2006) Reconceptualizing object authenitcity, *Annals of Tourism Research*, 33(1), pp. 65–86.

Saarinen, J. (1998) Social construction of tourist destinations: The process of transformation of the Saariselka tourism region in Finnish Lapland, in: G. Ringer (Ed) *Destinations: Cultural Landscapes of Tourism*, pp. 154–173 (London: Routledge).

Saarinen, J. & Kask, T. (2008) Transforming tourism spaces in changing socio-political contexts: The case of Parnu, Estonia, as a tourist destination, *Tourism Geographies*, 10(4), pp. 452–473.

Salvemos Puerto Viejo Costa Rica (2008) *YouTube – Salvemos Puerto Viejo Costa Rica*. Available at http://www.youtube.com/watch?v=PVEJFDzrilM (accessed 22 June 2011).

Schellhorn, M. (2010) Development for whom? Social justice and the business of ecotourism, *Journal of Sustainable Tourism*, 18(1), pp. 115–135.

Schollmann, A., Perkins, H. C. & Moore, K. (2001) Rhetoric, claims making and conflict in tourist place promotion: The case of central Christchurch, New Zealand, *Tourism Geographies*, 3(3), pp. 300–325.

Silver, I. (1993) Marketing authenticity in third world countries, *Annals of Tourism Research*, 20(2), pp. 302–318.

Smith, N. (1990) *Uneven Development: Nature, Capital, and the Production of Space* (Malden, MA: Blackwell).

Su, X. (2010) The imagination of place and tourism consumption: A case study of Lijang Ancient Town, China, *Tourism Geographies*, 12(3), pp. 412–434.

Su, X. & Teo, P. (2008) Tourism politics in Lijiang, China: An analysis of state and local interactions in tourism development, *Tourism Geographies*, 10(2), pp. 150–168.

Sundberg, J. (2003) Strategies for authenticity and space in the Maya Biosphere Reserve, Peten, Guatemala, in: K. Zimmerer & T. Bassett (Eds) *Political Ecology: An Integrative Approach to Geography and Environment-Development Studies*, pp. 50–69 (New York: Guilford).

Sywngedouw, E. (1997) Neither global nor local: "Glocalization" and the politics of scale, in: K. Cox (Ed) *Spaces of Globalization*, pp. 137–166 (New York: Guilford).

Tucker, H. (2007) Performing a young people's package tour of New Zealand: Negotiating appropriate performances of place, *Tourism Geographies*, 9(2), pp. 139–159.

United Nations World Tourism Organization (2005) Declaration on tourism and the millennium development goals, *Sustainable Development of Tourism e-bulletin*, p. 10. Available at http://www.worldtourism.org/sustainable/ebulletin/dec2005eng.htm (accessed 12 March 2011).

Urry, J. (1990) *The Tourist Gaze* (London: Sage Publications).

Vaccaro, I. & Beltran, O. (2007) Consuming space, nature, and culture: Patrimonial discussions in the hyper-modern era, *Tourism Geographies*, 9(3), pp. 254–274.

Vorhees, M. & Firestone, M. (2006) *Lonely Planet: Costa Rica* (London: Lonely Planet).

Wainwright, J. D. (2008) *Decolonizing Development: Colonial Power and the Maya* (Malden, MA: Blackwell).

Wang, N. (1999) Rethinking authenticity in tourism experience, *Annals of Tourism Research*, 26(2), pp. 349–370.

Wearing, S., Wearing, M. & McDonald, M. (2010) Understanding local power and interactional processes in sustainable tourism: Exploring village–tour operator relations on the Kokoda Track, Papua New Guinea, *Journal of Sustainable Tourism*, 18(1), pp. 61–76.

West, P. & Carrier, J. (2004) Ecotourism and authenticity: Getting away from it all? *Current Anthropology*, 45(4), pp. 483–498.
Young, M. (1999) The social construction of tourist places, *Australian Geographer*, 30(3), pp. 373–389.

Notes on Contributor

Eric Nost is a graduate student in the Geography department at the University of Kentucky.

(de)Constructing Place-Myth: Pitcairn Island and the *"Bounty"* Story

MARIA AMOAMO

Te Tumu School of Māori, Pacific and Indigenous Studies, University of Otago, Dunedin, New Zealand

ABSTRACT *This paper is concerned with the relationship between literature and the construction of place-myth relating to the story* Mutiny on the Bounty. *In 1790, nine British mutineers together with their Tahitian companions settled on Pitcairn Island where they remained hidden for nearly 20 years. The story of the mutiny is not myth but has served to mythologize Pitcairn through the various tropes of literature written about the* Bounty *saga. As literary place Pitcairn represented the image of a 'utopian paradise'. This discussion, through qualitative literary analysis and the process of textualization, evokes the idea of mapping, naming, and imagining islands. It identifies how the utopia/paradise place-myth of Pitcairn has persisted through time and become ultimately inseparable from its textual topography. But conversely, discussion exposes the paradoxical problem between myth and reality of islands and their representations. It highlights complex internal and external boundaries of identification that arise in the host visitor experience. Literary place-myth is rendered as powerful, persistent, mutable, and historically-rooted.*

Introduction

Islands are both physical, geographical formations and imaginative domains that have, historically, attracted much attention. According to Dening (2003: 203) islands continue to "please the imagination," it is perhaps the ludic element of islands as "small continents where there seem to be a near-magical inventiveness in making culture, order, out of Nature, chaos, all anew." A conventional image of the South Pacific is of an island paradise where an idyllic existence presides (Amoamo 2010). Artists, writers, poets, and adventurers have metaphorically represented islands as tokens of desire, places of possibility and promise, either an ideal inhabited island or else an empty island on which to start again (Howe 2000: 10). Such imaginings implied that, in isolation, utopian communities might exist, be established and evolve there. Hence, the storying of islands offers rich ground for the interface between literature, tourism and the construction of place-myth.

Pitcairn is one such island that evokes these imaginings. Central to this discussion is the construction of place-myth as it relates to Pitcairn Island and the story *Mutiny on the Bounty*. The trope of island paradise/utopia attached to Pitcairn founded on the *Bounty* story has a romantic cachet persisting for over two hundred years. The story is not myth, but has served to mythologize Pitcairn. Perceptions of "utopia" and "paradise" have persisted in popularized anthropology and geography, as well as tourism. Literary tourism, for example, trades on the motivation and interest of travelers to places associated with the lives of authors or related events or fictional characters in books (Anderson & Robinson 2002). Literary tourism sites fall into three broad categories: the factual site, the imaginative site, and the socially constructed site (Smith *et al.* 2010). This paper is concerned with Pitcairn as imaginative site. It examines tensions between place-myth, dichotomies of utopia/dystopia, and myth/reality that inform understandings of Pitcairn as tourist space/place through its representation in literature.

Qualitative literary analysis is the guiding principle of methodology supported by participant observation. This approach seeks to peel away textual layers and expose the construction of place-myth. The *textualization* of place, as viewed through the notion of layers, has not been fully explored in tourism research. Consequently, this article seeks to fill this gap. Discussion shows how the idea of mapping, naming, and imagining islands determine the way in which geographical place informs the location of culture. Descriptions like paradise and utopia reveal internal and external "layers" of meaning. The internal directs us toward the islanders in order to understand how distinctive identities develop and are experienced through thought and action. The external encompasses aspects like the tourist "gaze" (Urry 1990) and its relation to the "storying" of place. Discussion will also show how internal and external narratives contribute to the construction of place while creating their own dialectic of insider/outsider identities. These two aspects contend a correlation with power, myth and the tourist "gaze."

Myth and the Spatialization of Place

The texts examined in this paper attest to the fascination of past events to ascribe and (re)inscribe particular characteristics of place (Kolås 2004). Tetley and Bramwell (2002: 156) state: "it is writers who help to form the place myths that become the symbolic images and meanings that are broadly shared by many people." Thus, myth is part of a pre-established discourse through which readers conceptualize or understand a particular topic. In turn, this creates a storied landscape, a liminal landscape, and a place-myth. What's more, myth is seen as the appropriation of a historical image that survives as a mode of signification, what Barthes (1972) calls a metalanguage or second-order semiological system. It is at the order of second-level signification that myth is to be found. The latter requires context for understanding and the very act of representation is also an act of production. In other words, an image—in this case a literary place-image (of paradise/utopia) is being fashioned (Barke 2002).

According to Shields (1991) people's actions or practices also materially "spatialize" myths of place. Visitors seek out physical sites that represent myth, while the tourism industry promotes such sites, transforming myths in to global signs. An established meaning of myth that becomes part of the values and established discourse of the culture using it, predisposing the audience to believe in the illusions (Bourdieu 1992). The concept of social spatialization, thus, offers a way of talking about how place-images and place-myths form part of the wider formations of economic impact. Myth also exposes problems: remoteness and inaccessibility, ruggedness, and smallness, all the things that made Pitcairn Island an ideal refuge also made it domestically unsatisfactory (Sheppard 2004). Connell (2007: 118) is quick to point out, "islands were never paradise: even prior to colonization Pitcairn Island was depopulated several times."

Furthermore, he comments, "islands are places of discomfiting dialogues: utopian and dystopian, but pervasively utopian—places in which to construct social and spatial ideologies, reconfiguring landscapes, and peoples, as projections of outsiders', and more recently insiders', visions" (2003: 573). Therefore, this research focuses on the juxtaposition of myth and reality in the aftermath of the *Bounty* saga and how the image of paradise and utopia still dominates literature about Pitcairn. Linked processes of internal (insider) and external (outsider) narratives concurrently contribute to the construction of place-myth and have implications for those who reside in island places.

Pitcairn and the *Bounty* "Myth"

> It is Pitcairn's Island, the setting in 1790 for the final act of one of the greatest sea dramas of all time, the mutiny aboard His Majesty's Armed Transport *Bounty* on 28 April 1789. Inch for inch, it is the repository of more history – romantic history, bloody history, bogus history – than any other island in the Pacific (Ball 1973: 4).

Pitcairn is renowned as the refuge for the mutineers of H.M.S. *Bounty*. *Bounty's* mission, under the command of Lieutenant William Bligh was to collect breadfruit trees from Tahiti and transport them to the West Indies as food for slaves. As a result of the mutiny nine mutineers together with their Tahitian taios (female and male companions) landed on Pitcairn in January 1790. The position of the island was incorrectly charted by European explorer Philip Carteret in 1767, and so it offered a safe haven for the fleeing fugitives. Upon stripping the *Bounty* of all usable provisions the mutineers set fire to the ship, ensuring both isolation and entrapment. It could be argued that Pitcairn represented Howe's (2000) empty island on which to start again for the fugitives of this heinous act of piracy, a sort of Arcadia or Eden.

The new arrivals remained hidden from the outside world for nearly 20 years but any utopian vision was soon shattered. By 1800 violence and murder left only one mutineer, John Adams, alive with a number of women and hybrid children. Even the women had tried to build a craft to escape the island during this bloody period (Lummis 1997). Adams turned to the bible for redemption, nurturing a moral and God-fearing community that was fostered by like-minded patriarchs after his death. As news of their discovery in 1808 by American whaling ship *Topaz* reached Europe and America, the *Bounty* story unfolded. Word reached other nations that an idyllic community of young people lived on the remote rock, motivated by the Bible to live in peace, piety and harmony (Kirk 2008: 5). If the description could be believed, the people had formed a true Christian utopia.

It would be fair to say that Pitcairners have not paid much attention to documenting their history notwithstanding the *Bounty* heritage has prompted a wealth of externally written literature. It has been estimated some 1200 books, 3200 magazine and uncounted newspaper articles, documentary films, and three major Hollywood movies relating to the mutiny on the *Bounty* have accounted for Pitcairn's iconic status (Hayward 2006). The mythic notion of an island paradise is perpetuated in texts like:

- *Life and Death in Eden Pitcairn Island and the Bounty Mutineers* (Lummis 1997)
- *The Eventful History of the Mutiny and the Piratical Seizure of H.M.S. Bounty* (Barrow 1831)
- *Bounty Trilogy* (Nordhoff & Hall 1936)
- *Mutiny of the Bounty and the story of Pitcairn Island 1790–1894* (Young 1894)

During the 20th century a surfeit of both fiction and nonfiction continued to emerge. Collectively, such texts formulate the gaze over landscape and reveal how place-myth is both shaped and organized through discourse.

Pocock (1981: 15) comments that literature is the product of perception, or more simply, is perception. Literature is a powerful source of knowledge for tourists; a product of temporal and spatial ideologies, read in terms of conventions but mindful of the need to engage with reader's expectations. The writer articulates our own inarticulations about place and people providing thereby a basis for a new awareness, a new consciousness. Yet few writers have actually written about Pitcairn from personal visits due mainly to its remote locale. But another reason is that Pitcairners have fiercely guarded their privacy, restricting who visits and lives on the island. The founding motivation of the community *as* a refuge from the outside world has, to an extent fostered insularity together with strong religious doctrine and self-government. This creates the taxonomic distinction of insider/outsider, delineating boundaries of identification.

Barke (2002: 85) has commented that although the difference between fictional or nonfictional output is fundamental in a literary sense, the distinction may be less important in its relation to tourism. The story of the mutiny on the *Bounty* cannot be subsumed under the category literary tourism. However, the vast range of literature written on the subject indicates that the story motivates travelers to visit Pitcairn and forms part of a marketing strategy with commercial value (DeLyser 2003). However, literary tourists *per se* would not describe most visitors to Pitcairn. The majority are cruise ship or yacht passengers whose motivations are diverse and visits brief. Visitors who arrive on special interest group charters or travel by independent means are more likely to be influenced by literary texts and/or film media. For example, during the researcher's fieldwork in 2009 members of the Pitcairn Island Study Group (PISG) from the United Kingdom stayed for a week. The PISG website describes their purpose as "devoting itself to the study and history of the Pitcairn Islands, its people, and the mutiny" (www.pitcairnstudygroup.co.uk). For some of the group members it was "the realization of a boyhood dream," one member stating, "I've waited forty years for this." Most were well versed in the aforementioned literature and keen to associate (physical) place with (cognitive) text.

Tourist motives may be stimulated by real or fictional events, people or places, and the end product is the desire to go somewhere to see, experience or associate with a phenomenon one has read about, whether it is true or not. Myth serves to organize on the one hand, the tourist gaze (Urry 1990), its expectations and observations, and on the other hand, the workings of the community/place/space being gazed upon. An understanding of the link between myth and reality requires attention to the internal/external dialectic of myth-making, boundaries of identification, and the signifiers that become part of the cultural mythologies of places.

Methodology

The association of myth with the *Bounty* story has been outlined in the previous section and will be subject to further textual analysis. Discussion in the following sections reveals the problematic view of islands as bounded and essentialized sites of representation. Due to the extensive amount of literature relating to Pitcairn the following sections focus on texts written by authors' personal experience(s) defined as creative nonfiction. These texts represent the product of temporal and spatial ideologies and offer insight to an authentic Pitcairn experience whereby the emphasis is placed on historically located and contingent processes in which to examine place-myth and reality of place.

My background to approaching this topic is the combination of 18 months field experience(s) on Pitcairn Island (between 2008 and 2011) and 15 months extensive literature review relating to the study site. Therefore, the research methodology is grounded in ethnography. A comprehensive collection of fiction and nonfiction works has been reviewed relating to the *Bounty* story and Pitcairn's settlement. Visual media, such as documentaries, film, and the internet have collectively served to frame a certain spatialization of place. That is, an overall sense of social space typical of a time, place, or culture that allows us to appreciate change as intrinsic to peoples' ongoing *performative* actualizations of these spatial orders (Shields 1991). One influential internal source, from which excerpts are drawn, is *The Pitcairn Miscellany* (TPM). Published monthly since 1959, TPM serves as a social network to family, friends, and interested *Bounty* "buffs." It offers a rich contemporaneous account of Pitcairn life supported by islander's narratives as well as contributions from overseas readers. It therefore represents an authentic and trustworthy text as well as a source of vicarious adventure for its readers. A USA correspondent writes how "important the publication is for those faraway readers ... Pitcairn represents another world to interested "outsiders,, many of whom dream of one day visiting the island without hope of doing so" (TPM 1985).

The ethnographer's role as participant–observer involves various levels of textualization directed by experience (e.g., as member of the island tourism committee, assisting with heritage projects, and working in the medical clinic). Sociodemographic and descriptive information and characteristics of the physical setting as well as material culture was all recorded. During the busy cruise season (December–March), and yacht season (April–June) the researcher observed and interacted with tourists. To some extent, she could also partake in the opportunity to "be a tourist." Inclusion in social and community activities also raises the tension of being both "insider/outsider." In a sense, we could contend that "doing fieldwork" is not only an outwardly oriented social activity but also a psychological space in which memories and imaginations shape our interactions with informants, their lives, their histories, and their futures (Svasek 2010: 90).

Constructing Place: The Island as Icon in the Travel Imaginary

Pitcairn has often been described as one of the most remote islands in the world. Accessible only by sea, the nearest landfall is Mangareva in the Gambier Islands French Polynesia, a journey of two days by ship. Marginal places that have been "left behind" in the modern race for progress evoke both nostalgia and fascination (Shields 1991: 3). Pitcairn is both marginal in the sense of its remote geographic location and also as a site of illicit action represented by the very act of mutiny. This act marks the island and its inhabitants on the periphery of cultural systems of space in which places are ranked relative to each other. Critics have argued that places are more than simply geographic sites with definitive physical and textual characteristics; places are also settings (or locales) in which social relations and identities are constituted (Agnew 1987). Thus, the concept of place may refer to an individual's ability to develop feelings of attachment to particular settings based on a combination of use, attentiveness, and emotion—resulting in a layering of continually overlaid landscapes. Therefore, place provides individuals with a sense of belonging or alienation.

An example of this analogy is the culturally layered landscape of Pitcairn. Upon arrival the island was a blank slate on which to inscribe place names and suggest the mutineers and their descendants saw Pitcairn as a new independent world, not a replication of Britain or Tahiti. Nash (2009) has described place names as survey pegs of memory operating as a kind of mental map (or text) that functions in much the same way as a geographic map. Cognitive maps likely dominate local minds, whereas cartographic maps will be used by visitors, who then locate and associate the preconceived place names located in literature. In this respect, place names can be viewed as textual layers of information that may conceal hidden historical and mythological meanings.

The cultural landscape of Pitcairn tells of the relationships between people and place. Place names depict past events, reminders of people and actions. Lack of allusion to anything British found in other colonial outposts is notable, perhaps not surprising given the mutineers rebelled against such heritage in the very act of mutiny. Examples include "Bang on iron," the site of the *Bounty's* forge; "Isaac's Stone" is an offshore rock claimed by mutineer Isaac Martin. A Polynesian male who arrived on the *Bounty* was murdered at a place called "Timiti's Crack." Many places recall accidents and death, "Where Dan Fall," "McCoy's Drop," "Broken Hip" and "Where Minnie Off," or descriptors of man-made structures like "Big Fence," "Down the Grave," and "The Edge." "Christian's Cave" is perhaps the most iconic site situated high on the cliff-face overlooking Adamstown. Lead mutineer Fletcher Christian is reported to have spent many an hour "brooding" over his rebellious actions and that the cave offered a hideaway in case of discovery (Christian 1999). Visitors to the island often ascend the steep and treacherous route to the cave. The latter affords not only spectacular views but also represents how people's actions materially spatialize the myth of place by seeking out physical sites representative of myth.

Similarly, the "Hill of Difficulty" ascending from Bounty Bay to Adamstown is another well-known landmark. Upon arrival, author Ian Ball (1973: 159) said, "We faced the Hill of Difficulty, the adequately expressive name the pioneer Pitcairners gave to the grueling slog up the rough track sliced out of the cliff face. It leads one, panting and sweating, up to the first glimpse of level ground, The Edge, three hundred feet above the landing point." The researcher often observed cruise ship visitors refuse the quad bike ride; assuming they were keen to experience the difficulty of the hill. Perhaps, in doing so, they associated the experience with literary recollection. Notably, tourists actively sought out those who are descendants of the *Bounty* mutineers; the name Christian holds particular significance in this meeting. The present day host is thus temporally and spatially positioned; at once present in reality while recollected in the (literary) imaginary. Author Robert Kirk (2008: 232) describes Pitcairn people in tones reminiscent of Greek mythology stating, "They are the heirs of odyssean voyages, surging passions, of steamy romance." For Kirk, Pitcairn lies in "the public imagination" and that "the presence of the mutineer's pedigreed descendants perpetuates the island's status as an icon."

Many works of fiction have romanticized the story of the *Bounty* but Nicolson and Davies (1997) state, "much has been written about this romantic island but much of it has *been* romance." Textual analysis illustrates the continuity of conformity of similar literary tropes. Briefly castaway on the island in the mid 19th century, Walter Brodie's journal offers an idealized portrait of Pitcairn as the utopian picture of a familial community. Brodie described Pitcairn as "the realisation of Arcadia, or what we had been accustomed to suppose had existence only in poetic imagination – the golden age" (Smith 2003: 124). Upon visiting in 1878, Rear Admiral de Horsey of the *Shah* wrote of a people "whose greatest privilege and pleasure is to commune in prayer with their God, and to join in hymns of praise, and who are, moreover, cheerful, diligent, and probably freer from vice than any other community" (Young 1894: 206). Today, cruise ship passengers are often presented with the performative act of hymn-singing by the islanders; an act that reinforces the "utopian" and god-fearing image espoused by earlier literature.

Metaphoric discourses temporally and spatially perpetuate place-myth. To this end, literature is not a mirror of the world but part of a complex web of meanings possessing qualities that feed into a particular kind of tourist/travel experience. The result is a process of identification and differentiation. People are "placed" according to their putative affiliation with their place of origin (Shields 1991: 48) thus, distinguishing boundaries of identification and subjectivity. One example is the appropriation of the "pirate" motif by some island males. Motifs are often prevalent components of myth, particularly in the form of the individual hero. This display is motivated by a commercial imperative to sell a tourism product indeed, one Pitcairner has created the brand of "Pirate Pawl, his bodily accoutrements (tattooing and piercing) perpetuating the pirate image." What this practice reveals is the layering of cultural identity, commoditized *as* tourist attraction. In taking on the character of piracy/pirate islanders spatially perform place-myth. Perception, symbolic landscapes, and social identity are thus enforced and frames a certain way of reading landscape as an ideologically laden text. In this sense, place-myth operates as a second-order semiological system (Barthes 1972); already worked upon so as to make it suitable for communication. Connotation is determined by the form of the signifier that works through style and tone thus associating myth with ideology. These performative examples contribute to materially spatializing the myths of place and the signifiers that become part of the cultural mythologies of places.

Reading Place: The External Narrative

Various tropes of literature, such as travel writing, often use arrival scenes to "frame their narratives according to the 'I' who focuses the 'eye' through a lens oriented by their imagination or worldview" (Johnson 2010: 505). Johnson (2010: 509) notes "the 'gaze,' articulated through narrative may not reflect reality but instead may reflect what readers may want to see as apparently real." Johnson (2010: 511) identifies arrival scenes as defining moments in the travel experience, stating "one must cross a threshold and maintain a movement or passage that involves temporal and spatial dimensions of liminality." The awaited moment (of arrival) materializes and the travel writer tends to document it as a defining and sometimes, dramatic moment of the journey (Johnson 2010: 511) thus framing the rest of the story. The following arrival scenes frame authors' experience of Pitcairn, scripting the landscape to something familiar and thus illustrate how place-myth is (re)produced and maintained.

> Etched forever in my mind is the morning when Pitcairn's silhouette rose over the horizon straight ahead of the four-masted bark on which I sailed as a passenger. It was the fulfillment of a boyhood dream. I will always remember the friendliness and warmth and hospitality of the Pitcairners and the feeling, almost of awe, of finally being on the island itself after having visited it so often in my thoughts (Murray 1992: 15).

> Fifty years before I had read the story of this distant human habitation, and in my eager mind it had always been one of the wonder-places of the world. I had imagined it, dreamt about it, talked about it, but had never hoped to see the little speck of land so far out of the beaten track of ships and men . . . And yonder was Pitcairn! (Fullerton 1923)

> The numerous books I had read, the many pictures I had created from this reading, had shaped in my mind a Pitcairn that I couldn't bear to have altered by the inexorable impact of reality. But there it was at last before me, ready for me, with unguessed impressions and experiences to be added to my store (Shapiro 1936: 17)

The dream/reality experience is transferred to the physical form of Pitcairn *Island* framed by the experiential value derived from the history of a place and its literary representation. Place-myth is maintained through the semiotic act of "reading" place. The act is organic and actively situated, it illustrates the relationship between identity and the territory of a society, as the culture and identity of a society is manifested and perpetuated in its landscape (Huff 2008). Upon approaching the island Ball (1973: 149) wrote:

> It was at first a fog-colored smudge on the horizon. It enlarged gradually into the rich greens and chocolaty brown of the Pitcairn rock. Smudge-into-rock, it was no less welcome a sight to us on the storm-strewn deck of the Tahitian ketch *Maylis* than must have been presented one hundred and eighty-two years ago to another group, Fletcher Christian, his eight companions in mutiny . . . assembled expectantly along the weather rail of H.M.S. *Bounty.*

Ball (1973: 149) relates his own arduous passage to Pitcairn whereby they had "pitched, humped, corkscrewed a path southeast to our destination through a tropical storm ... the name Pitcairn will lodge forever in our memories as a synonym for haven." The researcher experienced exactly the same feelings upon her first arrival in 2008 after a tortuous 36-hour storm-ridden passage from Mangareva. Paradoxically, the first impression of Pitcairn in the early dawn was eerie and foreboding, albeit a welcome haven. Ball's account eludes to pre-*Bounty* (e.g., Carteret) and post-*Bounty* (e.g., mutineers) discoveries. His journey is portrayed as one of risk and unknown, interconnecting configurations of meaning from individual and shared relationships to, and conceptions and experiences of, given spaces. Such sentiments also exist at the level of myth, forming networks of meanings particular to individual cultures. Ball, whose motivation to visit Pitcairn included writing a re-interpretation of Bligh (whom has often been portrayed as a cruel Commander) is thus one who practices the place by giving it meaning through experience. We could construe Ball as a literary tourist in the sense that he had a deep, well informed interest *as* a writer but also *as* a tourist/writer who visits the literary heritage of a destination.

However, the same practice can be read as a layer of counter-narrative to popular imaginings of place depending on the purpose of visit. In more recent times, allegations and convictions of a number of Pitcairn men over sexual abuse have diluted the utopia myth to one of dystopia. Kathy Marks' (2008) book *Pitcairn Paradise Lost: uncovering the dark secrets of a South Pacific Fantasy Island* reveals how place-myth and sense of place are discursively manipulated. Notably, recent published titles (see Birkett 1997; Christian 1999) also appropriate the word "paradise" albeit its lexical use differs. Marks was a member of the media group that accompanied legal personnel to Pitcairn for the highly publicized "trials" in 2004. Her narrative exhibits those traits of the travel text that expose more about the author and their point of view than the place visited. The role as journalist/author links knowledge and power; the arrival scene exposes the latter whilst translating place to the readership.

> On our second day, a grey smudge appeared on the horizon: Pitcairn. The sight of it made my flesh tingle. It was quiet on deck. For the next five hours we watched as the island's distinctive silhouette emerged and the smudge turned into a solid chunk of rock. The loaf-shaped island stretched out before us, silent and aloof, its shores hammered by the relentless waves. Bounty Bay, a small, rock-strewn cove, was a mere chink in an armor of tall cliffs that enclosed Pitcairn almost completely ... thick vegetation and ochre-red rock exposed by gashes in the escarpments. (Marks 2008: 10)

Physical markers of landscape are used within predetermined lexical and metaphoric registers. The island setting embodies the "silent and aloof" armory of the people under investigation. Tone, nuance, allusion, and metaphor invert the image of paradise, acting as counter-narrative to earlier texts that frame Pitcairn as utopia. Such writer's tools provide context and evoke notions of place-myth; thus, the physicality of Pitcairn Island becomes ultimately inseparable from its textual topography. According to Marks, the paradise image is "truly lost," the "South Pacific Shangri-la," shrouded in myth becomes a "place of sinister secrets" exposing the apparent reality of Pitcairn to a new audience. As a result of the trials several Pitcairn men were convicted for historical offences and jailed on the island. Shields (1991: 256) notes that "even when the characteristics of a place change so radically that one would expect a change in the place-myth, this does not always take place." He argues that changes necessitate not just an adjustment of the myth, "cleaning out" the appropriate images and installing new ones, but a restructuring of the entire mythology and the development of new metaphors by which ideology is presented.

Myth and Reality Boundaries of Identification: The Inside Narrative

Pitcairn Island! The romance. The intrigue. The myth? What about the Pitcairn myth? Is there a Pitcairn myth? Yes, there certainly is. I have observed visitor after visitor come to Pitcairn with some sort of idea that it would be a step back to the garden of Eden. This is not reality. For the short-term visitor, on a passing yacht, reality is usually seen through rose coloured glasses and the myth is promulgated. The long-term visitors inevitably have to come to terms with reality and often leave before they intended: disappointed that Pitcairn is not full of perfect people. (TPM 1995)

I love Pitcairn, where one's existence can be lived this side of Eden according to God's plan, where the Gospel is free to reign … where there is liberty, where there is freedom to live out one's life of choice without being continually slaves to time. I love Pitcairn despite her problems and misfortunes in not having a doctor or dentist, and no stores, no outlet for island produce, no anchorage for vessels in the safety of a harbour, no beaches, and no song birds, but fortunate in that we have no dance halls, no intoxicating beverages, no tobacco and no taxes … and (I) would gladly yield up my life to preserve its freedom that our forefathers created out of chaos and rebellion, so that the future offspring of our children can every enjoy what our forebears left us" (TPM 1964).

Paradise is a mythological term drawn from imagination. The tourism industry has not been slow to capitalize on the former to inspire the latter. Travel literature (e.g., guidebooks, holiday brochures) perpetuate myths about island "paradises" and utopias, especially in the Polynesian islands, painting pictures for potential visitors, which, at least for many islanders, stand in stark contrast to their perception of their own existence (Cohen 1982; Harrison 2001: 13). As such, the place-myth of Pitcairn is misleading when empirically analyzed. According to Shields (1991: 61), "there is both constancy and a shifting quality to the construction of place-myth as the core images change slowly over time, displaced by radical changes in the nature of a place or may simply lose their connotative power. Others are invented, disseminated, and become accepted in common parlance."

The first quote above reflects the tourism industry's propensity to perpetuate global signs; the myth of island "paradise" evokes a set of established images that do not necessarily match reality. According to Cohen (1985: 99) "Mythological distance lends enchantment to an otherwise murky contemporary view." The efficacy of myth in this regard lies in its ahistorical character: it is beyond time. In addition, symbolism, a sense of belonging, and the complex nature of boundaries become indicative of what community "means." For Cohen community exists in the minds of its members as does the distinctiveness and reality of their boundaries. The second quote exemplifies this in that the writer's ideas and identity are reflected as a kind of palimpsest of continually overlaid landscape. Thus, individual and collective experiences are informed by an engagement and interpretation with place, and in turn these experiences create meaning for both local communities and visitors.

This section examines the "reality" of Pitcairn while recognizing that realities are numerous, varied, and partial, always contextual. To the outside world Pitcairn maintains an image of exclusivity and exoticness enforced primarily through the island's isolation and unique heritage. The island's inhabitants are descendants of *Bounty* mutineers, intrinsically linked to a storied landscape, a place-myth. Waldren's (1996) ethnographical study of the village of Deia on the island of Mallorca, contrasts the perception of space viewed from those on the "inside" and those from "outside," noting there is a distinct difference in how each group relates to, and perceives the village. Largely, the "outsiders" shared an idealized concept of landscape and timelessness somehow devoid of people. Waldren (1996: 39) says "for most who were not born or brought up there, Deia exists only as they perceive it, a paradise for rest and relaxation or an exotic landscape designed to test their creative abilities, to discover or soothe their soul." Whereas "for those who must wrest a living from the land the harshness of the landscape leaves little leisure for mere admiration."

Similar distinction can be made with Pitcairn. For islanders, the landscape must be cultivated, watered and fertilized to be productive. Feral goats constantly destroy gardens and contribute to erosion of the landscape. Extended periods of drought are more prevalent and the islanders constantly battle to catch and store sufficient water for domestic and agricultural use. Such conditions resulted in two evacuations (1831 and 1856). Strong easterly winds can wreck banana groves and destroy maturing vegetable plots whilst the introduction many decades ago of the fruit-fly pest is destructive to citrus trees. Oranges were once a major export commodity for the island. The sea is abundant with fish, but there is risk in negotiating the expanse of ocean; islanders fish from small wooden homemade "canoes" without life jackets and safety precautions. Pitcairners appreciate and resent their environment, it requires months of arduous labor and maintenance and waiting to collect and process the products. Work, personal histories, challenges, and memories of hard times affect each person's perception. Comparing internal and external narratives reveal how boundaries of identification are constructed and how island place/space is gazed upon by those inside and those outside.

The concept of place-myth is contextual and has much to do with the nature of local social organization and ideology as it does with geography (Waldren 1996: 55). The place of Pitcairn is not fiction, nor is it timeless and fixed, a bounded entity nor a mere physical space, it encompasses a range of challenges for those who reside there. One example of traveler motivation to experience "reality" is travel writer Dea Birkett who spent four months on Pitcairn Island. On a cold grey London day Birkett had visited a south end movie theatre, the Elephant, "in the hope of being transported to another place" (1997: 4). She had come to watch *"The Mutiny on the Bounty –* after 200 years, the truth behind the legend." Upon leaving the theatre Birkett (1997: 5) dwelt on the events of this (in)famous story:

> I walked over to the bus stop. The gorgeous isle still existed, somewhere, and could be visited. The *Bounty* story was not just a myth the Utopia the mutineers had searched for was a real place and the inhabitants were the inheritors of this mutinous dream.

Discussing islands Gillis (2004: 148) comments that "Today our most significant places are not those we dwell *in* physically but those we dwell *on* mentally." Birkett's *actual* experience exposed the reality of island life and myth did not match reality. The title of her book *Serpent in Paradise* perhaps indicates her transgression and misgivings ... she later comments "I had wanted to be immersed in the myth of the mutiny, become part of it, to live inside the dream I had formed at the Elephant" (1997: 278). Her spatial concept of place-image was bound to her notions of reality, truth, and causality. Birkett not only lied about her reason to visit Pitcairn (under the subterfuge of working for the British postal service) she also transgressed the insider/outsider boundary by entering into an intimate liaison with a married Pitcairn man. Her ostracism from the community grew day by day and after four months she was lonely and disillusioned. Toward the end of her book she states:

> Pitcairn had, almost since anyone knew of it, been more an idea than a geo- graphical entity. But such tiny islands have not only been promises, but also prisons. The most notorious penitentiaries – Alcatraz, Robben Island – have been surrounded by water. Islands are places upon which we can become trapped. Pitcairn had begun as my escape, but I had ended by escaping from Pitcairn (1997: 295).

Birkett's narrative highlights that understandings and concepts of space cannot be divorced from the real fabric of how people live their lives (Shields 1991). For tourists, as well as writers, islands (as place) often represent clear physical borders as well as psychological borders, which can be seen as an attraction in its own right for seeking to escape routine and responsibility (Rojek & Urry 1997). *Serpent in Paradise* is a work of creative nonfiction and also a travel text. Like Ball, Birkett is both literary tourist and literary author; motivated by story and setting: one who practices place. The book reveals the author's idiosyncratic "take" on places and people and is, undeniably, a genre of entertainment. Porter (1991) describes such travelers' tales as a form of cultural cartography that map and mediate the foreign that also involves a quest for authenticity. Of note is the way in which Birkett's travel writer subjectivity secures her position through various manifestations of the identity/difference logic, shaping the travel writer as a confident subject capable of negotiating, organizing and translating unfamiliar territory (Lisle 2006: 77). This includes a self-characterized by solitude and irony whilst projecting difference onto the local as "other." But as Birkett probes the layers of Pitcairn society, she discovers the facts differed from what she had *imagined*; she brought her preconceived ideas of Pitcairn and her forms of realism with her.

It could be said that the place-myth of Pitcairn has been perpetuated predominantly by external narratives, a continual and ongoing (re)collection of the story, transferred to both island and people. The islanders themselves have not embraced the myth to the same extent. They live the reality of isolation and isolation has its drawbacks. Electricity is supplied by diesel generator only ten hours a day; the import of basic supplies including diesel is constrained by high shipping freight charges and arrive only four times a year. Telecommunications are expensive and limited compared to other Pacific Islands. The islander's must constantly maintain machinery and equipment that is old and often fails. Pitcairner's still rely on the good will of a passing ship to evacuate a medical emergency. In 1981, the Editor of TPM wrote: "death has claimed another member of our small island family ... on Pitcairn, the loss is felt in wider terms ... the loss of skills and knowledge built up over the years and perhaps the loss of much needed manpower. Only 50 people on the island now." These same sentiments were reiterated when a death occurred during fieldwork in 2011.

An example of some ambivalence to the *Bounty* story was noted by Ball who found that on the anniversary of the mutiny (April 28) and even the landing on Pitcairn of the mutineers (15 January) neither date registered an important marker with the islanders. Instead he found the day most celebrated to be 23 January, the anniversary of the burning of the *Bounty*, known as "Bounty Day." On this day Pitcairners burn a replica of the *Bounty* ship in Bounty Bay, a ritual still practiced today. When Ball (1973: 353) asked one of the island elders about the lack of recognition of past events the reply was "we don't look back on those times much," Upon further investigation about the islanders' own interpretation of the mutiny he received vague replies that drew on the Hollywood movie versions: "oh, it was all in that Charles Laughton film – it was the cruelty of Bligh," or Nordoff & Hall's books, "it was all in the book by those two American fellows ... what were their names again? Of course, I don't know if it's *true* or not ... no one here really has strong feelings on it." The fact is Ball notes, the readership of *Bounty* literature likely "knows more about the story than the very ones who trace their descent from the whole adventure."

To substantiate such claims, Ball goes on to reveal that much of the tangible heritage (i.e., artifacts) remains off-island. Virtually all of the physical remnants of the *Bounty* have over time, been traded for more useful items such as flour, sugar, salt, and timber. For example, in 1937, Captain Irving of the yacht *Yankee* made an offer of a new vise and thirty dollars for H.M.S. *Bounty's* vise on behalf of a marine museum in the United States. It was decided to give it to him for the new one and take the thirty dollars, the Island Council minutes record (Ford 1996: 242). Even the move to start a museum on the island to house remaining items met with resistance. The current museum on Pitcairn only opened in 2005 and during the researcher's first year (2008–2009) only opened once for visitors. This appeared to be due to a lack of motivation rather than desire for monetary benefit (tourists pay $5.00 entry fee). Historical literature also refers to past arguments amongst islanders over individual ownership of artifacts and indeed, whether such items "belonged" in a museum; an issue not uncommon in the discourse of heritage tourism.

Conclusion: The Mutability of Place-Myth

> No place is a place until things that have happened in it are remembered in history, ballads, yarns, legends, or monuments. Fictions serve as well as facts (Urry 1995: 134).

Islands are places of fluidity and flux where utopian visions still persist. Utopia or paradise may not really exist, but the associative link between sign/signifier and signified still hold a central place in western cultures' mythical geographies. This discussion has examined the discursive construction of place-myth through literary analysis of selected texts as they relate to the story of Mutiny on the *Bounty*. It argues that place textualization viewed through the notion of layers, both narrative and physical, offers a more complete understanding of the construction of place-myth. Results reveal Pitcairn is a Pacific island inextricably bound to literary myth and imagination through various tropes of literature. In turn, the reality of how place is lived is exposed through juxtaposition of internal and external representations of place. External layers express notions of liminality (through arrival scenes) and the scripting of landscape. Excerpts from Murray, Fullerton, and Shapiro blend dream and reality through a sense of "reading" place; first organically (through literature), then actively (by visiting). In the case of Birkett, the imaginings of writers are promulgated (or not) by experience of place.

Moreover, writers organize sets of words, clauses, and paragraphs according to his or her intentions. In this way, content and meaning is mediated. Marks' discursively manipulates text in order to portray Pitcairn as dystopia rather than utopia. She (re)interprets landscape within predetermined lexical and metaphoric registers calling into question the construction of place-myth and indeed the very construction of metalanguage (Barthes 1972). Texts like TPM offer readers a layer of vicarious adventure, authentically supported by "insider" narratives whilst representing reality through the daily workings of the community/place/space being gazed upon.

Furthermore, Pitcairners spatialize place through their daily actions or practices, naming and mapping landscape. Place names tell of the relationship between people and place, symbolically, mythically and culturally. Islanders performatively practice place through acts of "piracy." The island's storied landscape continues to be discursively manipulated, performatively practiced and (re)produced. Thus, textualization *as process* offers rich ground for tourism analysis of the construction of place.

The expanse of literature written about the *Bounty* story has also ensured the *persistence* and *power* of place-image/myth. But the perception of "paradise" is not necessarily the view from within; the dichotomy between myth and reality is exposed when subject to scrutiny. In conclusion, what also becomes relevant in ascertaining the role of myth in relation to the *Bounty* story is its mutability. Pitcairn, as tourist space attests to the experiential value derived from the history of a place and its representation in literature. It is from such temporal and spatial perspective that literary accounts of Pitcairn have emerged, shrouded in language of real/unreal that has inspired writers for two centuries to attempt to unearth the true story of the mutiny or to relate the utopian vision of past and present on the island and its people. As a consequence such writings resonate with fancy and imagination, symbolic meanings, motifs, and mystery that will continually influence the movement, mobilities, and imaginings of the traveler/tourist/writer/reader.

References

Agnew, J. (1987) *Place and Politics: The Geographical Mediation of State and Society* (London: George Allen and Unwin).

Amoamo, M. (2010) Remoteness and myth making: Tourism development on Pitcairn Island, *Tourism Planning & Development*, 8(1), pp. 1–19.

Anderson, H. C. & Robinson, M. (Eds) (2002). *Literature and Tourism Reading and Writing Tourism Texts* (London: Continuum).

Ball, I. (1973) *Pitcairn: Children of the Bounty* (London: Gollancz).

Barke, M. (2002) 'Inside' and 'Outside' writings on Spain: Their relationship to Spanish tourism, in: H. C. Anderson & M. Robinson (Eds) *Literature and Tourism Reading and Writing Tourism Texts*, pp. 80–104 (London: Continuum).

Barrow, J. (1831) *The Eventful History of the Mutiny and Piratical Seizure of H.M.S. Bounty: Its Cause and Consequences*. Available at www.gutenberg.org/ebooks/14424 (accessed 07 October 2010).

Barthes, R. (1972) *Mythologies*, translated by Annette Lavers (New York: Hill and Wang).

Birkett, D. (1997) *Serpent in Paradise* (London: Picador).

Bourdieu, P. (1992) *Language and Symbolic Power* (Cambridge, England: Polity Press).

Christian, G. (1999) *Fragile Paradise* (Sydney: Doubleday).

Cohen, E. (1982) *The Pacific Islands from Utopian Myth to Consumer Product: The Disenchantment of Paradise* (Aix-En-Provence: Centre des Hautes Etudes Touristiques).

Cohen, A. P. (1985) *The Symbolic Construction of Community* (Chichester, Sussex, England: Ellis Horwood Limited).

Connell, J. (2003) Island dreaming: The contemplation of Polynesian paradise, *Journal of Historical Geography*, 29(4), pp. 554–581.

Connell, J. (2007) Islands, idylls and the detours of development, *Singapore Journal of Tropical Geography*, 28, pp. 116–135.

DeLyser, D. (2003) Ramona memories: Fiction, tourist practices, and placing the past in Southern California, *Annals of the Association of American Geographers*, 93(4), pp. 886–908.

Dening G. (2003) Afterword, in: R. Edmond & V. Smith (Eds) *Islands in History and Representation*, pp. 203–206 (London: Routledge).

Ford, H. (1996) *Pitcairn: Port of Call* (Angwin, CA: Hawser Titles).

Fullerton, W. Y. (1923) *The Romance of Pitcairn* (London: Carey Press).

Gillis, J. (2004) *Islands of the Mind* (New York: Palgrave MacMillan).

Harrison, D. (2001) Islands, image and tourism, *Tourism Recreation Research*, 26(3), pp. 9–14.

Hayward, P. (2006) *Bounty Chords Music, Dance and Cultural Heritage on Norfolk and Pitcairn Islands* (Eastleigh, UK: John Libbey Publishing).

Howe, K. R. (2000) *Nature, Culture, and History: The "Knowing" of Oceania* (Honolulu: University of Hawaii Press).

Huff, S. (2008) Identity and landscape: The reification of place in strasbourg, France, in: D. Knudsen, *et al.* (Eds) *Landscape, Tourism, and Meaning*, pp. 19–35 (Aldershot, Hampshire, England: Ashgate Publishing Ltd).

Johnson, P. (2010) Writing liminal landscapes: The cosmopolitical gaze, *Tourism Geographies*, 12(4), pp. 505–524.

Kirk, R. W. (2008) *Pitcairn Island, The Bounty Mutineers and their Descendants: A History* (Jeffersen, NC: McFarland & Co).

Kolås, A. (2004) Tourism and the making of place in Shangri-La, *Tourism Geographies*, 6(3), pp. 262–278.

Lisle, D. (2006) *The Global Politics of Contemporary Travel Writing* (Cambridge: Cambridge University Press).

Lummis, T. (1997) *Pitcairn Island: Life and Death in Eden* (Aldershot, England: Ashgate).

Marks, K. (2008) *Pitcairn: Paradise Lost: Uncovering the Dark Secrets of a South Pacific Fantasy Island* (Pymble, NSW: Harper Collins).

Murray, S. (1992) *Pitcairn Island: The First 200 Years* (La Canada, CA: Bounty Sagas).

Nash, J. (2009) Naming the sea offshore fishing grounds as place names on Pitcairn Island and Norfolk Island, *Shima: The International Journal of Research into Island Cultures*, 3(2), pp. 118–131.

Nicolson, R. & Davies, B. (1997) *The Pitcairners* (Auckland: Pasifika Press).

Nordhoff, C. & Hall, J. N. (1936) *The Bounty Trilogy* (Boston/Toronto: Little, Brown and Company).

Pocock, D. C. (Ed) (1981) *Humanistic Geography and Literature* (London: Croom Helm Ltd).

Porter, D. (1991) *Haunted Journeys: Desire and Transgression in European Travel Writing* (Princeton, NJ: Princeton University Press).

Rojek, C. & Urry, J. (Eds) (1997) *Touring Cultures: Transformations of Travel and Theory* (London: Routledge).

Shapiro, H. L. (1936) *Heritage of the Bounty: The Story of Pitcairn through Six Generations* (London: Victor Gollancz Ltd).

Sheppard, S. (2004) *Eden as Dystopia: The Failure of State Formation on Pitcairn Island*. Available at http://www.sais-jhu.edu/faculty/pecastaing/Dowloads/PitcairnSimon.pdf (accessed 06 January 2011).

Shields, R. (1991) *Places on the Margin Alternative Geographies of Modernity* (London: Routledge).

Smith, M., MacLeod, N. & Hart Robertson, M. (2010) *Key Concepts in Tourist Studies* (London: Sage Publications).

Smith, V. (2003) Pitcairn's 'guilty stock' The island as breeding ground, in: R. Edmond & V. Smith (Eds) *Islands in History and Representation*, pp. 116–132 (London: Routledge).

Svasek, M. (2010) "The Field" intersubjectivity, empathy and the workings of internalized presence, in: D. Spencer & J. Davies (Eds) *Anthropological Fieldwork: A Relational Process*, pp. 75–95 (Newcastle upon Tyne, UK: Cambridge Scholars Publishing).

Tetley, S. & Bramwell, B. (2002) Tourists and the cultural construction of Haworth's literary landscape, in: H. C. Anderson & M. Robinson (Eds) *Literature and Tourism Reading and Writing Tourism Texts*, pp. 155–170 (London: Continuum).

The Pitcairn Miscellany (1964) *Editorial*, 6(5), p. 1.

The Pitcairn Miscellany (1985) *Editorial*, 23(5), p. 1.

The Pitcairn Miscellany (1995) *Pastor Ponders in Closing*, 38(3), p. 2.

Urry, J. (1990) *The Tourist Gaze: Leisure and Travel in Contemporary Societies* (London: Sage Publications).

Urry, J. (1995) *Consuming Places* (London and New York: Routledge).

Waldren, J. (1996) *Insiders and Outsiders: Paradise and Reality in Mallorca* (Providence, RI: Berghahn Books).

Young, R. A. (1894) *Mutiny of the Bounty and Story of Pitcairn Island: 1790–1894* (Oakland, California: Pacific Press Publishing Company).

Notes on Contributor

Maria Amoamo is a postdoctoral fellow with a research interest in cultural, heritage and ethnic tourism and exploring issues of imagery, representation, and identity. Her current research focuses on small island development with regard to issues of vulnerability and resilience of Pacific Island communities in relation to tourism.

Residents' Attitudes towards Tourism Development in Cape Verde Islands

MANUEL ALECTOR RIBEIRO[*], PATRÍCIA OOM do VALLE[**]
& JOÃO ALBINO SILVA[**]

[*]Faculty of Economics, University of Algarve, Faro, Portugal
[**]Faculty of Economics, Research Center for Spatial and Organizational Dynamics (CIEO), University of Algarve, Faro, Portugal

ABSTRACT *The purpose of this study is to examine residents' attitudes and perceptions towards tourism development in the Cape Verde islands, a little-explored issue in the context of small islands' developing states, especially in Africa. Since the country is in the initial stage of tourism development, it is intended to show that residents predominantly share a positive attitude, which supports previous research. It is also intended to understand whether attitudes are homogeneously shared or instead tourism is differently perceived by residents. To address these objectives, a survey based on 492 questionnaires was applied to national residents in five counties that represent the major tourist areas of Cape Verde. The findings reveal that, in general, residents are optimistic about tourism. Yet, despite the overall positive attitude towards tourism, different segments of residents according to the way the tourism impacts are perceived could be identified. These segments report significant differences concerning socio-demographic characteristics and the degree of involvement in the tourism sector. This analysis provides important inputs for the planning process and sustainable development of tourism in the archipelago.*

Introduction

The Republic of Cape Verde is a small archipelagic state of volcanic origin, located in the Macronesia region of the North Atlantic Ocean, around 500 kilometres from Western Africa. Tourism is a relatively recent phenomenon in Cape Verde and it has shown a strong dynamic in the formation of both income and employment. Hence, it represented 21% of GDP in 2010 (Banco de Cabo Verde 2011), and the sector is continuing to grow, with diverse projects currently underway in the islands (Sarmento 2008; López-Guzmán *et al.* 2011). The exponential increase of visitors and the growing attention to this socioeconomic sector, classified as strategic by the

125

government, tourism-related business and the local community, have led to an intensification of research in the tourism sector in Cape Verde. This research has mainly focused on aspects of the tourism offer and demand, with some studies assessing tourists' motivations and satisfaction (Carvalho 2010; López-Guzmán *et al.* 2011).

For a destination to succeed, it has to satisfy or even surpass tourists' expectations, but tourism also has to be perceived as an activity that brings more benefits than inconveniences to local residents (Ap 1992; Gursoy & Rutherford 2004; Vargas-Sánchez *et al.* 2009). Tourists also visit places where people live, which increases the importance of incorporating community reactions into tourism planning and development, in order to minimize conflicts between 'hosts' and 'guests' (Zhang *et al.* 2006). The impact of tourism development on host communities has been attracting much attention in discussions concerning the sustainability of tourism, with some studies exploring tourist island regions of the Pacific (Choy 1992; Milne & Nowosielski 1997; Apostolopoulos & Gayle 2002), Caribbean (Wilkinson 1987; Weaver 1993; McElroy & de Albuquerque 1998; Apostolopoulos & Gayle 2002) and Mediterranean (Ioannides 1995; Akis *et al.* 1996; Boissevain 1996; Briguglio & Briguglio 1996; Lockhart 1997; Apostolopoulos & Gayle 2002). However, no studies have been found that examine residents' attitudes towards tourism on developing island states in the Atlantic Ocean such as Cape Verde.

The overall purpose of this study is to contribute to fill this research gap, which may be relevant in future political decisions related to tourism development in Cape Verde. The specific objectives of the study are twofold. First, to verify to what extent the paradigmatic findings of previous studies on the connection between the level of tourism development and residents' attitudes and perceptions towards tourism, such as those of Butler (1980) and Doxey (1975), also apply to the case of Cape Verde. These studies indicate that, in a destination where tourism development is still incipient, host communities predominantly have a positive attitude towards tourism, with a strong perception of its positive impacts and less awareness of its negative consequences. Secondly, this study intends to deepen the knowledge about how residents in Cape Verde perceive tourism in their country, by identifying and characterizing segments with different views concerning this theme.

This study provides an important analysis for scholars and tourism managers in developing destinations such as Cape Verde. In fact, by understanding residents' attitudes and perceptions towards tourism, policy makers in these regions will be better prepared to propose and implement adequate planning policies for the sustainability of tourism at the local, regional or national level. However, the interest of this study is not restricted to small island communities where tourism is in an initial phase. Actually, since tourism is a local phenomenon (Gunn & Var 2002), there are small regions taking the first steps towards tourism development even inside mature destinations. So, by approaching residents' attitudes in small communities where tourism development is still incipient, this study is also valuable for tourism planners of developed destinations.

Tourism in Cape Verde

Tourism has a strong potential in the Cape Verde islands, which are endowed with an enjoyable climate, white and black sand beaches, an abundance of submarine life and rugged landscapes, particularly unexplored. Along with these natural elements, Cape Verde is also notable for the hospitality of its inhabitants, named *Morabeza*, and for their great cultural diversity, and is associated with democratic stability, which are both facilitator characteristics for tourism development (López-Guzmán *et al.* 2011). Despite its wide-ranging tourism attractions, most tourists who choose Cape Verde as a destination are strongly motivated by its natural resources and the exotic appearance of the archipelago (Sarmento 2008).

Tourism in Cape Verde started in the 1960s after the construction of an international airport on the Island of Sal (Sarmento 2008). The construction of hostel Morabeza (now Hotel Morabeza) in 1967 marked the beginning of the island of Sal as a tourist destination, especially for sun and beach tourism. Tourism would accelerate with the stay of the South African Airways crew members in the island, with many flights to Europe and the United States of America (Directorate General of Tourism [DGT] 2009). However, the growth of tourism as an important economic activity in the development process of Cape Verde is fairly recent – since the late 1990s onwards – and was driven by several factors, such as the 'discovery' of the islands by investors in the tourism sector (first Italian and Portuguese, followed later by Spanish and English) and the assumption by successive governments that tourism would be one of the main vehicles of growth of the Cape Verdean economy (DGT 2009).

Over the past 11 years, the number of tourists in Cape Verde has grown by an average of 11.4% per year – higher than the growth rates of world tourism – rising from 145,000 tourists in 2000 to 381,831 in 2010 (National Institute of Statistics [NIS] 2011). In the same period, overnight stays increased from 684,700 to 2.342 million, an average annual growth of 14.5% in this period. In 2010 the main source of inbound tourists to Cape Verde came from the United Kingdom (25.0%), followed by Germany (15.2%), Italy (14.4%) and Portugal (12.0%) (NIS 2011).

The most explored touristic product in Cape Verde is the sun and sea, especially on the Island of Sal and, more recently, on the island of Boa Vista, after the opening of an international airport. The island of Sal hosts about 48.8% of the tourists who visit the archipelago. There is a concentration of tourism on this island, where more than 70% of the capacity of the tourist accommodation establishments is provided under the 'all inclusive' system (NIS 2011).

Presently, the majority of tourists visiting the country do it on charter flights mostly to the islands of Sal and Boa Vista, which are the two main tourist centres of the country (NIS 2011). There are currently four international airports that are connecting with regular flights to several European, African and American cities. It is noteworthy that over 60% of tourists entering Cape Verde do so in the form of charter flights. In parallel, cruise tourism is an industry that has been growing at a rapid rate over the past 2 years. It is estimated that, in 2012, approximately 50,000 tourists have visited Cape Verde through cruise tourism (DGT 2009). The *Porto Grande* in Mindelo, on the island of St. Vincent, is the main port of the country.

Nowadays tourism is considered strategic by the government and the economic agents of Cape Verde due to the income it provides, its ability to increase employment and the multiplier effects it provokes in several areas. Despite its potential, tourism development in the country faces difficulties, such as the lack of destination promotion, effective allocation of resources to the sector and the insufficient quality of some of the services provided. However, there is a real perception of the urgent need to overcome these problems by planning and implementing more effective tourism policies (Sarmento 2008).

Theoretical Background and Hypotheses

There is a considerable body of knowledge that focuses on residents' reactions to tourism, although with non-consensual conclusions. This section provides a comprehensive review of the literature and is not specific about destinations in the initial stage of tourism development. The reasons for this are twofold. First, the literature on the topic of island developing countries with similar characteristics to Cape Verde is very scarce and, therefore, the research background would be too limited. Secondly, since residents' attitudes change due to the level of development in tourism, it is important that policy makers and researchers of developing destinations are also aware of how residents perceive tourism in mature destinations. In fact, being more attentive to the costs that tourism development can bring, developing destinations will be better prepared to prevent those costs. Based on the literature review, some research hypotheses will be proposed.

Residents' Attitudes and Perceptions Towards Tourism

Residents' attitudes towards tourism have been extensively studied in recent decades in an attempt to understand the host communities' feelings about tourism development.

The tourism industry is dependent on the hospitality of the host community and, consequently, it should be developed according to their needs and desires (Lindberg & Johnson 1997; Gursoy & Rutherford 2004; Andriotis 2005; Alegre & Cladera 2009). Also, a favourable attitude by the host community is vital to the future success of a destination because it has a positive impact on visitors' satisfaction and loyalty (Snaith & Haley 1994; Swarbrooke 1995; Sheldon & Abenoja 2001; Valle *et al.* 2011). Andereck and Vogt (2000) and Sirakaya *et al.* (2002) claim that, without community support and the cooperation and participation of the host community, it is difficult to establish a sustainable tourism industry. The importance of the host community in supporting tourism development has therefore been widely recognized in the mainstream tourism literature (Akis *et al.* 1996).

The impacts of tourism development, their intensity and magnitude, vary from place to place, depending on the characteristics of each place, the activities developed there and the residents' and tourists' behaviour (van der Duim & Caalders 2002). The tourism impacts in host communities are usually classified as positive or negative, under the headings of economic, socio-cultural and environmental impacts.

The positive economic impacts include more investment, income tax revenues, job opportunities, increased infrastructure and tourism facilities in destination areas, and a rise in residents' living standards (Davis *et al.* 1988; Haralambopoulos & Pizam 1996; Andereck & Vogt 2000; Tosun 2002; Vargas-Sánchez *et al.* 2009). Regarding the negative economic impacts, the most quoted in the literature relate to the increasing price of goods and services, the overdependence on tourism, an increase in inflation rates and rise in land values, high propensity to import and the seasonality of production (Akis *et al.* 1996; Haralambopoulos & Pizam 1996; Brunt & Courtney 1999). However, the tourism industry has several positive socio-cultural impacts that include a range of features, from the promotion of cultural heritage, arts and handicrafts to the revitalization of local traditions (Brunt & Courtney 1999; Andereck *et al.* 2005). Tourism can also cause some negative socio-cultural impacts in the host community, such as the encouragement of cultural commercialization, prostitution, crime, drug addiction and gambling (Pizam & Pokela 1985; Cohen 1988; Ap 1992; Brunt & Courtney 1999).

On the environmental level, tourism can contribute to improve environmental re-sources, as it often demands the preservation of the natural heritage and improvement of public facilities (Akis *et al.* 1996; Andereck *et al.* 2005). However, tourism can also have significant negative environmental impacts, related to more traffic, water and noise pollution, vandalism, litter, erosion and depletion of natural resources (Ap & Crompton 1998; Ko & Stewart 2002; Andereck *et al.* 2005; Kuvan & Akan 2005).

Level of Tourism Development and Residents' Attitudes and Perceptions

Generally, there is an association between the level of tourism growth in a destination and local residents' awareness of the impacts of tourism (Pearce & Moscardo 1999). According to Doxey (1975), communities pass through a sequence of reactions as the impacts of tourism in their area of residence become more evident. So, an initial euphoria is followed by apathy, irritation or even antagonism. In this context, Butler (1980) also proposes a connection between tourism development and residents' attitudes towards tourists. Using his destination life-cycle model, he explains that as the number of visitors increases in a destination, residents who are overwhelmingly well disposed towards tourists tend to develop growing reservations about the long-term benefits of the presence of these visitors.

Other authors also argue that residents' attitudes towards tourism are more favourable in the early stage of development of the destination (Doxey 1975; Akis *et al.* 1996; Faulkner & Tideswell 1997; Upchurch & Teivane 2000; Pérez & Nadal

2005), and more negative in mature destinations (Doxey 1975; Faulkner & Tideswell 1997; Vargas-Sánchez *et al.* 2009). In this line of research, Smith and Krannich (1998) define a typology of four rural communities in the United States Rocky Mountain West with different experiences in terms of tourism growth, which includes '*tourism-saturated*', '*tourism-realized*' and '*tourism-hungry*' communities.

Studies on residents' attitudes towards tourism in African developing countries, such as Cape Verde, are extremely rare. Lepp (2007), in a study about Bigodi, Uganda, used qualitative methods to show that residents have positive attitudes towards tourism, mainly resulting from the premise that 'tourism creates community development, improves agricultural markets, generates income, and finally, that tourism brings random good fortune' (Lepp 2007: 876). Teye *et al.* (2002) instead found more ambiguous results. The setting for their study was Cape Coast and Elmina, Ghana, and they found that support for tourism development in these regions ranged from strong support to opposition to tourism development, depending on several factors such as the respondents' employment status and membership in community organizations.

As far as we reviewed, no studies on residents' attitudes and perceptions towards tourism in island developing African countries can be found. However, since significant previous research in different settings suggests a relationship between the level of tourism development and residents' attitudes towards tourism, the first research hypothesis is defined as follows:

H_1: Cape Verde is in an initial stage of tourism development and therefore residents have a positive attitude towards tourism, perceiving its positive impacts more strongly than its negative impacts.

Segmenting Residents Based on their Perceptions and Attitudes

Authors such as Lankford and Howard (1994) report that residents are not homogeneous in their attitudes towards tourism and are driven largely by perceptions of how tourism impacts their own lives and their community. In this sense, several studies have been developed using community segmentation, and cluster analysis in particular, as a way of better understanding residents' attitudes and perceptions towards tourism.

In their study, Davis *et al.* (1988) segmented residents in Florida identifying five groups of residents according to their attitudes, interests and opinions towards tourism, grouped as 'haters', 'lovers', cautious romantics', 'in-betweeners' and 'lover for a reason'. Madrigal (1995) found three nested segments of residents in two cities, which were named as 'lovers', 'realists' and 'haters'. Fredline and Faulkner (2000), in a study surrounding a major motorsport event in Gold Coast Indy, Australia, identified five segments, grouped as 'haters', 'lovers', 'ambivalent', 'moderately positive' and 'concerned for a reason'. William and Lawson (2001), in 10 New Zealand towns, identified four groups of residents as 'lovers', 'cynics', 'taxpayers' and 'innocents'. Andriotis and Vaughan (2003) found three groups of residents in Crete: 'advocates', 'socially and environmentally concerned' and 'economic skeptic'. In the Balearic Islands, Pérez and Nadal (2005) examined the host community's perceptions of tourism and five groups emerged from their data analysis: 'development supporters', 'prudent developers', 'ambivalent and cautious', 'protectionists' and 'alternative developers'.

In short, given earlier research which shows that, even at the same destination, residents may have different attitudes towards tourism, a second research hypothesis is formulated:

H_2: In the case of Cape Verde, in spite of an overall global attitude towards tourism, some specific segments of residents have a more positive attitude than others.

Factors Affecting Residents' Attitudes and Perceptions towards Tourism

In the last decades, numerous studies have been conducted to identify factors that influence residents' perceptions and attitudes towards tourism (McGehee & Andereck 2004). In the tourism literature, gender is viewed as one such factor. Martin (1995) observes that there is a significant relationship between attitude and gender, indicating that females have a more positive attitude to tourism than males. On the contrary, Mason and Cheyne (2000), in a study in New Zealand, found the opposite result. Other studies conclude that gender does not influence residents' attitudes towards tourism (Davis *et al.* 1988; Ryan & Montgomery 1994).

In like manner, age is also mentioned in the literature as a factor that can influence residents' attitudes towards tourism development, but although there is no consensus in the literature about its influence (Fredline & Faulkner 2000; Tomljenovic & Faulkner 2000; Weaver & Lawton 2001; Cavus & Tarinsevdi 2003; Harril 2004). The same applies to the education level (Haralambopoulos & Pizam 1996; Weaver & Lawton 2001; Teye *et al.* 2002; Andriotis & Vaughan 2003).

The degree of involvement in the tourism sector is another relevant issue in understanding residents' attitudes towards tourism development. This is related to the occupational status in the tourism sector, and a large number of studies (Johnson *et al.* 1994; Haralambopoulos & Pizam 1996; Weaver & Lawton 2001) have reported a significant relationship between attitudes and economic dependence on the tourism industry, suggesting that residents deriving more economic benefits from tourism were more favourable to the industry (Vargas-Sánchez *et al.* 2011). However, even though some other studies support this relationship (Martin *et al.* 1998; Vesey & Dimanche 2000; Harrill 2004), others reached the opposite conclusion (Smith & Krannich 1998; McGehee & Andereck 2004).

Hence, given previous studies showing that some socio-demographic variables and the degree of involvement in the tourism sector may influence residents' perceptions and attitudes towards tourism, two final research hypotheses are formulated:

H_3: The segments differ according to certain socio-demographic characteristics.

H_4: The segments differ depending on the degree of the residents' involvement in the tourism sector.

Methods

Instruments

This study relies on a questionnaire that was designed based on five previous studies: a survey of local residents developed to study the sustainability of tourism in the Azores, Portugal (Moniz 2006); a survey to analyse the sustainability of tourism in the Ugljan–Pasman Islands from the residents' perspective (Manning *et al.* 2001); a questionnaire to collect data on the attitudes and opinions of local residents towards tourism development (WTO 2004); a questionnaire used to analyse the degree of satisfaction of residents towards tourism in their counties of residence in the Algarve region, Portugal (Silva *et al.* 2001); and a questionnaire applied to local residents of the island of Madeira, Portugal (Martins 2000). However, a few adjustments were introduced to meet the aims of this study.

The questionnaire was divided into three parts, each composed of different measuring instruments. Part I included questions on socio-demographic characteristics: gender, age, marital status, number of persons in the household, county of residence, education level, tourism qualification (if applicable), occupation, working abroad (where, what and for how long), number of years living in the county and housing scheme. Part II inquired about the degree of residents' involvement in the tourism sector. Finally, Part III focused on residents' perceptions towards the impacts of tourism using 22 items measured on a five-point Likert scale (1 – *strongly disagree* to 5 – *strongly agree*). These items are listed in Table 2.

Data

The target population of this study was national residents living in Cape Verde who were 18 years of age or more. The survey was carried out in the counties of Tarrafal, Praia, Sal, São Vicente and São Filipe in August, September and October 2008. Figure 1 shows the geographic localization of Cape Verde and the five counties where the questionnaire was applied. According to Census 2000 (NIS 2001), the number of residents in this year was 431,989 individuals. As a first step, a sample of 384 residents was defined from these counties. The calculation of the sample size used the most conservative estimate for a single proportion (0.50), a confidence level of 95% and a margin of error of 4.5%. Moreover, the present study used the stratified sampling method, with the sample distributed in proportion to the population's distribution in the five counties, by gender and age group. As a second step, the sample dimension was proportionally corrected to 500 observations, in order to ensure that the county with fewest inhabitants (Sal) had a sample size of at least 30 observations.

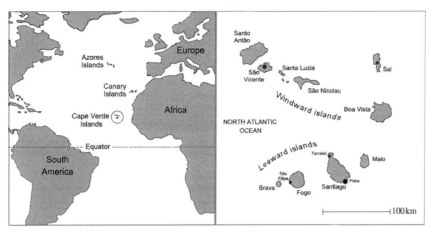

Figure 1. Cape Verde and the counties where the questionnaire was applied.

In the five countries, the questionnaire was applied in randomly selected popular places for residents (e.g. alongside the markets, in coffee shops and public parks), at predefined periods of time. In each place selected, all residents older than 18 years and willing to participate in the study had the opportunity to fill in the questionnaire. The questionnaire was hand-delivered/returned by two trained interviewers who informed respondents about the aims of the survey, the importance of answering all the questions and, whenever requested, clarified doubts on specific items. Data collection ended when the sampling size was reached, as well as the gender and age category strata. A total of 492 complete questionnaires were obtained, corresponding to 98.4% of the initially defined sample.

Therefore, the sample reflects the distribution of the target population in the selected islands, according to gender and age categories (NIS 2001). In the sample, 53% of respondents were female and 47% male. The average age is 40.6 years with a standard deviation of 2.07 years, with respondents ranging in age from 18 to 72 years. The majority of residents fall into the category of 'married/living with partner' (51%), followed by 'singles' (47%). Regarding the educational level, respondents were grouped into three categories: 'illiterate or with elementary education' (25%), 'high school' (52.8%) and 'medium or higher education' (22.2%). Most respondents (58.8%) have a professional activity, followed by students (19.4%), domestics (14.6%), unemployed (4.6%) and, finally, retired (2.6%). Table 1 characterizes the sample concerning the degree of involvement in the tourism sector.

Data Analysis Methods

The data analysis was organized into four phases. First, Categorical Principal Components Analysis (CATPCA), also known as non-linear principal components analysis,

Table 1. Frequency distribution of professional involvement degree in the tourism sector.

	Yes	No	Total
Do you earn your living through tourism?	19.2%	80.8%	100.0%
If yes, are you an entrepreneur in the tourism sector?	26.5%	73.5%	100.0%
Do you have direct contact with tourists as part of your work?	35.0%	65.0%	100.0%
Is tourism the main source of income of your household?	16.4%	83.6%	100.0%
Is any member of your household involved in tourism as a source of income or employment?	23.4%	76.6%	100.0%

was applied to the items used to measure residents' perceptions towards tourism in Cape Verde. This technique is particularly appropriate whenever the purpose is to reduce the dimensionality of a set of ordinal variables (such as those measured using Likert scales) into a smaller number of new variables that explain a considerable proportion of the original information (Meulman *et al.* 2004; Manisera *et al.* 2010). Cronbach alpha coefficients were used to examine the reliability of the retained components. Reliability coefficients above 0.6 are acceptable for an exploratory research (Churchill 1979). As an output of CATPCA, the scores of residents for each component were gathered. CATPCA, accompanied by descriptive statistics, was used to assess research hypothesis 1 (H_1).

Secondly, Multiple Correspondence Analysis (MCA) was applied to the set of components obtained through CATPCA, previously categorized based on their corresponding medians. MCA is an interdependence technique that, besides analysing several qualitative variables simultaneously, has the advantage of allowing their graphical representation through perceptual maps (Greenacre 2007). Perceptual maps simplify data interpretation, since they reveal similar variables or categories. Specifically, related categories are represented as points close together on the map and vice versa. MCA was used in this study because it is intended to identify homogeneous groups of residents in Cape Verde based on their perceptions of tourism impacts, and the perceptual maps can be very helpful to achieve this purpose. In this sense, particular attention has been given to the perceptual map that represents the categories of the variables, since it shows how these categories relate to each other, suggesting the existence of possible segments of residents regarding their attitude towards tourism. Thirdly, a cluster analysis was used to validate the segments of Cape Verdean residents suggested by the MCA's perceptual map (Lebart 1994; Carvalho 1998). Finally, the profile of each segment (or cluster) was described based on the variables used in the MCA (internal validation) but also in terms of the other variables included in the questionnaire (external validation). The sequential use of MCA and cluster analysis was used to evaluate research hypothesis 2 (H_2).

In order to differentiate the segments, the variable identifying the segment in which each responded was classified (the variable *segment membership*) was crossed with the variables previously used in the MCA, in order to understand the segments' profile regarding the attitude towards tourism (internal validation). In a second phase, the variable *segment membership* was crossed with other variables of the questionnaire with the purpose of deepening the knowledge of the profile of each segment of residents (external validation). The latter analysis was used to assess research hypotheses 3 and 4 (**H₃** and **H₄**).

Results

Results from CATPCA

For purposes of data reduction, CATPCA was applied to the set of 22 items in order to determine the principal components that best represent the perceptions about the positive and negative impacts of tourism, in the residents' perspective. Three components were retained, all presenting a Cronbach alpha higher than 0.6. All items load reasonably strongly on one component. Table 2 shows the results from CATPCA and some descriptive statistics: the percentage of responses in the response categories 'agree' plus 'strongly agree', and the most frequent response to each item.

Component 1 was labelled *Social, cultural and environmental benefits of tourism* because it includes items related to the general improvement in the standards of living and expresses a positive perception of the social, cultural and environmental impacts. High values for this component mean that respondents express beliefs in the general benefits of tourism for the county where they reside, regarding the improvement of several facets of everyday life. Table 2 shows that, excepting item 3, most respondents agree or strongly agree with the statements included in this component. Based on these results, we can conclude that Cape Verdeans have great faith in tourism as a means to improve their quality of life regarding a wide-ranging set of aspects. Component 2, referred to as *Costs of tourism*, includes variables related to environmental and social concerns. The results show that respondents, when confronted with the statements included in the component, expressed a positive attitude, not agreeing, in most cases, that tourism comes with substantial social and environmental costs. Lastly, Component 3, named as *Economic benefits of tourism*, includes items measuring the economic advantages of tourism with which residents express strong levels of agreement (higher than 60% in the sum of categories 'agree' and 'strongly agree').

Therefore, it can be concluded that respondents recognize that tourism brings economic benefits to the Cape Verdean economy. In addition, Cape Verdeans have great expectations from tourism, agreeing with its potential to improve the quality of life and as a source of economic growth. In contrast, residents do not view tourism as responsible for significant environmental or social costs. In short, residents in Cape Verde express a positive attitude towards tourism, thereby validating **H₁**.

Table 2. Attitude statements, *loadings* from CATPCA and descriptive statistics.

Components and items	Loadings	% agree + strongly agree/(mode)[a]
Social, cultural and environmental benefits of tourism (alpha = 0.655)		
Due to tourism there has been an improvement in infrastructure and public services (water supply, electricity, telephone, etc.)	0.606	58.0% (4)
Due to tourism the quality of life in my county has improved	0.599	53.0% (4)
I have access to better sporting, cultural and leisure facilities	0.589	30.4% (3)
Tourism has contributed to human resources development and introduction of new technologies in the country	0.577	68.4% (4)
Due to tourism there has been greater protection of the natural environment	0.575	68.0% (4)
Tourism helps to preserve the culture and encourages local handicrafts	0.551	85.6% (4)
Costs of tourism (alpha = 0.797)		
Tourism has exacerbated social inequalities	0.631	27.2% (2)
Tourism increases insecurity and crime	0.546	27.6% (2)
In general, tourists who come to Cape Verde do not respect our traditions	0.518	8.60% (2)
Hotel construction is affecting the environmental aesthetic quality	0.518	28.2% (2)
Tourism has caused the deterioration of places of historical and cultural interest	0.505	21.0% (2)
Residents have no access to major tourist attractions	0.502	14.8% (2)
Tourism has exacerbated the social problems of drugs, alcoholism and prostitution	0.498	35.2% (3)
Tourism disrupts the residents' behaviour	0.496	16.2% (2)
Tourists should pay more taxes for services that they use	0.495	36.4% (3)
Tourism has been responsible for changes in biodiversity and landscape	0.491	22.6% (2)
Tourism has contributed to the increase of environmental pollution	0.484	22.6% (2)
Due to tourism there is more trash in my county	0.458	8.80% (2)
I like tourists as long as they do not move here to stay	0.406	34.2% (3)
Economic benefits of tourism (alpha = 0.670)		
Tourism can create jobs for residents	0.513	81.2% (4)
Tourism increases residents' income	0.508	62.0% (4)
Due to tourism there are more business opportunities	0.501	73.2% (4)

[a]2 – *disagree*; 3 – *neither agree or disagree*; 4 – *agree*.

Results from MCA

Before applying MCA, the scores of the residents for each component were gathered and the three components were categorized based on their medians. Three categorical variables resulted from this procedure, with the same name as the original components, each one with two categories: 'equal to or lower than the median' versus 'above the median'. Thus, in the categorized variable *Social, cultural and environmental benefits of tourism*, residents with an individual score higher than the median were classified as having a more positive attitude towards these sets of benefits that tourism can bring to the Cape Verdean population. By contrast, residents with an individual score equal to or lower than the median were considered as expressing a less positive attitude towards these benefits. The same reasoning was applied in relation to the categorized variable *Economic benefits of tourism*. Regarding the categorized variable *Costs of tourism*, residents with an individual score higher than the median were classified as expressing a less positive attitude towards tourism, taking the view that tourism can have several social and environmental costs (and vice versa).

Applying MCA to the three categorized variables, two dimensions were retained, accounting for 74.84% of the total variance (the first dimension accounts for 43.27% and the second dimension accounts for 31.57% of variance). MCA enables us to explore the joint relationship among the three categorized variables through the perceptual map representing the categories of the variables. This map suggests the existence of three segments of residents regarding their attitude towards tourism (Figure 2). As can be seen in Figure 2, the categories 'above the median' of the variables *Social, cultural and environmental benefits of tourism* and *Economic*

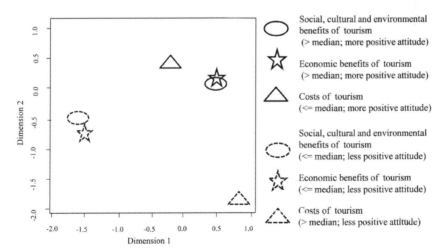

Figure 2. Perceptual map from MCA (joint plot of category points).

benefits of tourism are represented in the upper right-hand quadrant, as well as the category 'equal to or lower than the median' of the variable *Costs of tourism*. As previously explained, these categories express a more positive attitude towards tourism. This combination of categories suggests the existence of a segment of residents with an overall favourable attitude towards tourism, considering its diverse impacts. In the lower right quadrant is represented the category 'above the median' of the variable *Costs of tourism*. This situation suggests the existence of a group of residents who recognize these costs, i.e. with a less favourable attitude towards tourism. Finally, on the left-hand side of the map are represented the categories 'equal to or lower than the median' with regard to the variables *Social, cultural and environmental benefits of tourism* and *Economic benefits of tourism*. This aspect indicates the existence of a third segment of residents composed of individuals who are more sceptical in terms of the positive impacts of tourism.

Results from Cluster Analysis

Cluster analysis was used in this study in order to validate the three segments suggested by the perceptual map produced by the MCA and to allow, subsequently, its characterization. This analysis used Ward's clustering method and the squared Euclidean distance as a measure of dissimilarity. An observation of the dendrogram, not presented in this study, clearly suggests three segments. The three-segment solution was validated by the method *k-means* which indicates that the centroids of the three segments are significantly different regarding the variables used as the basis of segmentation, i.e. the two dimensions resulting from MCA (ANOVA tests: $p = 0.000$). Table 3 shows the number of residents included in each segment and the coordinates of each centroid in each dimension of MCA, which will be represented in the perceptual map. As can be observed, segment 1 is the largest ($n = 270$; 55.6% of respondents), followed by segment 3, ranked as middle size ($n = 134$; 26.8%), and finally segment 2 ($n = 88$; 17.6%).

Figure 3 displays the centroids of the three segments (dark squares) in the perceptual map produced by MCA. As can be seen, the location of the centroids suggests the existence of three segments with features referred to in the previous paragraph: the centroid of segment 1 on the upper right-hand quadrant; that of segment 2 on the

Table 3. Final segment centres and number of residents in each segment.

Dimensions from MCA	Segments		
	Segment 1	Segment 2	Segment 3
Dimension 1	0.38	1.03	−1.46
Dimension 2	0.71	−1.85	−0.27
Number of residents (segment dimension)	270 (55.6%)	88 (17.6%)	134 (26.8%)

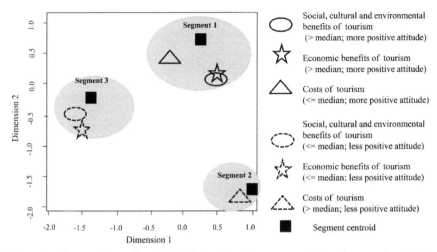

Figure 3. Perceptual map from MCA (joint plot of category points) and segment centroids.

lower right-hand quadrant; and of segment 3 on the left-hand part of the perceptual map. This analysis allows us to define the existence of groups of residents in Cape Verde based on their attitude towards the impacts of tourism in the islands, some of them with a more positive attitude than others, which gives support to H_2.

*Profiling the Segments (*Internal Validation*)*

As expected, a significant dependence relationship was found between *segment membership* and each categorical variable used in the MCA (chi-square tests of independence: p = 0.000). This result means that the segments are significantly different as regards the three variables of attitude that led to the segmentation, which gives internal validity to the three-segment solution. Table 4 shows the distribution of residents included in each segment (percentages within segments) by the response levels of the categorical variables used in the MCA. The percentages presented in the table are within segments. Based on the analysis of this table, names were given to each segment: segment 1 – optimistic residents; segment 2 – rational residents; segment 3 – indifferent residents.

Segment 1, 'optimistic residents', is the largest group (n = 270, 55.6%). It includes individuals who recognize fewer negative impacts of tourism and more positive impacts. As shown in Table 4, this group clearly shows a more positive attitude with regard to the variables *Social, cultural and environmental benefits of tourism* and *Economic benefits of tourism* (100% present values in these variables above the median). Simultaneously, 100% of individuals who belong to this segment recognize less the existence of the costs of tourism. In general, this group shows a clearly positive attitude towards tourism, which justifies the attributed designation.

Table 4. Distribution of variables used by MCA in the three-segment solution.

Variables used in the MCA	Segments			Total
	Segment 1 'Optimistic'	Segment 2 'Rational'	Segment 3 'Indifferent'	
Social, cultural and environmental benefits of tourism				
Less positive attitude[a]	0.0%	6.8%	61.9%	17.8%
More positive attitude[b]	100.0%	93.2%	38.1%	82.2%
Total	100.0%	100.0%	100.0%	100.0%
Costs of tourism				
More positive attitude[b]	100.0%	0.0%	97.8%	81.8%
Less positive attitude[a]	0.0%	100.0%	2.2%	18.2%
Total	100.0%	100.0%	100.0%	100.0%
Economic benefits of tourism				
Less positive attitude[a]	0.0%	9.1%	64.2%	18.8%
More positive attitude[b]	100.0%	90.9%	35.8%	81.2%
Total	100.0%	100.0%	100.0%	100.0%

[a]'Above the median'.
[b]'Equal to or below the median'.

Segment 2, 'rational residents', is the smallest group (n = 88, 17.6%). This name was proposed because this segment includes residents who generally have a reflective attitude regarding the benefits and costs of tourism in Cape Verde. As shown in Table 4, this group has a more moderate vision of tourism, clearly recognizing its potential benefits, but also noticing the potential problems. For almost all the individuals included in this segment, tourism brings benefits to both residents and the country. However, this group is unanimous in expressing concern over the costs of tourism, recognizing that it brings social and environmental costs.

Segment 3, 'indifferent residents', ranked middle in group size (n = 134, 26.8%). This group includes residents who, in most cases, recognize less the benefits of tourism – either in social, cultural and environmental terms (61.9%) or in economic terms (64.2%) – but also they do not consider that this activity will bring significant costs (97.8%). In short, this segment includes residents who show some passivity or apathy towards the touristic phenomenon: most of them neither shows a strong belief in its benefits nor perceives substantial negative social and costs.

Profiling the Segments (External Validation)

In this second stage, segments were analysed to determine whether they differ with regard to the following variables: socio-demographic characteristics and degree of involvement in the tourism sector. The percentages within segments can be seen in Tables 5 and 6. Only the variables significantly discriminating the groups will be presented and described (chi-square tests of independence: $p < 0.1$).

Table 5. Socio-demographic characteristics by segments (percentages within segments).

Socio-demographic characteristics	Segments		
	Segment 1 'Optimistic'	Segment 2 'Rational'	Segment 3 'Indifferent'
Gender			
Male	47.8%	56.8%	38.1%
Female	52.2%	43.2%	61.9%
Age group			
18–34 years	53.6%	48.9%	52.2%
35–54 years	28.4%	38.6%	29.9%
>54 years	18.0%	12.5%	17.9%
Marital status			
Single	45.7%	47.7%	50.0%
Married/living with a partner	52.5%	52.3%	47.8%
Other	1.8%	0.0%	2.2%
County of residence			
Tarrafal	8.6%	8.0%	6.7%
Praia	42.4%	31.8%	59.0%
Sal	5.8%	14.8%	0.7%
São Vicente	33.1%	30.7%	19.4%
São Filipe	10.1%	14.8%	14.4%
Education level			
Primary school	22.6%	30.7%	26.1%
Secondary school	54.7%	42.1%	56.0%
Medium or higher education	22.6%	27.3%	17.9%
Tourism qualification			
Yes	10.4%	26.1%	14.2%
No	89.6%	73.9%	85.8%
Occupational status			
Employed	57.2%	61.4%	59.7%
Unemployed	5.0%	3.4%	5.2%
Housewife	14.7%	12.5%	15.7%
Student	20.1%	22.7%	15.7%
Retired	2.9%	0.0%	3.7%
Working abroad			
Yes	8.3%	10.2%	12.7%
No	91.7%	89.8%	87.3%
Housing scheme			
Own house	63.3%	60.2%	73.1%
Rented house	34.5%	37.5%	24.6%
Other situation	2.2%	2.3%	2.2%

Table 5 shows that the segments are different as regards certain socio-demographic variables, thereby supporting H_3. Segment 1, 'optimistic residents', represents the highest percentage of residents in the age category 18–34 years (53.6%) and married/living with a partner (52.5%). As for the education level, 22.6% of residents in

Table 6. Frequency distribution of professional involvement degree in the tourism sector by segment.

| | Segments | | |
Degree of involvement in the tourism sector	Segment 1 'Optimistic'	Segment 2 'Rational'	Segment 3 'Indifferent'
Do you earn your living through tourism?			
Yes	19.1%	22.7%	17.2%
No	80.9%	77.3%	82.8%
Total	100.0%	100.0%	100.0%
Do you have direct contact with tourists as part of your work?			
Yes	36.0%	47.7%	24.6%
No	64.0%	52.3%	75.4%
Total	100.0%	100.0%	100.0%
Is tourism the main source of income of your household?			
Yes	15.8%	19.3%	15.7%
No	84.2%	80.7%	84.3%
Total	100.0%	100.0%	100.0%
Is any member of your household involved in tourism as a source of income or employment?			
Yes	23.4%	28.4%	20.1%
No	76.6%	71.6%	79.9%
Total	100.0%	100.0%	100.0%

this segment have primary education, 56% secondary education and 22.6% medium or higher education. This segment has the smallest number of residents with studies in tourism (10.4%). Segment 2, 'rational residents', has the highest percentages of males (56.8%) and aged from 35 to 54 years (38.6%), while the age groups 18–34 years (48.9%) and older than 54 years (12.5%) have less weight than in the other two segments. In this segment, 52.3% of individuals are married/live with a partner, 27.3% have medium or higher education and 26.1% have 'studies in tourism'. These results may explain the attitude expressed towards tourism, which is essentially a considered attitude, recognizing that tourism brings benefits but also involves costs. Segment 3, 'indifferent residents', has the highest percentages of females (61.9%), singles (50%), and residents who live in the municipality of Praia (59%). Regarding the education level, 'secondary education' has a higher weight than in the other two segments (56%) and 'primary education' is more prominent than in segment 1 (26.1%). Regarding studies in tourism, segment 3 lies in between the other two segments. This segment reports the highest percentage of residents who have worked abroad (12.7%).

Concerning the degree of involvement in the tourism sector, Table 6 shows significant differences among segments, thereby supporting H_4. Actually, the degree of involvement is much higher in segment 2, in which 27.7% of the residents earn their living through tourism, 47.7% have some direct contact with tourists as part of their work and 28.4% have at least a close family member professionally involved in the tourism sector. The highest professional involvement of this group in the tourism sector, together with other factors mentioned above, namely a higher level of educa-tion and a higher weight of tourism studies, may explain the rational attitude towards tourism that is shared by the residents of this segment. In segment 3, there is the op-posite situation, since 75.4% of the individuals in this segment have no contact with tourists as part of their work, only 17.2% make their living through tourism, 15.7% find in tourism the main source of income of the household and only 20.1% have some household member professionally involved in the sector. This situation might be a possible cause for the indifference towards tourism expressed by the residents included in this segment.

Discussion and Conclusions

The first conclusion of this study is that, in general, residents in Cape Verde express an optimistic view about tourism, recognizing its positive impacts more than its negative consequences. This result is in accordance with the previous research in the field, specifically studies by Doxey (1975) and Butler (1980), reporting that, in destinations in the early stage of tourist development, residents tend to express a positive attitude towards tourism. Using the terminology of Upchurch and Teivane (2000), residents in Cape Verde may be classified in the 'embracement phase' in terms of tourism. Similarly, the findings of this study are consistent with Doxey's (1975) Irridex Model and Cape Verde should be within the *'euphoria'* stage of tourism development. This result does not mean that residents in Cape Verde see tourism as the only option for economic development. Instead, two specific reasons can justify this result. On the one hand, since the 17th century, the ports of this country have received numerous sailors of different origins (Åkesson 2004), meaning that residents are very used to interacting with different people and different cultures. To Cape Verdeans, being visited now by tourists is just an extension of old habits and customs. In addition, in almost every family of this country, there is one family member who has already emigrated, mainly to the USA, Portugal, France, The Netherlands, Italy, São Tomé and Principe, Angola, etc. (Carling 2004; Åkesson 2011). Therefore, Cape Verde inhabitants are very receptive to other cultures and know how important it is for a visitor to be warmly received in a foreign country.

The second conclusion to stand out is that, despite an overall enthusiastic attitude towards tourism, three segments of residents could be identified, suggesting different perspectives according to the way the tourism impacts are perceived. This finding aligns with previous studies, namely those of Gursoy *et al.* (2009) and Lankford and Howard (1994), which show that, even in the same destination, residents may have dissimilar attitudes towards tourism development. In the current research, the seg-ments were designated as 'optimistic residents', 'rational residents' and 'indifferent residents'. Indeed, the segments have a very different dimension, with the 'optimistic residents' including the largest percentage of respondents and the 'rational residents' clearly the group with lower expressivity.

Segment 1 perceives the costs of tourism less and strongly recognizes its positive benefits, clearly revealing a positive attitude towards tourism and showing great optimism regarding the importance that tourism will play in the future of Cape Verde. This segment finds a counterpart in the segment named 'lovers' in the studies of Davis *et al.* (1988), Fredline and Faulkner (2000) and William and Lawson (2001), and, similarly, in the 'advocates' segment in Andriotis and Vaughan (2003) or even in the 'development supporter' segment in the analysis conducted by Pérez and Nadal (2005).

Segment 2, the least expressive, also shows a positive attitude, although less optimistic than the previous group, but a more reflective and aware vision of the current state of tourism in Cape Verde. Residents included in this segment are concerned about the costs and negative impacts caused by tourism. However, they show a positive attitude towards the economic benefits of tourism, recognizing that it brings several benefits both for the residents and for the country. Regarding previous research, residents in segment 2 can be compared to those classified as 'in-betweeners' in Davis *et al.* (1988), as 'realists' in Madrigal (1995), as 'prudent developers' in Pérez and Nadal (2005) and as 'socially and environmentally concerned' in Andriotis and Vaughan (2003). The balanced view of this group of residents may be explained by two types of factors that can contribute to this more thoughtful and reflective assessment. On the one hand, in this segment, students and individuals with a superior academic qualification have a higher level of expression. On the other hand, it comprises more residents who are professionally involved in the tourism sector, and recognize not only its potential, but also the problems it can bring.

Residents included in segment 3 do not recognize significant positive impacts of tourism in these islands, but they also do not consider that tourism is responsible for substantial environmental and socio-cultural costs. In short, this segment includes residents who show some passivity or indifference towards the touristic phenomenon: the majority do not believe strongly in the benefits but do not perceive its potential adverse effects either. Compared to previous research, this segment is more similar to the group found in Fredline and Faulkner (2000) (the 'ambivalent') or in William and Lawson (2001) (the 'innocent').

Overall, results of the cluster analysis show that the majority of Cape Verdeans held a positive attitude towards tourism in Cape Verde since segment 1, 'optimistic residents', is the largest. Concomitantly, no residents' group was found to be very critical or pessimistic about the current state of tourism development in the country. Most of the analysed individuals express, in contrast, optimism about the future of tourism in the country, supporting its development. This result is encouraging regarding the growth of tourism in Cape Verde and should be used to foster a desirable tourism industry in the country. In this sense, several policies could be developed that would involve the host community participating actively in the tourism development process. First, it would be important to invest in more and better technical and college education in tourism, taking advantage of the enthusiastic attitude shared by most residents and giving the natural privileged conditions of the country to tourism development. It would be important for the focus of education not to be restricted to improving the hospitality industry in the region, but also to better prepare Cape Verdeans to manage tourism-related companies and to increase their entrepreneurship and leadership capabilities. This is an essential aspect to ensure that a significant part of the economic benefits that tourism can bring would stay in the country. Secondly, in order to increase the involvement of the local communities in the tourism development process, it would be very important if policy makers in Cape Verde were able to support, technically and financially, small businesses related to tourism. Thirdly, the positive attitude shared by most residents towards tourism could be translated into pro-tourism behaviours. Cape Verdeans naturally know how to be affable hosts: it is the '*Morabeza*' way. However, it is important that they are incentivized to be guides of their own heritage and culture, inviting tourists to share their habits, taste their gastronomy, know their handcrafts, etc.

Cape Verde is an island destination, with weaknesses and vulnerabilities, whose attractiveness relies on 'an integrated set of natural, geographical and socio-cultural conditions' (Pena 2003: 118) that responds, at a higher level, to the needs of important segments of demand. Therefore, on the one hand, it should pursue a sustainable tourism development option that preserves the unique environmental and geographical conditions that attract tourists to the country, while allowing local communities to be safeguarded in social, environmental and cultural respects. In this sense, it is important to involve the local communities in slow, small-scale and mainly locally owned tourism projects, with a strong focus on resources protection. On the other hand, the projects proposed to foster the development of tourism in the local communities of the archipelago should be regularly gauged, allowing tourism planners to obtain important inputs for the planning process and development of tourism on the islands.

This study did not intend to be an exhaustive work on residents' attitudes towards tourism. Its limitations should be mentioned in order to provide guidelines for further research. First, no previous study was conducted, nor was any *focus group* with Cape Verdean tourism *opinion leaders* realized that could provide some early indicators of attitudes, which could later be validated by the instrument used for the data collection. Thus, the attitude items used in the empirical study were drawn only from the literary references specified in the methodological section. Secondly, the empirical study that supports this work was conducted at a single moment in time, in the summer of 2008. It is suggested that in the future further studies should be carried out to allow a comparison with the results presented here. A further study should try to add new attitude items to the analysis, which might allow its improvement and enable the discovery of new components that influence residents' attitudes towards tourism. A future study should also investigate how the current large external tourism operator investment is compatible with projects aiming at a sustainable tourism development and how these companies should interact with residents. In short, it is suggested that studies be repeated in the future, in order to monitor and compare residents' attitudes towards tourism in subsequent stages of the life cycle of the touristic activity, as suggested by Doxey (1975) and Butler (1980).

Acknowledgements

This paper is partially financed by FCT — Foundation for Science and Technology.

References

Åkesson, L. (2004) Making a life: Meanings of migration in Cape Verde, unpublished Ph.D. thesis, University of Gothenburg, Sweden.

Åkesson, L. (2011) Remittances and relationships: Exchange in Cape Verdean transnational families, *Ethnos*, 76(3), pp. 326–347.

Akis, S., Peristianis, N., & Warner, J. (1996) Residents' attitudes to tourism development: The case of Cyprus, *Tourism Management*, 17(7), pp. 481–494.

Alegre, J. & Cladera, M. (2009) Analysing the effect of satisfaction and previous visits on tourist intentions to return, *European Journal of Marketing*, 43(5/6), pp. 670–685.

Andereck, K., Valentine, K., Knopf, R. C., & Vogt, C. A. (2005) Residents' perceptions of community tourism impacts, *Annals of Tourism Research*, 32(4), pp. 1056–1076.

Andereck, K. & Vogt, C. (2000) The relationship between residents' attitudes toward tourism and tourism development options, *Journal of Travel Research*, 39(1), pp. 27–36.

Andriotis, K. (2005) Community groups' perceptions of and preferences for tourism development: Evidence from crete, *Journal of Hospitality & Tourism Research*, 29(1), pp. 67–90.

Andriotis, K. & Vaughan, R. D. (2003) Urban residents' attitudes toward tourism development: The case of crete, *Journal of Travel Research*, 42(2), pp. 172–185.

Ap, J. (1992) Residents' perceptions on tourism impacts, *Annals of Tourism Research*, 19(4), pp. 665–690.

Ap, J. & Crompton, J. L. (1998) Developing and testing a tourism impact scale, *Journal of Travel Research*, 37(2), pp. 120–130.

Apostolopoulos, Y. & Gayle, D. J. (2002) *Island Tourism and Sustainable Development: Caribbean, Pacific, and Mediterranean Experiences* (Westport, Conn: Praeger).

Banco de Cabo Verde (2011) *Relatórios do Conselho de Administração. Relatório e Contas 2010.* (Cidade da Praia: Banco de Cabo Verde).

Boissevain, J. (1996) 'But we live here!': perspectives on cultural tourism in Malta, in: L. Briguglio, R. Butler, & D. Harrison (Eds) *Sustainable Tourism in Islands and Small States: Case Studies*, pp. 220–240 (London: Pinter).

Briguglio, L. & Briguglio, M. (1996) Sustainable tourism in the Maltese islands, in: L. Briguglio, R. Butler, D. Harison, & W. L. Filho (Eds) *Sustainable Tourism in Islands and Small States: Case Studies*, pp. 162–179 (London: Pinter).

Brunt, P. & Courtney, P. (1999) Host perceptions of sociocultural impacts, *Annals of Tourism Research*, 26(3), pp. 493–515.

Butler, R. W. (1980) The concept of a tourist area cycle of evolution: implications for management of resources, *Canadian Geographer/Le Géographe canadien*, 24(1), pp. 5–12.

Carling, J. (2004) Emigration, return and development in Cape Verde: The impact of closing borders, *Population, Space and Place* 10(2), pp. 113–132.

Carvalho, A. (2010) A Imagem de Cabo Verde como destino turístico no mercado do destino português, unpublished Master's thesis, University of Aveiro, Aveiro.

Carvalho, H. (1998) Variáveis qualitativas na análise sociológica: exploração de métodos multidimensionais, unpublished Ph.D. thesis, ISCTE, Lisboa.

Cavus, S. & Tanrisevdi, A. (2003) Residents attitudes toward tourism development: A case study in Kusadasi, Turkey, *Tourism Analysis*, 7(3-4), pp. 259–269.

Choy, D. J. L. (1992) Life cycle models for Pacific island destinations, *Journal of Travel Research*, 30(3), pp. 26–31.

Churchill, G. A. (1979) A paradigm for developing better measures of marketing constructs, *Journal of Marketing Research*, 16(1), pp. 64–73.

Cohen, E. (1988) Tourism and AIDS in Thailand, *Annals of Tourism Research*, 15(4), pp. 467–486.

Davis, D., Allen, J., & Cosenza, R. M. (1988) Segmenting local residents by their attitudes, interests, and opinions toward tourism, *Journal of Travel Research*, 27(2), pp. 2–8.

Directorate General of Tourism [DGT] (2009) *Tourism Development Strategic Plan for Cape Verde* (Praia, Cape Verde: Directorate General of Tourism).

Doxey, G. V. (1975) A causation theory of visitor-resident irritants: Methodology and research inferences. Paper presented at the Sixth Annual Conference Proceedings of the Travel Research Association, San Diego, CA.

Faulkner, B. & Tideswell, C. (1997) A framework for monitoring community impacts of tourism, *Journal of Sustainable Tourism*, 5(1), pp. 3–28.

Fredline, E. & Faulkner, B. (2000) Host community reactions: A cluster analysis, *Annals of Tourism Research*, 27(3), pp. 763–784.

Greenacre, M. J. (2007) *Correspondence Analysis in Practice*, 2nd ed. (Boca Raton, Florida: Chapman & Hall/CRC).

Gunn, A. C. & Var, T. (2002) *Tourism Planning. Basics, Concepts, Cases*, 4th ed. (New York: Routledge).

Gursoy, D., Chi, C. G., & Dyer, P. (2009) An examination of locals' attitudes. *Annals of Tourism Research*, 36(4), pp. 723–726.

Gursoy, D. & Rutherford, D. G. (2004) Host attitudes toward tourism: An improved structural model, *Annals of Tourism Research*, 31(3), pp. 495–516.

Haralambopoulos, N. & Pizam, A. (1996) Perceived impacts of tourism: The case of samos, *Annals of Tourism Research*, 23(3), pp. 503–526.

Harrill, R. (2004) Residents' attitudes toward tourism development: A literature review with implications for tourism planning, *Journal of Planning Literature*, 18(3), pp. 251–266.

Ioannides, D. (1995) A flawed implementation of sustainable tourism: The experience of Akamas, Cyprus, *Tourism Management*, 16(8), pp. 583–592.

Johnson, J. D., Snepenger, D. J., & Akis, S. (1994) Residents' perceptions of tourism development, *Annals of Tourism Research*, 21(3), pp. 629–642.

Ko, D. W. & Stewart, W. (2002) A structural equation model of residents' attitudes for tourism development, *Tourism Management*, 23(5), pp. 521–530.

Kuvan, Y. & Akan, P. (2005) Residents' attitudes toward general and forest-related impacts of tourism: The case of Belek, Antalya, *Tourism Management*, 26(5), pp. 691–706.

Lankford, S. & Howard, D. (1994) Developing a tourism impact attitude scale, *Annals of Tourism Research*, 21(1), pp. 121–139.

Lebart, L. (1994) Complementary use of correspondence analysis and cluster analysis, in: M. J. Greenacre & J. Blasius (Eds) *Correspondence Analysis in the Social Sciences*, pp. 162–178 (San Diego: Academic Press).

Lepp, A. (2007) Residents' attitudes towards tourism in Bigodi village, Uganda, *Tourism Management*, 28(3), pp. 876–885.

Lindberg, K. & Johnson, R. L. (1997) Modeling resident attitudes toward tourism, *Annals of Tourism Research*, 24(2), pp. 402–424.

Lockhart, D. G. (1997) Tourism to Malta and Cyprus, in: D. G. Lockhart & D. Drakakis-Smith (Eds) *Island Tourism: Trends and Prospects*, pp. 152–180 (London and New York: Pinter).

López-Guzmán, T., Borges, O., & Cerezo, J. M. (2011) Community-based tourism and local socio-economic development: A case study in Cape Verde, *African Journal of Business Management*, 5(5), pp. 1608–1617.

Madrigal, R. (1995) Residents' perceptions and the role of government, *Annals of Tourism Research*, 22(1), pp. 86–102.

Manisera, M., van der Kooij, A. J., & Dusseldorp, E. (2010) Identifying the component structure of satisfaction scales by nonlinear principal components analysis, *Qualitative Technology and Quantitative Management*, 7(2), pp. 97–115.

Manning, E. W., Clifford, G., Klaric, Z., & Vereczi, G. (2001) *Workshop on Sustainable Tourism Indicators for the Islands of the Mediterranean, Kukljica*. Island of Ugljan, Croatia. 21–23 March, 2001. Final Report, Madrid: World Tourism Organization.

Martin, B., McGuire, F., & Allen, L. (1998) Retirees' attitudes toward tourism: implications for sustainable development, *Tourism Analysis*, 3(1), pp. 43–51.

Martin, S. R. (1995) Montanans' attitudes and behavioral intentions toward tourism: implications for sustainability, in: S. McCool & A. Watson (Ed) *Linking Tourism, the Environment, and Sustainability*, pp. 69–76. (Intermountain Research Station, Ogden, USA: National Recreation and Park Association).

Martins, J. F. (2000) Attitudes of residents towards tourism in Madeira, unpublished Ph.D. thesis, University of Surrey, Guildford.

Mason, P. & Cheyne, J. (2000) Residents' attitudes to proposed tourism development. *Annals of Tourism Research*, 27(2), pp. 391–411.

McElroy, J. L. & de Albuquerque, K. (1998) Tourism penetration index in small Caribbean islands, *Annals of Tourism Research*, 25(1), pp. 145–168.

McGehee, N. & Andereck, K. (2004) Factors predicting rural residents' support of tourism, *Journal of Travel Research*, 43(2), pp. 131–140.

Meulman, J. J., Van der Kooij, A. J., & Heiser, W. J. (2004) Principal components analysis with nonlinear optimal scaling transformations for ordinal and nominal data, in: D. Kaplan (Ed) *The Sage Handbook of Quantitative Methodology for the Social Sciences*, pp. 49–72 (London: SAGE).

Milne, S. & Nowosielski, L. (1997) Travel distribution technologies and sustainable tourism development: The case of South Pacific microstates, *Journal of Sustainable Tourism*, 5(2), pp. 131–150.

Moniz, A. I. A. (2006) A sustentabilidade do turismo em ilhas de pequena dimensão: o caso dos Açores, unpublished Ph.D. thesis, Universidade dos Açores, Açores.

National Institute of Statistics (NIS) (2011) *Análise Dos Principais Resultados -Movimentação de Hóspedes em 2010* (Cidade da Praia: Instituto Nacional de Estatísca).

Pearce, P. L. & Moscardo, G. (1999) Tourism community analysis: Asking the right questions, in: Douglas G. Pearce & Richard Butler (Eds) *Contemporary Issues in Tourism Development*, pp. 31–51 (London and New York: Routledge).

Pena, J. R. (2003) *Um Programa de Acções Estratégicas Para Reforçar a Competitividade do Turismo em Portugal* (Lisboa: Economia & Prospectiva, Ministério de Economia).

Pérez, E. A. & Nadal, J. R. (2005) Host community perceptions a cluster analysis, *Annals of Tourism Research*, 32(4), pp. 925–941.

Pizam, A. & Pokela, J. (1985) The perceived impacts of casino gambling on a community, *Annals of Tourism Research*, 12(2), pp. 147–165.

Ryan, C. & Montgomery, D. (1994) The attitudes of Bakewell residents to tourism and issues in community responsive tourism, *Tourism Management*, 15(5), pp. 358–369.

Sarmento, E. M. (2008) *O Turismo Sustentável Como Factor de Desenvolvimento das Pequenas Economias Insulares: O Caso de Cabo Verde* (Lisboa: Edições Universitárias Lusófonas).

Sheldon, P. J. & Abenoja, T. (2001) Resident attitudes in a mature destination: The case of Waikiki, *Tourism Management*, 22(5), pp. 435–443.

Silva, J., Mendes, J., & Guerreiro, M. (2001) *Construção de Indicadores de Avaliação da Qualidade no Turismo* (Lisboa: Projecto de Investigação da Universidade do Algarve, Direccção Geral do Turismo).

Sirakaya, E., Teye, V., & Sönmez, S. (2002) Understanding residents' support for tourism development in the central region of Ghana, *Journal of Travel Research*, 41(1), pp. 57–67.

Smith, M. D. & Krannich, R. S. (1998) Tourism dependence and resident attitudes, *Annals of Tourism Research*, 25(4), pp. 783–802.

Snaith, T. & Haley, A. (1994) *Tourism: The State of the Art* (London: John Wiley and Sons).

Swarbrooke, J. (1995) *The Development and Management of Visitor Attractions* (Oxford: Butterworth-Heinemann).

Teye, V., Sönmez, S., & Sirakaya, E. (2002) Residents' attitudes toward tourism development, *Annals of Tourism Research*, 29(3), pp. 668–688.

Tomljenovic, R. & Faulkner, B. (2000) Tourism and older residents in a sunbelt resort, *Annals of Tourism Research*, 27(1), pp. 93–114.

Tosun, C. (2002) Host perceptions of impacts: A Comparative Tourism Study, *Annals of Tourism Research*, 29(1), pp. 231–253.

Upchurch, R. S. & Teivane, U. (2000) Resident perceptions of tourism development in Riga, Latvia, *Tourism Management*, 21(5), pp. 499–507.

Valle, P., Mendes, J., Guerreiro, M., & Silva, J. A. (2011) Can welcoming residents increase tourist satisfaction? The case of Algarve, Portugal, *ANATOLIA: An International Journal of Tourism and Hospitality Research*, 22(2), pp. 260–277.

Van der Duim, R. & Caalders, J. (2002) Biodiversity and tourism: Impacts and interventions, *Annals of Tourism Research*, 29(3), pp. 743–761.

Vargas-Sánchez, A., Plaza-Mejía, M. d. l. Á., & Porras-Bueno, N. (2009) Understanding residents' attitudes toward the development of industrial tourism in a former mining community, *Journal of Travel Research*, 47(3), pp. 373–387.

Vargas-Sánchez, A., Porras-Bueno, N., & Plaza-Mejía, M. d. l. Á. (2011) Explaining residents' attitudes to tourism: Is a universal model possible? *Annals of Tourism Research*, 38(2), pp. 460–480.

Vesey, C. M. & Dimanche, F. (2000) Urban Residents' Perceptions of Tourism and Its Impacts, Unpublished manuscript (LA, USA: University of New Orleans).

Weaver, D. B. (1993) Model of urban tourism for small Caribbean islands, *Geographical Review*, 83(2), pp. 134–140.

Weaver, D. B. & Lawton, L. J. (2001) Resident Perceptions in the Urban-Rural Fringe, *Annals of Tourism Research*, 28(2), pp. 439–458.

Wilkinson, P. F. (1987) Tourism in small island nations: A fragile dependence, *Leisure Studies*, 6(2), pp. 127–146.

Williams, J. & Lawson, R. (2001) Community issues and resident opinions of tourism, *Annals of Tourism Research*, 28(2), pp. 269–290.

World Tourism Organization (WTO) (2004) *Indicators of Sustainable Development for Tourism Destinations: A Guidebook* (Madrid: World Tourism Organization).

Zhang, J., Inbakaran, R. J., & Jackson, M. S. (2006) Understanding community attitudes towards tourism and host-guest interaction in the urban-rural border region, *Tourism Geographies*, 8(2), pp. 182–204.

Notes on Contributors

Manuel Alector Ribeiro is a PhD student in the Tourism Programme of the University of Algarve, Portugal. His current research interests include residents' attitudes and behavior towards tourism development.

Patrcia Oom do Valle received her PhD degree in Quantitative Methods Applied to Economics and Business (specialization in Statistics) from the University of Algarve, Portugal. She is Professor at the Faculty of Economics, University of Algarve, and member of the Research Centre for Spatial and Organizational Dynamics (CIEO). Her current research interests include applied statistics and modeling in the areas of tourism and environment.

João Albino Silva received his PhD degree in Economics from the Technical University of Lisbon, Portugal. He is Professor and President of the Scientific Commission at the Faculty of Economics, University of Algarve, Portugal, and a member of the Research Centre for Spatial and Organizational Dynamics (CIEO). His current research interests include economics of tourism, regional development, and tourism destinations and sustainability and governance in tourism.

Slow Tourism at the Caribbean's Geographical Margins

BENJAMIN F. TIMMS[*] & DENNIS CONWAY[**]

[*]Social Sciences Department, California Polytechnic State University, San Luis Obispo, USA
[**]Department of Geography, Indiana University, Bloomington, USA

ABSTRACT *The Caribbean tourism industry owes much of its success to beneficial geographical site and situation factors. Yet these geographical advantages have also contributed to the mass tourism-related pressures of economic dependency, social division and environmental degradation. We argue geographically marginal locales in the Caribbean have the potential to develop alternative tourism models that ameliorate these negative repercussions. With its conceptual roots originating from the slow food movement and theoretically rooted in Herman Daly's 'soft growth' development, we propose slow tourism as a viable soft growth model that is a more culturally sensitive and sustainable genre of alternative tourism. This new model and its locational appropriateness appears eminently suitable since it diversifies and revitalizes mature tourism offerings, redirects tourism away from 'hard growth' maxims, and thereby contributes to more sustainable tourism ensembles. In a maturing industry that requires innovation, revitalization and significant change in offerings if it is to survive and prosper, we argue the best places to promote slow tourism lies in the Caribbean's overlooked geographical margins where diversity and authenticity still persist.*

Introduction

The Caribbean tourism industry owes much of its success to beneficial geographical site (amenity) and situation (accessibility) factors, both of which have contributed to tourism's position as the dominant economic sector in the region. Traditionally the favourable site factors for islands in the Caribbean have been described as the tropical 'three S's' of sunlight, sand and sea so sought after by mass tourists from temperate latitudes (Davenport & Jackiewicz 2008). Situation factors refer to the accessibility of Caribbean destinations for these same tourists, noting the relative geographical proximity to tourism markets in North America and Western Europe in comparison to other tropical tourist destinations (Dodman 2009).

Having such a geographically advantageous tourism industry holds many development benefits, including being a major source of foreign exchange earnings, provider of employment, and stimulator of linkages with other sectors of island economies, such as agriculture (Timms 2006; Rhiney 2009). However, these positive geographical characteristics and the resultant embracing of mass tourism by most Caribbean islands have also resulted in an assortment of economic, social and environmental problems. Amongst them is the continuation of economic dependency that has plagued Caribbean societies since the colonial plantation era, through post-colonial transitions and into the present post-1980s neo-liberal crisis (Conway & Timms 2003; Duval & Wilkinson 2004; Pattullo 2005). In its most recent neo-liberal form, based on liberalized trade and privatization, this legacy renders island economies dependent. Also, because each competes intra-regionally for foreign tourist markets, their vulnerability to the vagaries of the global economic system increases, while their autonomy is diminished. Further exacerbating these economic concerns are high levels of capital leakage, whereby foreign ownership or control of tourism ensembles repatriates profits and sources inputs, such as food and management, from abroad. As a result, foreign exchange earnings are reduced and extra-sectoral linkages continue to determine Caribbean tourism's development paths (Momsen 1998).

Furthermore, the region's continued incorporation into a global order in which mass tourism adheres to the dictates of neo-liberal capitalist policies of de-regulation has resulted in a lack of concern for social equity and social justice. This has produced unacceptable social divisiveness and a widening of inequalities and class-stratification in many Caribbean insular societies that have reached advanced states of tourism penetration (Thomas 1991; McElroy & de Albuquerque 1998; Potter *et al.* 2004). Other negative social impacts include the spread of cultural imperialism with the demonstration effect altering local cultural norms and reorientating household resource allocations toward consumptive, rather than productive, activities. In relation, tourism also contributes to the rise of hedonistic activities, such as gambling, drugs and prostitution (Maingot 1994) while replicating the master–slave legacy of the plantation era through the tourist–servant relationship (Potter *et al.* 2004).

Tourism has been implicated in the creation, or exacerbation of, a host of environmental problems. Long-haul airline travel has recently come under scrutiny, as it is the greatest contributor of carbon dioxide emissions of any tourism activity (Hall 2009). Unacceptable levels of environmental degradation of coastal zones have accompanied the unfettered embracing of mass tourism by Caribbean small-island states, thereby increasing their vulnerability to natural hazards, such as floods, hurricanes and even volcanic eruptions (Commonwealth Secretariat 1991; Watts 1995; Walsh 1998; Baldwin 2000; Pelling & Uito 2001; Boruff & Cutter 2007; Wilkinson 1999). In addition, many islands may have over-reached, or are approaching, their tourism carrying capacity, as increased influxes of wealthy resource-intensive tourists have taxed Caribbean water, food and waste disposal capacities. The result has been a whole-scale transformation of both the natural and cultural landscapes of Caribbean islands dependent on mass tourism, which in turn threatens the very geographical site factors upon which tourism in the Caribbean depends.

In light of the many concerns just noted, there has been a necessary re-evaluation of mass tourism in the Caribbean from a sustainability perspective (Conway & Timms 2003; Duval & Wilkinson 2004; Weaver 2004; Pattullo 2005). Here we not only join these critics but go a step further to argue that geographically marginal locales in the Caribbean – both regionally and internally – have considerable potential as appropriate sites to develop sustainable tourism models that minimize, or avoid altogether, mass tourism's negative repercussions while maximizing local community benefits and contributing to overall sustainable development. Underlying this challenging reappraisal of conventional Caribbean tourism, we also propose that future tourism in the region be more sustainable by concentrating on quality considerations and being risk-averse through a community development focus on participatory planning, co-management and small-scale tourism – not tourism growth and development *per se*.

To achieve this goal we propose slow tourism as a viable model for the Caribbean's geographical margins with the same development potential as the philosophically related slow food movement (Conway & Timms 2010). More broadly referred to as the slow movement, it is the antithesis to the fast and unsustainable life of modern industrial society through advocating a return to a more sustainable slow life based on savouring experience, rather than maximizing consumption. Like its precursor, the slow tourism model we propose for geographically marginal locales in the Caribbean offers a more sustainable tourism product that is less alienated (and alienating), more culturally sensitive, authentic and a better-paced experience for hosts and tourists alike. The goals we set for our slow tourism model coalesce with those of other alternatives to mass tourism, such as eco-tourism, community tourism and pro-poor tourism (amongst others) in that they are, or should be, all development-from-below initiatives that have sustainability built into their *praxis*. However, slow tourism advances the alternative tourism genre by adopting Herman Daly's concept of 'soft growth' where emphasis is placed on advancing development (quality) instead of promoting physical growth (quantity) (Daly 1990; 1991; 2008). As such, slow tourism promotes equitable economic and social benefits to local communities, limits environmental pressures, and serves the growing demand for responsible tourism sought after by a more consciously motivated cohort of travellers – all hallmarks of a progressive sustainable development model for the Caribbean.

This paper first focuses on the contributions of geographical site and situation factors to mass tourism's development in the Caribbean and its most attractive coastal zones. Paradoxically, these same factors that contributed to the industry's early 'hard growth' development also brought about geographical marginality in interiors and less-accessible coastal and insular regions, which nowadays can serve as advantageous locales for fostering alternative tourism efforts that follow sustainability maxims. Accordingly, in the third section we propose slow tourism as a 'soft growth' alternative model that embraces the best notions of progressive 'development-from-below' theories and environmental sustainability objectives (Daly 1990; 1991; Conway 1993; Klak 2007). We view slow tourism as a derivative of the globally successful slow food movement, since it adheres to similar philosophical tenets and follows soft growth principles in stressing 'quality of life' considerations as opposed to the 'fast and furious' pursuits of contemporary practices in too many peoples' everyday lives.

In an industry that has undergone constant change from inception to maturation in its passage through Butler's (1980; 2004) Tourism Area Life Cycle (TALC), the need to maintain its competitiveness and undertake upgrading strategies to revitalize its offerings (ECLAC 2008), slow tourism offers a new vision and a new alternative perspective to sustain and maintain Caribbean tourism in the future. It may well be that the best locales to find and promote such an alternative tourism model are the overlooked geographical margins where diversity and authenticity exist and opportunities await discovery and appropriate development.

The Role of Geography in Tourism Development Trajectories

Site: The Importance of Place

Site refers to the physical characteristics of a location, such as soil types, topography, climate and other amenities. For Caribbean tourism the positive geographical site factors have been traditionally surmised as the tropical 'three S's' of abundant sunlight, attractive white sand beaches and azure seas (Davenport & Jackiewicz 2008). For the first of these site factors, sun, the ideal tropical location ensures more direct incoming solar radiation than found in temperate latitudes while the Caribbean dry season with bright sunshine is a striking juxtaposition, albeit seasonally complementary, to the grey dreariness of winter in the major tourist markets in Europe and North America.

There are also regional differences in sunshine due to the orographic process of forced uplifting of warm and moist air masses, resulting in heavy precipitation on the windward slopes of mountains and islands. The higher Windward Islands of the Lesser Antilles (Figures 1, 2) receive greater amounts of cloud and rainfall and, hence, less sunshine, than the lower elevation Leeward Islands. Orography also plays an important part in the internal sunshine offerings of the Greater Antilles whereby northeast coasts and mountains generate greater orographic effects while the southwestern coasts, in contrast, generally lie in the rain-shadow of the central mountains and, hence, are much drier while receiving greater amounts of sunshine. There is a compromise to be made for mass tourism, however, in that greater amounts of rain equate to more tropical green vegetation which many temperate tourists value as representing an idealized exotic 'Garden of Eden' (Grove 1995), as opposed to the dry tropical savannah landscapes of the southwestern coasts. As a result, we most often see mass tourism developments on the north coast of the Greater Antilles islands

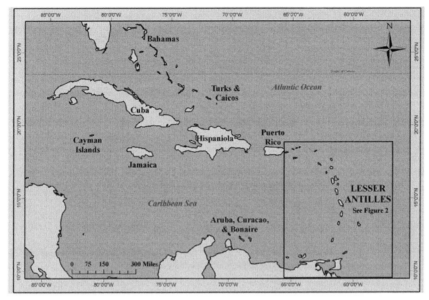

Figure 1. The Caribbean. *Source:* ESRI (2011).

which receive more rainfall than the southwest, yet have more sun than the northeast; in effect, striking a balance between sunshine and foliage.

The second of the three S's, attractive white sand beaches, is also due to the tropical location of the Caribbean's coral reefs. Over time, these reefs have been weathered, with the eroded coral creating elegant white sand beaches. Ideal beach availability also differs regionally, whereby the older Leeward Islands of the Lesser Antilles have had more time for coral reefs to be weathered and deposited as white sand beaches. The Windward Islands of the Lesser Antilles are younger and volcanic, with the mountainous terrain and higher precipitation amounts leading to greater deposition of eroded material from inland. The Windward Island of Dominica perhaps stands as the extreme example of the difference, with black sand beaches resulting from the volcanic origin of the island. In contrast, the Leeward Island of Antigua has extensive white sand beaches owing to its large coral reefs, which both provide white sand granules and protect the beaches from erosion.

The final of the 'three S' site factors, the azure Caribbean Sea, also owes its attractiveness and warmth to the tropical location. Typically, there is a preference for sites with shallow and calm water. Coral reefs not only help provide this, but offer diving opportunities and, as previously discussed, are responsible for the white sand beaches. Obviously, the interior of islands do not benefit from proximity to these attractive seashores, but even the coastlines vary in quality of sea conditions due to local geographies and their near-shore environments. For example, the coastlines

155

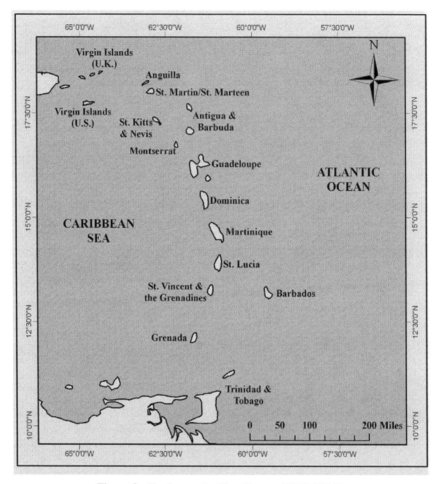

Figure 2. The Lesser Antilles. *Source:* ESRI (2011).

facing the Caribbean Sea tend to have more amenable conditions than those facing the Atlantic Ocean, which often are rougher and colder in water temperature.

There are compromises between all three of these physical site factors that contribute to the general pattern of mass tourism development in the Caribbean. In the Greater Antilles, mass tourism developments tend to occur on northern coastlines, where the aforementioned balancing of foliage and sunshine prevail. For the Windward Islands of the Lesser Antilles the majority of the mass tourism developments are on the west coast bordering the Caribbean Sea, and in a slight rain-shadow of the mountainous interiors. Even in the Leeward Islands, with few exceptions, the

156

majority of mass tourism development also has occurred on the western coastlines that border the calmer, and warmer, Caribbean Sea.

Situation: The Importance of Location

Geographical situation factors, which refer to the location of a locale relative to another, are most applicable in terms of market accessibility and competition. For the Caribbean as a region the geographical proximity to the world's major tourist markets in North America and Europe place it at a great advantage over other tropical locations, such as Southeast Asia, the South Pacific or equatorial Africa. Within the Caribbean region, differences in geographical proximity exhibit distance decay whereby locales closest to the USA and, to a lesser degree, Europe attract the majority of tourists, while those further away receive less.

For example, the Greater Antilles dominate in absolute number of tourist arrivals, by a large margin. While the greater size of the Greater Antilles islands contributes to this trend, it is less of a factor for the islands of the Lesser Antilles as exhibited by the application of a tourism penetration index. This index consists of the number of hotel rooms per square kilometre, daily visitor density per 1,000 population and per capita visitor spending (McElroy & de Albuquerque 1998). Recent data for the tourism penetration index showed that islands which lie closer to the US mainland, such as St Maarten, the Cayman Islands, the US and British Virgin Islands and Anguilla, have higher tourism penetration index scores than those lying further away, namely Trinidad and Tobago, Grenada, St Vincent and Dominica (Parry & McElroy 2009) (Table 1).

Beyond the simplicities of geographical proximity lies the situation factor of connectivity; most notably direct air service from North America and Europe. Those lacking direct air service require an extra flight to connect, which increases time, cost and distance (Klak & Flynn 2008). Direct air service for St Lucia has contributed to its higher tourism penetration index than neighbouring St Vincent or nearby Dominica, both of which lack this important accessibility factor (Conway & Jemiolo 1991). Even within islands this holds true as areas close to, or easily accessible from, airports tend to have more developed tourist industries than outlying areas that are difficult or expensive to reach (Padilla & McElroy 2005). One prime example of this intra-island accessibility function is Jamaica where the mass tourism industry on the north coast is connected internationally by the airport in Montego Bay and, internally, by the north coast highway. The southwestern coast lacks these situation amenities, which has limited the scope of tourism development there (Dodman 2009). Similarly, the Cedros Peninsula in the far south of Trinidad has always been a disadvantaged remote location without integration into the national settlement and highway systems, with a predictable lack of tourism development being one consequence.

The amenable geographical site and situation factors contribute to the selection of tourism development locations which, in a positive feedback loop, are prioritized

Table 1. Indicators for selected Caribbean islands, 2009

Caribbean subdivision	Island/Country	Land area (km²)	Population (000)	Population density (people/km²)	Tourism penetration index	Tourist expenditures ($US million)
Greater Antilles	Cuba	109,820	11,477	105	—	2,359
	Dominican Republic	48,320	9,824	203	—	4,176
	Haiti	27,560	9,720	353	—	54
	Jamaica	10,831	2,847	263	—	1,1976
	Puerto Rico	8,870	3,979	449	—	3,535
Leeward Islands	Virgin Islands (UK)	151	25	165	0.745	552
	Virgin Islands (US)	346	110	317	0.390	1,520
	Anguilla	91	15	162	0.255	102
	St Maarten	34	37	1101	0.920	633
	Antigua & Barbuda	442.6	87	196	0.147	334
	St Kitts and Nevis	261	50	191	0.104	126
	Barbados	430	286	664	0.151	1,184
Windward Islands	Montserrat	102	5	50	0.026	7
	Dominica	751	73	97	0.025	72
	St Lucia	616	161	261	0.098	311
	St Vincent & the Grenadines	389	104	268	0.035	96
	Grenada	344	108	313	0.030	99
	Trinidad & Tobago	5,128	1,229	240	0.002	397
Outlying Islands	Bahamas	10,010	310	31	0.177	2,501
	Turks & Caicos	948	24	25	0.405	304
	Cayman Islands	264	50	190	0.327	530

This categorization of Windward and Leeward islands differs from common convention by basing division on geological history with higher elevation inner-arc volcanic islands labelled as Windward while lower elevation extinct volcanic islands of the outer-arc are labelled Leeward. Trinidad & Tobago are included as Windward due to their higher elevations and greater orographic effects, even though they lack the same volcanic history as the other Windwards.
Source: CIA (2011), CTO (2011) and McElroy and Parry (2010).

in infrastructure development leading to greater access and, hence, more tourism development. However, there is also a negative feedback loop in that increased mass tourism developments can lead to the previously discussed economic, social and environmental problems that detrimentally affect the tourism industry's health both in the short and long term (Butler 1980; 2004; de Albuquerque & McElroy 1992).

Marginality: Geographical Limitation or Advantage?

Since the onset of mass tourism in the late 1960s and early 1970s, geographically marginal locations in the Caribbean, which are less endowed with the traditional amenable tourism site and situation factors, have commonly been overlooked by mass tourism developers and planners. Most islands' tourist industries have undergone growth and transformation so that just about all of them are in the later stages of their tourism life cycles (ECLAC 2008). Yet unevenness still prevails in most islands' tourism landscapes and geographically marginal locales now provide spaces for alternative forms of tourism to take root and develop; particularly in diverse, remoter locales in the Caribbean – be it ignored smaller islands or remote sections of larger ones. The time has come, then, to create and promote new models of sustainable tourism in these under-developed locales that maximize local benefits while avoiding the negative pitfalls so frequently attributed to mass tourism.

For example, ecotourism has become a prominent form of alternative tourism that is reliant on natural areas relatively undisturbed by human activities. It is partly because of their marginal locations, especially lack of accessibility, that a greater amount of 'pristine' nature remains (Timms 2008). And, in turn, it is this very marginality that has limited mass tourism development, leaving alternative tourism models such as ecotourism as the main options for these locales, as exemplified by Dominica (Weaver 1991; Klak & Flynn 2008). Further, marginality plays a similar role within islands, such as the remoteness of the Toco-Matura–Grande Rivière region in the northeast of Trinidad, which has helped in the local development of a community co-managed ecotourism model centred on the preservation of breeding sites for the endangered leatherback turtle (James & Fournillier 1993; Harrison 2007). However, it is important to note that the primary goal of ecotourism is environmental sustainability, although some proponents have argued for the inclusion of economic and social sustainability (Weaver 2004; Klak 2007).

Similarly, community-based tourism is reliant on maintaining and improving local community development (Milne & Ewing 2004). Places like Treasure Beach, Jamaica, situated on the marginal southwest coast of the island, is an example where alternative tourism offerings are based on the attractiveness, hospitality and safety of the local community. Here the tourism industry, then, is a major stakeholder in maintaining, improving and promoting the local community through creating and funding community development groups, sponsoring health and youth sporting programmes, assisting fishing cooperatives and even organizing disaster relief assistance (Conway

& Timms 2010). Though this alternative tourism's social goals are focused on the local community, its reach does not implicitly include environmental sustainability.

The same applies to other alternatives as well, such as heritage tourism's defined focus on cultural attributes (Prentice 1993; Nuryanti 1996; Pulsipher 1999) and pro-poor tourism's defined interest in poverty reduction (Renard 2001; Torres & Momsen 2004; Lewis & Brown 2007). All of these alternative tourism models, which are attempting to maintain and/or improve local conditions in the face of increasing global pressures brought by modern industrial society, are related in their calls for sustainability. Following the Bruntland Commission's call, there is common agreement that environmental sustainability can be defined as the ability to 'create economic and social benefit for now without sacrificing the well-being of future generations and the land on which they live' (Pattullo 2005: 246).

We would more explicitly include environmental sustainability while adding the concept of resilience to shocks – such as natural disasters or economic crises – to the definition. In order to achieve this latter refinement, we build upon Weaver's (2004: 440) definition of ecotourism whereby 'qualifying products must be primarily nature-based, focused on the provision of learning opportunities, and managed in such a way as to maximize the likelihood of environmentally and socio-culturally sustainable outcomes, including positive benefits for local communities'. This comprehensive and holistic definition accommodates and includes, rather than distinguishes between, a range of selected new tourism alternatives.

Adopting this definition as a starting point, we develop an inclusive alternative model titled 'slow tourism' that encompasses the environmental sustainability concerns of ecotourism, addresses the social and cultural sustainability interests of community-based tourism and pro-poor tourism, and advances economic sustainability ideals such as maximizing local linkages through agri-tourism. As such, slow tourism contributes to the advancement of the alternative tourism genre by coalescing the goals of these related tourism models through the adoption of Herman Daly's concept of 'soft growth' to philosophically identify, and combat, the core problems relating to the saturation of mass tourism resulting from its unsustainable hard growth axioms.

Slow Tourism as an Alternative Genre

The Hard Growth of Mass Tourism

At its core, slow tourism stands as the antithesis to mass tourism – with the latter focused on the economic growth paradigm leading to an improved Gross Domestic Product (GDP) through expanding market share. The adoption of neo-liberal economic capitalistic polices in the Caribbean has further encouraged the invitation of large-scale foreign-owned tourism developments to increase the numerical size of visitors and thereby provide material returns and monetary accumulations as a desired optimal consequence. For example, Jamaica's mass-tourism-dominated north coast has seen the addition of over 8,000 rooms solely from invited Spanish firms between 2001 and 2010 (JAMPRO 2010). In the spring of 2011, it opened a cruise ship terminal in Falmouth to accommodate the world's largest cruise ship to increase the number of day-trippers (Flemming 2011), even though they spend up to 17 times less than stay-over visitors (Potter *et al.* 2004).

Such massive tourism expansion demonstrates the modern capitalistic focus on what Herman Daly (1990) has labelled hard growth. Hard growth involves a continuous increase in size and scale, as exhibited by an economic focus on increasing GDP through increased production, which is eventually constrained by natural limits (Hall 2009). However, island ecosystems are limited in their ability to both provide natural resources for hard growth and to serve as an environmental sink for the generated waste (McElroy & de Albuquerque 1991; Goodland 1992; Conway & Lorah 1995). It is argued that the limits to hard growth have been surpassed in many of the region's islands based on the untenable axiom of an ever-growing economy based on hard growth in what are essentially closed ecosystems (Vitousek *et al.* 1995).

The reliance on these imported external inputs, along with foreign ownership of many mass tourism complexes, also facilitates capital leakage, with estimates ranging from 40 to 85 percent of tourist revenues leaving the islands (Potter *et al.* 2004; Pattullo 2005). Such importation also increases the pressure on the natural resource base by increasing the flow of matter and energy through the typical small island ecosystems, with waste disposal already becoming the most visible of problems in this regard. And, if the scale of impacts is broadened beyond individual Caribbean island ecosystems, the quantitative increase in tourist numbers also negatively affects the global environment. The vast majority of these increased tourists arrivals will do so via air transport, which increases carbon dioxide emissions (Hall 2009).

On a more philosophical level, mass tourism is also reflective of the socio-cultural changes that capitalist hard growth principles have prompted. While wealth generation has created a growing number of people with time for leisure, the quickening pace of activity is now shrinking both space and scarcity of time for leisure activities (Morello 2004). Further, this has created a focus on the quantity of leisure activity consumption in a shorter amount of time by a multitude of alienated, and alienating, mass tourist acolytes that 'mistake frenzy for efficiency' (Irving 2008: 44). Indeed, the mass commodification of tourists' leisure spaces is a result of time scarcity during holidays, as much as there are time–space compressions of the modern workday life (Harvey 1989). In sum, the hard growth paradigm of mass tourism has resulted in negative economic, environmental and social repercussions, which exhibit a lack of sustainability over the long term.

Slow Tourism as a Soft Growth Alternative

In light of the unsustainable nature of hard growth, Daly (1990) promotes an alternative of soft growth that entails qualitative improvements in efficiency. The difference between these two components is analogous to the difference between growth and development, whereby 'growth is a quantitative increase in physical scale, while development is qualitative improvement or unfolding of potentialities. An economy can grow without developing, or develop without growing, or do both, or neither' (Daly 1991: 402). Soft growth, then, is not directly dependent on the natural resource base nor on the external throughputs of the global industrial complex and commercial commodity chains. Instead, it promotes economic development, rather than mere growth, by relying on the use of local resources and increasing efficiency.

One cognizant, and specific, example of soft growth in response to mass-consumptive society has been the slow food movement (Petrini 2001; Stille 2001; Kummer 2002; Irving 2008). In the same vein of thought as soft growth, slow food calls for a reversal in peoples' living practices in general, and their eating habits specifically, from the quickened pace of 'fast life' resulting from modern industrial society based on hard growth principles to one which emphasizes experience (quality) over mere consumption (quantity). This movement particularly targets 'fast food' as symbolic of the powerless position in which people find themselves in today's hectic and stressful world, with slow food preparation, organization and enjoyment symbolizing its antithesis (Pietrykowski 2004).

Slow food has spurred many other derivatives that are collectively referred to as the 'slow movement'. One salient offshoot is the advocacy of slow travel as an alternative to mass tourism's fast-paced, escapist vacation. Embracing similar sentiments to slow food's culinary focus, it concentrates on the enjoyment of the journey rather than just physical travel as a mode of transport to a destination. Gardner (2009: 11) expands upon this concept in claiming '[s]low travel engineers time, transforming it into a commodity of abundance rather than scarcity'. A similar derivative of the slow food movement's genesis is the concept of slow cities as an alternative approach to contemporary urban development (Mayer & Knox 2006). Slow cities bring to the fore a focus on local resources, emphasizing social, cultural and economic strengths and the importance of region-based heritages. The movement aims to improve urban sustainability and address the interdependencies between the environment, economy and equity (Campbell 1996).

Building upon the slow food movement and its city and travel progeny, we propose a slow tourism derivative that combats the conundrum of time–space compression that mass tourism creates by advocating a return to more sustainable slow livelihoods based on savouring experience, rather than maximizing consumption. Further, borrowing from Gardner's (2009) slow travel notions, we reiterate that slow tourism also is about making the decision to slow down by enjoying the process of travel; in effect reversing time–space compression through creating quality time and benefitting from 'quality leisure', meeting the rising demand of a maturing cohort of more time- and experience-seeking travellers (Conway & Timms 2010; Timms & Neill 2011). Promotion of sustainability is also paramount, not only from an environmental perspective but also culturally by countering the loss of local distinctiveness as it relates to leisure, sense of place, and conviviality through understanding others' cultures and developing common interests between hosts and 'tourists as guests'.

Economically, slow tourism aims to develop softly through reducing capital leakage as opposed to merely 'growing' a destination through increasing tourist arrivals. This increases tourism efficiencies through quality enhancements, such as local provisioning of agricultural products and beverages, handicrafts, furnishings and service activities. At the community and household levels, handicrafts, food production, service and retail stores, and a diverse assortment of locally owned and managed accommodation establishments provide much-needed income for the entrepreneurial minded. Being petty-commodity producers, such small informal sector operations have cost structures, economic relations and motivations based on familial and/or household relations (Wheelock 1992). It has been demonstrated that smaller locally owned tourism enterprises purchase a substantially larger percentage of their goods, such as food, from local sources than do large foreign-owned enterprises (Momsen 1998). While this is partly attributable to economies of scale for larger foreign-owned establishments, it also has to do with improved local relationships (Timms 2006).

Additionally, the focus on quality over quantity creates greater resilience to economic shocks through a community development focus and not tourism growth and development *per se*. Hence, productive activities are orientated toward local consumption patterns with tourism demand accommodated by responsive increases in production. And maximizing local multipliers contributes to diversified, articulated, resilient and less dependent local economies capable of reorientating production toward local needs during global economic shocks, such as global food crises, which creates a more competitive position for local farmers in relation to rising costs of imported foodstuffs (Timms 2009). In concert, the associated recent global economic recession and resultant decrease in visitor numbers and expenditures can be combated through such reorientation of production, be it agriculture or other sectors, toward domestic markets as rising import costs create an opportunity for local producers.

Such micro-economic flexible responses to marginality would also have positive impacts on social sustainability. In these complementary activities, the balance of social power and economic decision making shifts from the formal to the informal (complementary) economy. This can broaden rural household and family economic roles from activities dominated by men to incorporate activities managed by women as significant and important to household survival and reproduction (Momsen 1994). Further, they supplement household incomes, add flexibility to the survival strategies open to members, and help maintain rural farming endeavours, such as 'Antillean gardens', food-forest plots and smallholdings (Berleant-Schiller & Pulsipher 1986; Hills 1988; Brierley 1991). Hence, the positive benefits of slow tourism's soft growth potential advances the interests of the under-privileged and powerless in the oft-forgotten marginal villages and scattered communities, which addresses the goals of both community tourism and the poverty reduction aims of pro-poor tourism (Renard 2001; Torres & Momsen 2004).

The adoption of soft growth importantly addresses, and is based upon, concerns over environmental sustainability. Capturing a greater share of capital spent by tourists allows destination economies to develop while minimizing the resource demands that increased numbers of tourists would require. Island ecological systems require greater conservation efforts, and the replacement of the hard growth maxims of mass tourism and its derivatives with soft growth policies and practices would contribute greatly to this cause (Conway & Timms 2003). And, from a global environmental change perspective, maximizing the returns from small-scale tourism establishments as opposed to expanding the number of rooms in large resorts would reduce the potential carbon dioxide contributions of tourism by lowering the expansion of air travel service the latter would require (Hall 2009).

One caveat, however, is that the slow travel movement calls for the avoidance of air travel (whenever possible) and promotes slower and more environmentally friendly alternative modes of transport (Dickinson 2007). Unfortunately, Caribbean tourism is dependent on air travel and the alternative, cruise ships, lies outside the slow tourism paradigm of local inclusiveness and reducing capital leakage. Ferries and sailboat travel can be promoted, and included, in a slow tourism model but are quite limited in their scope, and certainly not a viable alternative to long-haul air travel to and from the main markets. But, as mentioned earlier, focusing on quality over quantity can partially counter, or ameliorate the rise in number of air passengers, reducing the environmental footprint (Hall 2010). Also, the Caribbean's greater proximity to major markets in Europe and the USA relative to other tropical destinations in Asia, the Pacific and Africa reduces the environmental impact from airline carbon dioxide emissions.

A second concern is that this localized small-scale slow tourism model cannot be the panacea for all of tourisms problems throughout the Caribbean region as a whole. Hall (2010) argues for the need of a global steady-state tourism, also based on Daly's (2008) work, but notes that it is not palpable at the moment to tourism planners. We agree in the context of mass tourism-saturated locales, although they can promote more soft forms of growth through focusing on maximizing returns from existing accommodation 'spaces' by filling unoccupied rooms and reducing seasonal variations in occupancy rates. More importantly, however, we also believe that our concept of slow tourism can be advanced in those geographically marginal locations where diversity persists and considerable potential awaits; and have argued this geographical and contextual aspect of uneven development earlier. It also needs to be stressed further that slow tourism encourages new ideas about how to grow *locales* in more conscious and measured ways so that inclusive alternatives are formed from the existing cultural hearths of local practice and communal/familial knowledge that have always existed in the many overlooked, marginal and out of the way peripheries of Caribbean islands.

Implementing Slow Tourism in the Caribbean's Geographical Margins

As discussed, it is geographically marginal locations in the Caribbean, and elsewhere for that matter, where alternatives to mass tourism, such as slow tourism, have available spaces for appropriate slow growth development. But without careful planning and implementation, slow tourism could very well serve as a 'Trojan horse', identifying and opening these areas to the hard growth axioms of mass tourism (Butler 1990). In some cases, this has been the experience of eco-tourism as it can be co-opted as a marketing product for mass tourism, resulting in environmental and socio-economic stress (Carrier & Macleod 2005). Or, in another case, the 'disneyfication' of cultural tourism, such as is currently occurring in Falmouth, Jamaica, where historical Georgian architecture is being modernly retrofitted to appeal to the new influx of cruise ship visitors that the newly operational cruise ship terminal is now delivering. Therefore, we provide a few lessons for implementing slow tourism in geographically marginal locations based on the example of Treasure Beach, Jamaica (Figure 3). Treasure Beach is a loosely organized series of small fishing villages on the marginal southwest coast of the island. Lacking the relative geographical site and situation factors of easy accessibility, white sand beaches, tropical wet climate and associated vegetation and calm seas has limited its appeal to mass tourism developers and left it free to develop a unique form of alternative tourism that, while not specifically evolving with slow tourism as a specific goal, followed a trajectory based on slow tourism ideals (Hawkins 1999).

The first lesson is to keep tourism establishments small scale, with a focus on developing the quality of a locale as opposed to a focus on merely growing a locale. In order to do so, development must be carefully planned and managed, which

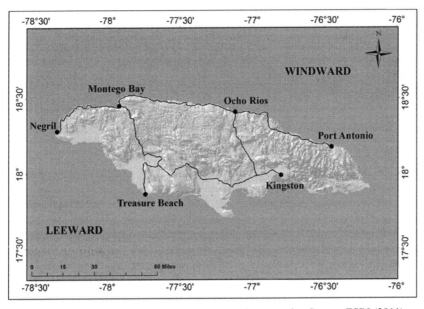

Figure 3. Jamaica's major tourist sites, roads and topography. *Source:* ESRI (2011).

requires cooperative partnerships between local stakeholders and local government planning efforts (Scheyvens & Momsen 2008). In the past two decades, neo-liberal restructuring has forced states to focus on hard growth promotion of mass tourism, but has also called for decentralization of government functions to the local level that is argued to address more appropriately local situations and concerns (Ribot 2004). Social scientists tend to agree, and have long advocated for empowering local communities in development decision making and management, particularly as they are the proximate stakeholders in its success (Ostrom 1990; Conway & Timms 2003). In Treasure Beach this has resulted in local legislation limiting tourist accommodations to 15 rooms per acre (half the density for Jamaica as a whole) to deliberately exclude mass tourism development. Further, local stakeholders in Treasure Beach's tourism industry have fought to limit the scale of expansion of water utilities to an adjacent area targeted for mass tourism development for the same purpose (Jason Henzell, personal communication, 2007). Such targeted planning is essential to ensure that tourism development is guided and controlled to reflect local concerns, and minimizes environmental pressures on the local resource base.

A second related lesson is to keep the control of slow tourism local to ensure that benefits accrue to local communities through tourism multipliers, and not let it be repatriated abroad, which is more likely with larger foreign-owned tourism enterprises (Momsen 1998; Timms 2006). The vast majority of tourism establishments in Treasure Beach are owned and run by local families, including restaurants, accommodations and tour operators. These locally owned establishments procure much of their supplies locally from fishing cooperatives, farming cooperatives and markets, and craftspeople. Even the small resort Jake's in Treasure Beach, which recently became part of the larger Chris Blackwell's consortium Island Outpost, has developed relationships with the local agricultural cooperative, Treasure Beach Ital Farmers Association. It purchases seafood from local fishermen, meats from local ranchers and uses local building materials and workers as an intentional strategy to develop the local community (Jason Henzell, personal communication, 2007). Hence, a greater percent of the tourist's expenditures remain in the local community, stimulating the local economy and spreading benefits more equitably.

A third suggestion is to include a diversity of establishments at multiple price points to promote democratization of the benefits of a slow tourism product. The importance of this diversity increases the possible sources of tourists and encourages more small-scale local establishments (Timms & Neill 2011). One concern of alternative tourism is the limited, and specific, demand for these offerings that can be considered elitist (Whelan 1991). However, in Treasure Beach there is a variety of tourism establishments, including higher-end chic small resorts and villas, mid-priced guesthouses and even budget backpacker establishments, which attract a diversity of visitors that seek out a more community-orientated tourism experience while combating critiques of elitism in alternative tourism. Further, Treasure Beach has created its own web-portal that promotes a slower tourism product, including searches for local accommodations, restaurants, tour operators, and serves as a web presence for local community development organizations and schools (TreasureBeach.net 2011).

This last point relates to our final lesson, the slow tourism product should be a true partnership with the local community that develops the quality of tourism and local community symbiotically and reinforces the slow growth focus on development over growth. In Treasure Beach this is accomplished in several ways, including the aforementioned web-portal that benefits both tourism and community. One specific example for Treasure Beach is the donation of $US1 for every occupied hotel room to local community development groups that promote health and literacy campaigns, sponsor local sports teams and even provide disaster relief assistance, as occurred after Hurricane Ivan in 2004 and Hurricane Dean in 2007 (Conway & Timms 2010). Since the slow tourism model has a stake in the local community, the benefits of slow tourism contributed back to ensure a thriving local community as it is part of the slow tourism product. Other examples of such soft growth slow tourism in marginal locales in the Caribbean await study, and promotion, to test and develop our theoretical claims (Conway & Timms 2010). As the concept of slow tourism is still in its early stages of development, it is a prime topic for more research and development.

Conclusions

Geographical marginality and the geographical dimensions of place disadvantages, which can be recast for alternative tourisms' advantage, have not been considered previously as important considerations in the evolution and maturation of Caribbean tourism industrial mixes. With many Caribbean islands' tourism life cycles being in their latter stages (ECLAC 2008), and in need of revitalization and renewal if they are not to founder and become stagnant, as Butler's (2004) TALC general model predicts, it behoves planners and tourism promoters in the Caribbean to recognize the value and necessity of encouraging the widening of their tourism sector's diversity to include new and appropriate tourism forms that are more sustainable economically, socially and environmentally. Here we argue that slow tourism can serve this goal in marginal locations through its philosophical basis in slow growth development.

Being practical and realistic about the difficulties of launching slow tourism in such previously overlooked and underdeveloped locales, the modest pace and limited scale of development of slow tourism that we envisage occurring will limit its ability to be the panacea for all of the Caribbean tourism industry ills. However, it can be a partner to many Caribbean islands' conventional sun, sand and sea tourism offerings to not only provide a more comprehensive tourism product (Timms & Neill 2011), but ameliorate the often-produced uneven landscapes that mass tourism's penetration has caused, or exacerbated (Scheyvens & Momsen 2008). Slow tourism initiatives in the remoter locales can also serve as a model for other forms of new tourism alternatives by adopting soft growth forms of development (Conway & Timms 2010).

Further, lessons learned from slow tourism could influence the adoption of more soft growth practices for the mass tourism industry as well, decreasing its negative economic, social and environmental impacts while maximizing local benefits. For example, instead of building more rooms or adding more cruise-ship terminals, Caribbean islands can maximize the benefits of their existing tourism capacities and its supportive infrastructure while at the same time seeking to address the unevenness of regional economic well-being that commonly persists even in the smallest of islands. Cutting down on capital leakage and stimulating local enterprises is a worthwhile goal which carries tremendous potential to grow local economies in a more socially, economically, and environmentally sustainable manner (Timms 2006). The current volatility in the global economic order, and the failure of neo-liberalism to overcome the inevitable structural crises that plunge such capitalist geo-economic systems into severe downturns (Harvey 2003), shows that there is an even greater need to find more sustainable forms of tourism in the Caribbean that stimulate local economies and are less vulnerable to external market shocks than the current hard growth mass tourism industry (Timms 2009).

One final reflection deserves noting in regards to this re-evaluation of the Caribbean tourism industry and our advocacy of a place in the future mix for slow tourism. Common, if despondent, findings of early tourist development models envisaged three stages of evolution with the possibility of the final stage dominated by mass tourism stagnation and its associated negative social, economic and environmental consequences (Butler 1980; de Albuquerque & McElroy 1992; McElroy & de Albuquerque 1998). Importantly, however, McElroy and de Albuquerque (2002) remind us that it is unfettered hard growth beyond the second transitional stage of tourist penetration and rapid expansion into the third saturation stage that bodes ill for Caribbean tourisms' continued vitality.

We argue that geographically marginal locations, both regionally and within islands, that have yet to progress past the first or second stages, are prime locations to disregard quantitative hard growth development and adopt the quality of soft growth development through slow tourism. In order to do so, however, the development of slow tourism must be carefully planned and managed with the full participation of local stakeholders. And, this entails government and legislative support (Scheyvens & Momsen 2008), such as the cooperative partnership that occurred in Treasure Beach, Jamaica. If not, the slow tourism brand could very well be co-opted as a marketing tool for the mass tourism industry to employ in capturing a niche market and develop along the rather uncontrollable, evolutionary trajectories of past explanatory models.

Slow tourism, based on the slow movement's philosophical bases and following a soft growth trajectory, stands as the antithesis to mass tourism as potentially sustainable socially, economically and environmentally. Hence, it coalesces the goals of many other alternative tourisms – the environmental prospects of ecotourism (Weaver 2004; Klak 2007), the poverty-reduction goals of pro-poor tourism (Torres & Momsen 2004), the linkage-induced stimulation effects of agri-tourism (Momsen

1998; Collins 2000; Timms 2006), the cultural aspects of heritage tourism (Pulsipher 1999), the egalitarian efforts of community tourism (Milne & Ewing 2004), amongst others. The generalizable strength of its humanistic ethical position lies in its stress on quality considerations rather than quantity realizations. The former, therefore, becomes the preferred way forward for all stakeholders through advancing soft growth over hard growth and focusing on the adoption of this alternative, participatory, inclusive model in geographically marginal locations throughout the Caribbean (Conway & Timms 2010). As such, it caters to the growing numbers of contemporary globally experienced tourists who are seeking a heightened quality of life in their visits that offers variety, uniqueness and thorough enjoyment in the easy-paced, and local community tourism leisure-environments without imposing undue demands on their local host communities as their guests. Indeed, it moves the focus of tourism back to the 'original meaning of words such as 'holidays' (holy days), 'vacances' (in French, 'empty days') or 'recreation' (Matos 2004: 96).

References

Baldwin, J. (2000) Tourism development, wetland degradation and beach erosion in Antigua, West Indies, *Tourism Geographies*, 2(2), pp. 193–218.
Berleant-Schiller, R. & Pulsipher, L. D. (1986) Subsistence cultivation in the Caribbean, *New West Indies Guide*, 3(1), pp. 1–40.
Boruff, B. J. & Cutter, S. L. (2007) The environmental vulnerability of Caribbean island nations, *Geographical Review*, 97(1), pp. 24–45.
Brierley, J. S. (1991) Kitchen gardens in the Caribbean, past and present: their role in small farming development, *Caribbean Geography*, 3(1), pp. 15–28.
Butler, R. W. (1980) The concept of a tourist area cycle of evolution: implications for management of resources, *Canadian Geographer*, 24(1), pp. 5–12.
Butler, R.W. (1990) Alternative tourism: pious hope or Trojan horse?, *Journal of Travel Research*, 28(3), pp. 40–45.
Butler, R. W. (2004) The tourism area life cycle in the twenty-first century, in: A. A. Lew, C. M. Hall & A. M. Williams (Eds) *A Companion to Tourism*, pp. 159–169 (New York: John Wiley).
Campbell, S. (1996) Green cities, growing cities, just cities? Urban planning and the contradictions of sustainable development, *Journal of the American Planning Association*, 62(3), pp. 296–312.
Caribbean Tourism Organization (CTO) (2011) Statistics and market research. Available at http://www.onecaribbean.org/statistics/countrystats/ (accessed 1 February 2011).
Carrier, J. & Macleod, D. V. L (2005) Bursting the bubble: the socio-cultural context of ecotourism, *Royal Anthropological Institute*, 11, pp. 315–334.
Central Intelligence Agency (CIA) (2011) The world factbook. Available at https://www.cia.gov/library/publications/the-world-factbook/index.html (accessed 1 February 2011).
Collins, P. (2000) Agro-tourism – a sustainable approach to economic growth, in: *Proceedings: Agrotourism Conference*, Trinidad and Tobago, Inter-American Institute for Co-operation in Agriculture.
Commonwealth Secretariat (1991) *Sustainable Development: An Imperative for Environmental Protection* (London: Economic Affairs Division, Commonwealth Secretariat).
Conway, D. (1993) The new tourism in the Caribbean: reappraising market segmentation, in: D. Gayle & J. Goodrich (Eds) *Tourism Marketing and Management in the Caribbean*, pp. 167–177 (London: Routledge).

Conway, D. & Jemiolo, J. (1991) Tourism, air service provision and patterns of Caribbean airline offer, *Social and Economic Studies*, 40(2), pp. 1–45.

Conway, D. & Lorah, P. (1995) Environmental protection policies in Caribbean small islands: some St. Lucia examples, *Caribbean Geography*, 6(1), pp. 16–27.

Conway, D. & Timms, B. F. (2003) Where is the environment in Caribbean development thinking and praxis?, *Global Development Studies*, 3(1–2), pp. 91–130.

Conway, D. & Timms, B. F. (2010) Re-branding alternative tourism in the Caribbean: the case for 'slow tourism', *Tourism and Hospitality Research*, 10(4), pp. 1–16.

Daly, H. E. (1990) Sustainable growth: an impossibility theorem, *Development*, 3/4, pp. 45–47.

Daly, H. E. (1991) Sustainable growth: A bad oxymoron, *Environment and Carcinogenic Reviews*, 8(2), pp. 401–407.

Daley, H. E. (2008) *A Steady-State Economy* (London: Sustainable Development Commission).

Davenport, J. & Jackiewicz, E. L. (2008) Spaces of tourism, in: E. Jackiewicz & F. Bosco (Eds) *Placing Latin America: Contemporary Themes in Human Geography*, pp. 97–113 (Lanham, MD: Rowman & Littlefield).

de Albuquerque, K. & McElroy, J. L. (1992) Caribbean tourism styles and sustainable strategies, *Environmental Management*, 16, pp. 615–632.

Dickinson, J. (2007) *Slow Tourism Travel for a Lower Carbon Future.* Available at http://www.bournemouth.ac.uk/icthr/PDFs/rgs_report.pdf (accessed 31 August 2009).

Dodman, D. (2009) Globalization, tourism and local living conditions on Jamaica's north coast, *Singapore Journal of Tropical Geography*, 30(2), pp. 204–219.

Duval, D. T. & Wilkinson, P. F. (2004) Tourism development in the Caribbean: meaning and influences, in: D. Duval (Ed.) *Tourism in the Caribbean: Trends, Development, Prospects*, pp. 59–80 (London: Routledge).

Economic Commission for Latin America and the Caribbean (ECLAC) (2008) *Tourism Life Cycle, Tourism Competitiveness, and Upgrading Strategies in the Caribbean* (Port of Spain, Trinidad and Tobago: ECLAC).

ESRI (Environmental Systems Resource Institute) (2011) *ArcMap 10* (Redlands, CA: ESRI).

Flemming, B. (2011) Falmouth Pier Docks History, *Jamaica Gleaner*, 19 February 2011. Available at http://jamaica-gleaner.com/gleaner/20110219/news/news1.html (accessed 29 March 2011).

Gardner, N. (2009) A manifesto for slow travel, *Hidden Europe*, 25, pp. 10–14.

Goodland, R. (1992) The case that the world has reached its limits: More precisely that current throughput growth in the global economy cannot be sustained, *Population & Environment*, 13(3), pp. 167–182.

Grove, R. H. (1995) *Green Imperialism: Colonial Expansion, Tropical Island Edens and the Origins of Environmentalism, 1600–1860* (Cambridge: Cambridge University Press).

Hall, C. M. (2009) Degrowing tourism: décroissance, sustainable consumption and steady-state tourism, *Anatolia: An International of Tourism and Hospitality Research*, 20(1), pp. 46–61.

Hall, C. M. (2010) Changing paradigms and global change: from sustainable to steady-state tourism, *Tourism Recreation Research*, 35(2), pp. 131–145.

Harrison, D. (2007) Cocoa, conservation and tourism: Grande Rivière, Trinidad, *Annals of Tourism Research*, 34(4), pp. 919–942.

Harvey, D. (1989) *The Condition of Postmodernity* (Oxford: Basil Blackwell).

Harvey, D. (2003) *The New Imperialism* (Oxford: Oxford University Press).

Hawkins, M. (1999) Tourism and place in Treasure Beach, Jamaica: imagining paradise and the alternative, Doctoral Dissertation, Department of Geography, Louisiana State University.

Hills, T. (1988) The Caribbean food-forest: ecological artistry or random chaos?, in: J. S. Brierley & H. Rubenstein (Eds) *Small Farming and Peasant Resources in the Caribbean*, pp. 1–28 (Winnipeg, Canada: Department of Geography, University of Manitoba).

Irving, J. (2008) *Welcome to Our World: Companion Slow Food.* Available at http://www.slowfoodusa.org/downloads/local_chapter_resources/COMPANION_ENG.PDF (accessed 16 September 2011).

Jamaica Promotions Corporation (JAMPRO) (2010) Look out Dubai, here's Jamaica! Available at http://www.jamaicatradeandinvest.org/index.php?action=investment&id=34&oppage=5&opid=6 (accessed 26 August 2010).

James, C. & Fournillier, K. (1993) *Marine Turtle Management in Northeast Trinidad – A Successful Community Based Approach towards Endangered Species Conservation* (Laventille, Trinidad Tobago: Forestry Division, Government of Trinidad and Tobago).

Klak, T. (2007) Sustainable ecotourism development in Central America and the Caribbean: Review of debates and conceptual reformulation, *Geography Compass*, 1(5), pp. 1037–1057.

Klak, T. & Flynn, R. (2008) Sustainable development and ecotourism: general principles and an Eastern Caribbean case study, in: E. L. Jackiewicz & F. J. Bosco (Eds) *Placing Latin America: Contemporary Themes in Human Geography*, pp. 115–136 (Lanham, MD: Rowman & Littlefield).

Kummer, C. (2002) *The Pleasures of Slow Food* (San Francisco: Chronicle Books).

Lewis, A. & Brown, T. (2007) Pro-poor tourism: a vehicle for development in Trindad and Tobago. Paper presented at the Conference in Crisis, Chaos and Change: Caribbean Development Challenges in the 21st Century, St Augustine, Trinidad and Tobago.

Maingot, A. P. (1994) *The United States and the Caribbean: Challenges of an Asymmetrical Relationship* (Boulder: Westview Press).

Matos, R. (2004) Can slow tourism bring new life to alpine regions?, in: K. Weiermair & C. Mathies (Eds) *The Tourism and Leisure Industry: Shaping the Future*, pp. 93–103 (New York: The Haworth Hospitality Press).

Mayer, H. & Knox, P. L. (2006) Slow cities: sustainable places in a fast world, *Journal of Urban Affairs*, 28(4), pp. 321–334.

McElroy, J. L. & de Albuquerque, K. (1991) Tourism styles and policy responses in the open economy-closed environment context, in: N. P. Girvan & D. Simmons (Eds) *Caribbean Ecology and Economics*, pp. 143–165 (Barbados: Caribbean Conservation Association).

McElroy, J. L. & de Albuquerque, K. (1998) Tourism penetration index in small Caribbean islands, *Annals of Tourism Research*, 25(1), pp. 145–168.

McElroy, J. L. & de Albuquerque, K. (2002) Problems for managing sustainable tourism in small islands, in: Y. Apostolopoulos & D. J. Gayle (Eds) *Island Tourism and Sustainable Development: Caribbean, Pacific and Mediterranean Experiences*, pp. 15–31 (London: Praeger).

McElroy, J. L. & Parry, C. E. (2010) The characteristics of small island tourist economies, *Tourism and Hospitality Research*, 10(4), pp. 315–328.

Milne, S. & Ewing, G. (2004) Community participation in Caribbean tourism: problems and prospects, in: D. T. Duval (Ed.) *Tourism in the Caribbean: Trends, Development, Prospects*, pp. 205–217 (London: Routledge).

Momsen, J. H. (1994) Tourism, gender and development in the Caribbean, in: V. Kinnaird & D. Hall (Eds) *Tourism: A Gender Analysis*, pp. 106–120 (New York: John Wiley).

Momsen, J. H. (1998) Caribbean tourism and agriculture: new linkages in the global era?, in: T. Klak (Ed.) *Globalization and Neoliberalism: The Caribbean Context*, pp. 115–134 (Lanham, MD: Rowman & Littlefield).

Morello, G. (2004) Spacing and timing in leisure activities, in: K. Weiermair & C. Mathies (Eds) *The Tourism and Leisure Industry: Shaping the Future*, pp. 69–81 (New York: The Haworth Hospitality Press).

Nuryanti, W. (1996) Heritage and postmodern tourism, *Annals of Tourism Research*, 23(2), pp. 249–260.

Ostrom, E. (1990) *Governing the Commons: The Evolution of Institutions for Collective Action* (Cambridge: Cambridge University Press).

Padilla, A. & McElroy, J. L. (2005) The tourism penetration index in large islands: the case of the Dominican Republic, *Journal of Sustainable Development*, 13(4), pp. 353–372.

Parry, C. E. & McElroy, J. L. (2009) The supply determinants of small island tourist economies, *The ARA (Caribbean) Journal of Tourism Research*, 2(1), pp. 13–22.

Pattullo, P. (2005) *Last Resorts: The Cost of Tourism in the Caribbean* (London: Cassell Latin American Bureau).

Pelling, M. & Uito, J. I. (2001) Small island developing states: natural disaster vulnerability and global change, *Environmental Hazards*, 3(2), pp. 49–62.

Petrini, C. (2001) *Slow Food: The Case for Taste* (New York: Columbia University Press).

Pietrykowski, B. (2004) You are what you eat: the social economy of the slow food movement, *Review of Social Economy*, 62(3), pp. 307–321.

Potter, R. B., Barker, D., Conway, D. & Klak, T. (2004) *The Contemporary Caribbean* (Harlow, UK: Pearson Education Limited).

Prentice, R. (1993) *Tourism and Heritage Attraction* (London: Routledge).

Pulsipher, L. M. (1999) 'Here where the old-time people be': reconstructing the landscapes of the slavery and post-slavery era in Montserrat, West Indies, in: J. B. Haviser (Ed.) *African sites: Archaeology in the Caribbean*, pp. 9–37 (Princeton, NJ: Markus Wiener).

Renard, Y. (2001) *Practical Strategies for Pro-poor Tourism: A Case Study of the St. Lucia Heritage Tourism Programme* (London: Overseas Development Institute).

Rhiney, K. (2009) Towards a new model for improved tourism-agriculture linkages? The case of two farmers' co-operatives in Jamaica, *Caribbean Geography*, 15(2), pp. 142–159.

Ribot, J. C. (2004) *Waiting for Democracy: The Politics of Choice in Natural Resource Decentralizations* (Washington: World Resources Institute).

Scheyvens, R. & Momsen, J. H. (2008) Tourism and poverty reduction: issues for small island states, *Tourism Geographies*, 10(1), pp. 22–41.

Stille, A. (2001) Slow food: An Italian answer to globalization, *The Nation*, August, 21/27, pp. 11–16.

Thomas, G. A. (1991) The gentrification of paradise: St. John's Antigua, *Urban Geography*, 12(5), pp. 469–487.

Timms, B. (2006) Caribbean agriculture-tourism linkages in a neoliberal world: problems and prospects for St. Lucia, *International Development Planning Review*, 28(1), pp. 35–56.

Timms, B. (2008) The parallax of landscape: situating Celaque National Park, Honduras, in: D. C. Knudsen, M. M. Metro-Roland, A. K. Soper & C. E. Greer (Eds) *Landscape, Tourism, and Meaning*, pp. 95–108 (Aldershot, UK: Ashgate).

Timms, B. (2009) Development theory and domestic agriculture in the Caribbean: recurring crises and missed opportunities, *Caribbean Geography*, 15(2), pp. 101–117.

Timms, B. & Neill, S. (2011) Cracks in the pavement: conventional constraints and contemporary solutions for linking agriculture and tourism in the Caribbean, in: R. Torres & J. Momsen (Eds) *Tourism & Agriculture: New Geographies of Consumption, Production, and Rural Restructuring*, pp. 104–116 (London: Routledge).

Torres, R. & Momsen, J. H. (2004) Challenges and potential for linking tourism and agriculture to achieve pro-poor tourism objectives, *Progress in Development Studies*, 4, pp. 294–318.

TreasureBeach.net. (2011) Homepage. Available at http://treasurebeach.net/guide/ (accessed 19 January 2011).

Vitousek, P. M., Loope, L. & Andersen, H. (1995) *Islands: Biological Diversity and Ecosystem Function* (Berlin: Springer-Verlag).

Walsh, R. P. D. (1998) Climatic changes in the Eastern Caribbean over the past 150 years and some implications in planning sustainable development, in: D. F. M. McGregor, D. Barker & S. Lloyd-Evans (Eds) *Resource Sustainability and Caribbean Development*, pp. 51–68 (Kingston, Jamaica: The University of the West Indies Press).

Watts, D. (1995) Environmental degradation, the water resource and sustainable development in the Eastern Caribbean, *Caribbean Geography*, 6(1), pp. 2–15.

Weaver, D. B. (1991) Alternative to mass tourism in Dominica, *Annals of Tourism Research*, 18, pp. 414–432.

Weaver, D. B. (2004) Manifestations of ecotourism in the Caribbean, in: D. T. Duval (Ed.) *Tourism in the Caribbean: Trends, Development, Prospects*, pp. 172–186 (London: Routledge).

Wheelock, J. (1992) The household in the total economy, in: P. Ekins & M. Max-Neef (Eds) *Real-life Economics: Understanding Wealth Creation*, pp. 124–135 (London: Routledge).

Whelan, T. (Ed.) (1991) *Nature Tourism* (Washington, DC: Island Press).

Wilkinson, P. F. (1999) Caribbean cruise tourism: Delusion? Illusion?, *Tourism Geographies*, 1(3), pp. 261–282.

Notes on Contributors

Benjamin F. Timms is Assistant Professor of Geography at California Polytechnic State University in San Luis Obispo, California. He studies sustainable tourism development in the Caribbean with a focus on maximizing economic linkages between tourism and local industries.

Dennis Conway is Professor Emeritus of Geography at Indiana University, Bloomington, Indiana. He has co-authored seven books and over 120 publications on Caribbean urbanization, transnational migration, economic development and alternative tourism models.

Index

INDEX